The Absolute Comic

The Absolute Comic

by Edith Kern

New York   Columbia University Press   1980

Library of Congress Cataloging in Publication Data
Kern, Edith G   1912–
    The absolute comic.

    Bibliography: p.
    Includes index.
    1. Comic, The.   2. Comedy—History and criticism.
I. Title.
BH301.C7K47   809'.917   80-10478
ISBN 0-231-04908-0

Columbia University Press
New York   Guildford, Surrey

Contents

Acknowledgments

I WISH to express my sincere thanks to the following institutions for having made this study possible: the Guggenheim Foundation, whose fellowship propitiated my research on this subject; the Radcliffe (now Bunting) Institute for having elected me a fellow and made available to me its own and Harvard University's vast resources; the National Endowment for the Humanities for having provided me with the opportunity of preparing and conducting, under its auspices, a year-long seminar for college teachers on "Comedy as a Fantasy Triumph."

The enthusiasm expressed by Professor W. G. Moore of Oxford University with regard to my analyses of Molière's work has been an inspiration to me and makes me regret even more deeply his untimely death.

I am also grateful to Richard Hayes for the careful reading of my manuscript.

E. K.

The Absolute Comic

one
laughter
and
Tears

> DAUGHTER: Daddy, are these conversations serious?
>
> FATHER: Certainly they are.
>
> D: They're not a sort of game that you play with me?
>
> F: God forbid . . . but they are a sort of game that we play together.
>
> D: Then they're *not* serious! . . . I don't understand.
>
> F: Yes. The point is that the purpose of these conversations is to discover the "rules." It's like life—a game whose purpose is to discover the rules, which rules are always changing and always undiscoverable. (Bat*M:* 14, 20)

LAUGHTER and tears are so exclusively human that their essences have remained almost as enigmatic to the human mind as that mind itself. Man's eye, Giambattista Vico maintained somewhere, cannot see itself—except as its mirror image. But such elusiveness becomes a challenge to play the game of discovering the "rules, which rules are always changing and always undiscoverable." A never ending stream of thinkers have engaged in this game, perhaps first among them Aristotle. With regard to tears and the tragic, the thoughts he expressed in his *Poetics* are still considered valid by many, although new insights are being gained that are apt to affect and possibly alter them. Aristotle's analyses of laughter and the comic, on the other hand, have been considered inadequate and his ideas concerning the relationship between laughter and tears remain largely unexplored. Yet recent findings in folklore and anthropology seem to imbue his scant statements with meanings that have escaped intervening centuries. In their light, his brief historical mention of religious rites as the common origin of tragedy and comedy seems to regain fundamental significance and has led to the assumption that there existed a comic as well as a tragic scapegoat—an implication that the great turn-of-the-century analysts of the comic, Bergson and Freud, ignored.

True representatives of their time, Bergson and Freud were more concerned with the mechanisms of wit and laughter than with comedy's more ancient and more recent elements of farce that reveal its kinship with the tragic. We have the precious testimony of their contemporary, the perceptive French critic Lanson (Lan*M, passim*), that in France (though certainly not exclusively in that country) theater audiences winced at that time at Molière's farcical episodes and maintained an icy silence when his Imaginary Invalid, for instance, kept count of his bowel movements, his laxatives, and his enemas. Such rejection and even suppression of what today we consider traditional elements of farce in the work of so great a playwright suggest not only that the game of finding the "rules" of the comic is not yet over but also that its "rules" have been changing so that—like the *Vexierbild* game so popular in the salons of seventeenth-century Germany—it seems but a "teasing image" that appears to the beholder now in one way, now in another, and whose different structures he can never perceive simultaneously.

At the beginning of his ingenious study on laughter, Bergson asked himself: "What does laughter mean? What is the basal element in the laughable? What common ground can we find between the grimace of a merry-andrew, a play upon words, an equivocal situation in a burlesque, and a scene of high comedy?" (Ber*L:* 61). He concluded above all that laughter comes from superiority—a concept expressed with more or less clarity by almost all who have tried to ascertain the essence of laughter, and he held the equally widespread belief that laughter is liberating. But while he was highly successful in discovering these and similar common denominators for all laughter, Bergson failed to recognize the dichotomy within laughter itself, a dichotomy which the poet Baudelaire had observed several decades earlier and which clearly indicates that laughter has a history conforming to the Hegelian pendulum pattern. It swings from what the poet called the "grotesque," "carnivalesque," or "absolute comic" to the "significative." Baudelaire found the absolute comic, or farce, highly creative from an artistic point of view, the significative comic mainly imitative and mimetic (Bau*L*: 143–44). Considering all laughter in essence satanic, he believed nevertheless that neither laughter nor tears would have been conceivable before the Fall, since both involve ugly physiognomic convulsions incongruent with paradise and its harmony. What makes laughter particularly satanic is, according to him, the presence, on the part of the laugher, of that same arrogance and sense of superiority that occasioned the fall of Satan and that depends upon the moral and physical abasement of its object. Yet, to the poet, the significative comic is the more satanic of the two, since it is predicated upon the superiority of man over his fellow man, whereas the absolute comic represents rather man's triumph over nature. Aside from its religious overtones, Baudelaire's analysis shows so much kinship with insights into laughter more recently arrived at that it is well worth our while to look at some of his arguments.

Baudelaire thought the significative comic, in its extreme, to be expressive of and appealing to lucid thought and to have a sense of utility about it. He believed the absolute comic to serve no particular end, but to require intuition to grasp it (Bau*L*: 144). To illustrate what he had in mind when speaking of the absolute comic, he gave a spirited description of English mimes he had seen performing in the style of the Italian commedia dell'arte theater:

The English Pierrot swept upon us like a hurricane, fell down
like a sack of coals, and when he laughed his laughter made the
auditorium quake; his laugh was like a joyful clap of thunder.
He was a short, fat man, and to increase his imposingness he
wore a beribboned costume which encompassed his jubilant person as birds are encompassed with their down and feathers, or
angora with their fur. Upon his floured face he had stuck,
crudely and without transition or gradation, two enormous
patches of pure red . . . when he laughed his mouth seemed to
run from ear to ear. As for his moral nature, it was . . . heed-
lessness and indifference, and consequently the gratification of
every kind of greedy and rapacious whim. . . . And everything
. . . was the dizzy height of hyperbole. Pierrot walks past a
woman who is scrubbing her doorstep; after rifling her pockets,
he makes to stuff into his own her sponge, her mop, her bucket,
water and all! As for the way in which he endeavored to express
his love to her, anyone who remembers . . . the monkeys in
their famous cage at the Jardin des Plantes can imagine it for
himself. Perhaps I ought to add that the woman's role was taken
by a very long, very thin man, whose outraged modesty emit-
ted shrill screams. It was truly an intoxication of laughter—
something both terrible and irresistible. (BauL: 147–48)

Though fully aware of the violence and immorality inherent in this comic, Baudelaire admired it; he especially admired
the French masters of grotesque farce, first among them Rabelais, who had made it a part of their art. Callot's famous seventeenth-century etchings of commedia dell'arte figures, entitled
"Balli di Sfessania," seemed to him a perfect expression of its
spirit and were cherished by him, although Sfessania must have
evoked for him the grotesque celebrations of ancient saturnalia
and the carrying in procession of absurdly distorted obscene
figurines—possibly of a sacred nature. (The name Sfessania was
believed to have been derived from Fascenna, a town so
famous in antiquity for the lewdness of its songs that Horace,
when mentioning phallic license, spoke of *Fescennina licentia*.)
The poet regretted, indeed, that some of the carnivalesque interludes of Molière's comedies—those, for instance, of his

Bourgeois gentilhomme (Would-Be Gentleman) and his *Malade imaginaire* (Imaginary Invalid)—were no longer performed and were altogether disregarded by nineteenth-century stage directors because of their farcical nature. These interludes are even less known today, but because they are important in Baudelaire's conception of the absolute comic as compared to the significative, we must briefly dwell on some of their features here.

Le Bourgeois gentilhomme and *Le Malade imaginaire*—like several other comedies by the great playwright—are interspersed with interludes of song and dance, culminating at the end of each comedy in a scene that represents a fulfillment of the protagonist's aspiration in a manner totally illogical and surpassing his most ambitious dreams. In each play the fantastic triumph is justified by the statement that it is carnival, when everything is possible and permitted. This is how the Invalid's brother explains to his niece the masquerade he has prepared for her father, who unwittingly is to play its main part: "It's not so much making fun of him as playing up to his fancies. And it's all among ourselves. We can each take a part and so give the play for each other's amusement. After all, it's carnival time. Come along, let us go and get things ready" (Mo*II:*274).

Since each of the comedies was, or was intended to be, presented during actual carnival time, the author playfully fused fact and fiction and thereby stressed art as art and not as an imitation of life. Real life was drawn into the "frame" of his fictional reality in the manner of Velasquez' famous painting *Las Meninas,* wherein the painter and his work become the center while all else is reflected reflection. In *Le Bourgeois gentilhomme* (Mo*WG*), the protagonist, M. Jourdain, ruthlessly exploited by young noblemen whom he woos in order to become socially acceptable, is granted all that had been denied him in a scene similarly "framed" as being carnivalesque. Before the eyes of the spectators, he is miraculously transformed into a Turkish paladin, as dervishes whirl about him, as chants in Lingua franca (that Pidgin English of the Mediterranean) are proffered in his honor, and dancing tailors remove his ordinary clothes to replace them with others befitting his newly acquired high rank. In the process of this fantasy elevation, he is abased and physically abused in all sorts of ways: pushed about, punched, and made to kneel down. Slapstick accompanies the moments of his greatest triumph, so that he is made the butt of laughter just when he believes himself most admired, although all others, onstage and in the audience, know that all is but make-believe.

The interludes in *Le Malade imaginaire* are fantasies on the ancient theme of *carpe diem,* forming a delightful counterpoint melody to the Invalid's perpetual imaginary suffering; but the comedy ends with a carnival scene during which he is gloriously inducted into the medical brotherhood. Having passed an absurd medical examination, he has the degree of doctor conferred upon him and is presented with all the appropriate regalia, while medical instruments of gigantic proportions are carried about him and he is assured in song and dance that he will henceforth live forever, immune to death. Hymns are sung in his honor, promising him a millennium of eating, drinking, bleeding, and killing. During Molière's lifetime, the Invalid's triumph had particular poignancy: the playwright acted the part and was a real, not an imaginary, invalid, mockingly defying death and yet very soon its victim, because he died during the comedy's fourth performance. But to some of his contemporaries this victory of fantasy hardly heightened the comedy's interest or its human and artistic complexity. They saw it above all as blasphemy and did not hesitate to say so. Was Molière not defying religion and all it stood for when, in the part of the Invalid, he played dead in order to discover his "wife's" true feelings? Was he not displaying bad taste in having the Invalid speak of matters pertaining to the body and the effect of the medicines he had to take? Was not the Invalid's farcical victory over death sacrilegious in the extreme? Joining forces with his rivals, these detractors made it impossible for Molière to present his play first before the king at Versailles, where he had intended to stage it during the carnival season. They continued to persecute him even beyond his death.

What was there, then, about such farce that so appealed to Baudelaire that he believed it more significant than the comic he called significative? What made it, on the other hand, still so odious and embarrassing even to French audiences of the nineteenth and early twentieth centuries that they suppressed it? Why did Bergson largely ignore it when he composed his essay on laughter, which is so strongly based on an analysis of Molière's work? Baudelaire's use of the terms grotesque and carnivalesque in describing it may well give us a clue: The laughter of the English mimes and of the Molière interludes is that of carnival. The episodes are, from the point of view of art, creative and not mimetic. They reveal man as *homo ludens,* as does the work of some of the modern writers we will glance at. There emanates from them a conception of man's place in the universe quite different from that of so-called realism. To judge such work by the standards of significative comedy, by criteria of social refinement, morality, or even "character" means to misunderstand work and author alike. There is no stress here on individuals facing their world and shaping it or being shaped by it. We are confronted rather with representatives of mankind who remind us of the motto of Panurge, one of Rabelais' characters: "All are fools. Solomon says that the number of fools is infinite; nothing can be added to infinity, and nothing can be subtracted from it, as Aristotle proves. And I should be a raging fool if, being a fool, I did not consider myself one" (RG:415). Since Baudelaire's absolute comic is that of popular festivities of the Middle Ages and the Renaissance, it is violent and immoral by realistic standards and yet liberating in a sense that transcends such realism. But whether we appreciate it and understand the authors who created it in the past as well as those who do so today depends largely upon our grasp of its nature. A giant step toward its understanding was recently taken by Mikhail Bakhtin, the Russian critic and scholar, in a study devoted to the grotesque in the world—real and fictional—of Rabelais (BakR.).

Bakhtin's findings cannot but affect our reading of such authors as Boccaccio, Chaucer, and Molière, or of contemporary authors of farce or the absolute comic. In their light we come to recognize, within the seemingly lighthearted and heedless laughter of farce, philosophical and psychological depths previously unsuspected. Bakhtin's analyses make us see the carnivalesque as a vision of man *sub specie aeternitatis*—quite in contrast to bourgeois notions of the individual's importance and his obligation to standards of propriety. Baudelaire—as Nietzsche was to be a few decades later—was among the few thinkers in an increasingly scientific era to admit to the existence of the irrational within man, without feeling any need to apologize; it is as if Bakhtin—though quite unwittingly—set out to provide us with the scholarly data to support Baudelaire's intuitive understanding of farcical laughter. To Bakhtin, carnival laughter "is, first of all, a festive laughter. Therefore it is not an individual reaction to some isolated 'comic' event. Carnival laughter is the laughter of all the people. Second, it is universal in scope; it is directed at all and everyone, including the carnival's participants. The entire world is seen in its droll aspect, in its gay relativity" (BakR: 11). He rightly considered such laughter ambivalent—gay and triumphant but also mocking and deriding, asserting and denying, burying and reviving (BakR: 12). When Bakhtin speaks of carnival and its laughter he has in mind, however, all the great folk festivals of the Middle Ages and the Renaissance: the Feast of Fools, the Feast of the Ass, and the Easter and Christmas Laughters known to the Christian world, yet closely akin to the Saturnalia and other ancient festivities and theatrical performances.

In his attempt to make us understand again the halfforgotten idiom of farce, Bakhtin explains that:

> Celebrations of a carnival type represented a considerable part of the life of medieval men, even in the time given over to them.

Large medieval cities devoted an average of three months a year to these festivities. The influence of the carnival spirit was irresistible: it made a man renounce his official state as monk, cleric, scholar, and perceive the world in its laughing aspect. Not only schoolmen and minor clerics but hierarchs and learned theologians indulged in gay recreation as relaxation from pious seriousness. "Monkish pranks" (Joca monacorum) was the title of one of the most popular medieval comic pieces. Confined to their cells, monks produced parodies or semiparodies of learned treatises and other droll Latin compositions (BakR: 13). Laughter penetrated, we are told, "the highest forms of religious cult and thought" (BakR: 13), and this is attested to by an enormous number of Latin manuscripts extant.

The result of such festive periods was a temporary suspension (both ideal and real) of all hierarchical rank and the admission of extraordinary forms of communication. Speech and gesture were those of the marketplace: frank and free and disallowing any and all distance between those who came into contact with one another. All habitual norms of decency and etiquette were abandoned. All this is amply reflected in the work of Rabelais, with its abundance of imagery "of the human body with its food, drink, defecation, and sexual life" (BakR: 18) as well as the exaggerated forms that such bodily images there assume. But Bakhtin reminds us also that references to the body were, in this context, not felt to be obscene but had rather a "positive, assertive character" (BakR: 19). While they were meant to degrade and bring down to earth all that was too high, too spiritual, too ideal, and too abstract, they were viewed, nevertheless, in their cosmic aspect of life coming into existence and decaying. Such bodily images, Bakhtin insists, had little to do with "the body and its physiology in the modern sense of these words," because the body was not individualized. "The material bodily principle is contained, not in the biological individual, not in the bourgeois ego, but in the people, a people who are continually growing and renewed. This is why all that is bodily becomes grandiose, exaggerated, im-

measurable" (Bak*R:*19), and why "degradation here means
. . . the contact with earth as an element that swallows up and
gives birth at the same time. To degrade is to bury, to sow,
and to kill simultaneously, in order to bring forth something
more and better" (Bak*R:*21). It is in this sense that "carnival's
hell represents the earth which swallows up and gives birth"
and is "often transformed into a cornucopia; the monster,
death, becomes pregnant" (Bak*R:*91).

As is well known and pictorially recorded in Brueghel's
canvases, hell was an essential part of the setting for carnival,
and being able to laugh about it, removed, during carnival, all
fear of it. His creative fantasy made man the victor over his
fears just as the Imaginary Invalid, in the carnival scene, was to
be victorious over the death whose threat perpetually dogged
him. Bakhtin proclaims such carnivalesque laughter not only
"a victory over mystic terror of God, but also a victory over
the awe inspired by the forces of nature, and most of all over
the oppression and guilt related to all that was consecrated and
forbidden (mana and taboo). It was the defeat of divine and
human power, of authoritarian commandments, of death and
punishment after death, hell and all that is more terrifying than
the earth itself" (Bak*R:*90–91). Indeed, this fantasy defeat of
authority itself acquired religious overtones when, in secu-
larized versions of the Feast of Fools, "the solemn decorum of
cathedral services would be suddenly turned upside down as
the inferior clergy heard the glad tidings that 'He hath put
down the mighty from their seats, and exalted them of low
degree' (Deposuit potentes de sedes: et exaltavit humiles)
(Bar*S:*25). Rabelais' Pantagruel expresses a similar sentiment
when he declares that God "often wishes his glory to be mani-
fested in the confounding of the wise, the humbling of the
mighty, and the raising up of the simple and humble"
(R*G:*408).

The social importance of such feasts has not escaped histo-
rians and anthropologists, and Enid Welsford describes them as
follows:

The great seasonal festivals in Christian Europe have a twofold aspect: on the one hand they are occasions for solemn worship, on the other hand they are wild times of feasting, lawlessness and buffoonery. Shrovetide is a season when a good Christian confesses his sins, but it is also the Carnival, when the sober citizen will put on a mask and adopt the behaviour of the fool; the Christmas season was once an equally wild time. . . . But not only were the festivals treated as seasons of lawlessness and buffoonery when all revellers behaved foolishly, they were also marked by the performance of certain traditional dances and games, the performers of which were grotesquely disguised and regarded as fools. (WF:70)

The dances and games Welsford alludes to are the English mummery plays and morris dances as well as the German *Fastnachtspiele* that combine scapegoat rites with celebrations of nature's changing seasons in such a way that the fool as central figure is frequently killed and later resurrected. Since these more formalized presentations seem to have been inserted into otherwise spontaneous and unruly manifestations of the revellers, they may explain the barely marked transition from popular festivals to stage performances. Bakhtin's study of Rabelais is among the first to shed light on the transition of carnivalesque expression from popular festivities to farcical narratives and theater of the Middle Ages and the Renaissance. It has thereby provided us with new insights:

"Carnival," Bakhtin maintains, "celebrated temporary liberation from the prevailing truth and from the established order; it marked the suspension of all hierarchical rank, privileges, norms, and prohibitions. Carnival was the true feast of time, the feast of becoming, change, and renewal. It was hostile to all that was immortalized and completed" (BakR:10). It was the enemy of all that represented pompous authority, incapable of recognizing its own imperfections and evanescence. It laughed at rigidity and at the individual's exaggerated notion of his own importance, considering him but a link in the great dance of death. Its spirit is echoed in farce and in the entire work of Rabelais, who laughingly condemned all those incapable of acknowledging their own foolishness by laughing at themselves. He mockingly called them *agelasts,** beings incapable of understanding that in the course of nature the old (winter) must give way to the young (spring), so that all pomposity and clinging to social hierarchy is ultimately overturned. In the spirit of carnival, Rabelais clownishly uncrowns the old, while triumphantly welcoming the new (RG:11).

A veritable despository of the carnivalesque comic, Rabelais' work reflects in many of its episodes a grotesque turning upside down of the world and a view of man as a mere link in the dance—not so much of death as of life. To realize this is to see meaning in some of his episodes dealing with birth and death that might otherwise seem merely burlesque and possibly embarrassing. When Gargamelle gives birth to Gargantua, for instance, the baby rises from her bowels to her ears—a carnivalesque turning upside down of the world. But Gargantua's own wife dies when their son Pantagruel is born, and the father first mourns his wife Badebec, "newly dead," yet rejoices in his son "newly born, and so big and handsome [that] . . . his mind was troubled with the doubt whether he ought to weep in mourning for his wife, or laugh out of delight at his son" (RG:177). His lamentations for his good wife are grotesque, stressing only her physical and sexual qualities: "Ah, Badebec, my darling, my little coney—hers was a good three acres and two roods in size for all that—my tenderling, my codpiece, my shoe, my slipper, never shall I see you again . . . And as he spoke he bellowed like a cow. But when Pantagruel

---

* Rabelais seems to have created the word. In his *Dictionnaire de la Langue française au XVIe siècle* (Paris: Champion, 1925), Huguet lists *agelaste* and *agelastes* with exclusive reference to Rabelais: *Agelaste*—La calumnie de certains Canibales, misantropes, agelastes, avoit tant contre moy esté atroce et desraisonnée, qu'elle avoit vaincu ma patience. Rabelais IV, à Odet de Chastillon. *Agelastes*—poinct ne rians, tristes, facheux. Rabelais, IV, Briefve Declaration.—Ils ne furent onques tant sévère Caton, ne Crassus l'ayeul tant agelaste . . . qui n'eût perdu contenance. Rabelais, V, 24.

came into his mind, he suddenly began laughing like a calf"
(RG: 177). In this moment where life and death compete, it is
decidedly life that wins out. Gargantua has the fire blown up,
the candles lit, and the toast for soup cut up, as he decides that
"it's better to weep less and drink more" (RG: 178). He does
not even join the priests at his wife's funeral but rather stays
home to rock his son. The epitaph he composes in his wife's
honor is an ambivalent carnivalesque uncrowning as well as a
song of praise, for he realizes that death is inescapable and that
"the same fate hangs over our heads! God care for those who
remain alive! I must think of finding another" (RG: 179). It is
not Badebec the individual that counts but Badebec as mother
and wife, and in this function she can be replaced by another.
As often in carnivalesque celebrations, moreover, praise min-
gles with abuse.

Such degradation of the old, to which Gargantua here
gives verbal expression, was symbolized during popular festivities by means of clothes worn upside down or trousers slipped
over one's head, with the shift from top to bottom suggesting
the defeat of old age, death, or winter; and that from bottom to
top, new life, youth, and spring. The intake and elimination of
food constituted a similar symbolism with regard to life and
death and their simultaneous and ambivalent association with
both womb and tomb. Life and death were seen as being in
perpetual flux, not only within the all-embracing rhythm of the
seasons but also with regard to the ambivalence of the meaning
of each. In this perspective upon life, the value of the individual
was minimal and his degradation therefore symbolic and impersonal, whether in festive play or literature. Suffering, both
physical and emotional, became thus neutralized, as it were,
and failed to evoke empathy within the spectator, since no one-
to-one relationship was established and all were both spectators
and participants in this world of universals.

Carnivalesque festivities were, of course, largely impro-
vised, and the calendar itself set limits to all overindulgence in
food and drink that accompanied them. In cities of the Rhine-

land, the "spirit of carnival," *Hoppeditzchen,* is even today carried to its grave at the end of the season of festivities and his coffin followed by a solemnly dressed group of "mourners." Yet the liberating force of carnivalesque laughter—felt to be so innocent by Baudelaire—was sometimes considered offensive by authorities and the philosophy that informed it suspect. Baudelaire's contemporaries were not the only ones to reject it. Medieval Feasts of Fools with their parodies of the sacred and their irreverence—even if clearly temporary—toward all worldly and clerical power often made these powers uneasy as to whether to welcome their make-believe as therapeutic or to feel threatened by their potential of turning from play to reality. On the whole, however, the festive juxtaposition of the sacred with the obscene, a carnivalesque turning upside-down of the world, was not only accepted but even indulged in by authorities of the Middle Ages and the Renaissance, who devised as many apologies for them as there were occasional outbursts of prohibitions against them. Only Reformation and Counter-Reformation could dampen the popular joy in temporary irreverence by giving parody the meaning of satire and fantasy that of actuality. For, as Bakhtin tells us, even as late as 1444, for instance, the formidable Paris School of Theology circulated a letter describing such feasts as gay diversions, necessary

> so that foolishness, which is our second nature and seems to be inherent in man might freely spend itself at least once a year. Wine barrels burst if from time to time we do not open them and let in some air. All of us men are barrels poorly put together, which would burst from the wine of wisdom, if this wine remains in a state of constant fermentation of piousness and fear of God. We must give it air in order not to let it spoil. This is why we permit folly on certain days so that we may later return with greater zeal to the service of God. (BakR: 75).

Bakhtin reminds us that Rabelais, whose work so richly reflects the popular spirit of carnival, did not eliminate from his

1524 edition the daring travesties of sacred texts, although he expurgated from it for reasons of prudence certain allusions to the Paris School of Theology, the Sorbonne (BakR:86). Rabelais could discover nothing offensive in the fact that Panurge, in seeking advice from Friar John as to whether he should marry or not, couched his words in the form of the litany, in praise of the male sexual parts, repeated 153 times and accompanied by the same number of flattering epithets (BakR:416). Nor could he or his contemporaries apparently see any wrong in his using Christ's last words on the cross—"sitio" (I thirst) and "consummatum est" (it is finished)—in a literal sense as applying to food and drink and thereby debasing them; or in his transforming the invitation "venite adoremus" (come, let us adore) into "venite apotemus" (come, let us drink) (BakR:86).

But it is only too obvious that none of this laughter could be acceptable to the weakening lines of authority in the times of the Reformation and Counter-Reformation. While, according to Bakhtin, Rabelais' language and style clearly influenced the first French translation of the Bible in 1535; while his work was read instead of the Bible at assemblies of French joyous societies (BakR:77, 101–2); while Montaigne, as late as 1580, could peruse Rabelais' writings and those of Boccaccio with intense pleasure (BakR:65)—society was nevertheless soon to take issue with the absolute comic of this writer who extolled the virtues of eating and drinking wine, who paid homage to the powers of nature that govern the human body, and who failed to take individual and social decorum seriously. Bakhtin recalls that in the latter part of the seventeenth century, the French satirist La Bruyère severely censored Rabelais' "filth," while admiring his humanistic ideas. To illustrate how widely held was this view in eighteenth-century France, the Russian scholar quotes a note Voltaire wrote before 1758:

> Rabelais in his extravagant and unintelligible book let loose an extreme jollity and an extreme impertinence; he poured out erudition, filth and boredom; you will get a good story two pages long, at the price of two volumes of nonsense. Only a few ec-

centric persons pride themselves on understanding and esteem-
ing this work as a whole; the rest of the nation laughs at the
jokes of Rabelais and holds his book in contempt. He is
regarded as chief among buffoons; we are annoyed that a man
who had so much wit should have made such wretched use of it;
he is a drunken philosopher who wrote only when he was
drunk. (BakR:116–17)

It is obvious that Voltaire could neither appreciate the absolute comic nor grasp its underlying philosophy; he was, in
that sense as in many other ways, the heir of French classicism.
For the trouble Molière encountered should not be explained
entirely—as it has frequently been—on the basis of personal
rivalries and animosities; it must be seen also as a clash between
imagination nourished by a tradition of the absolute comic and
a growing desire of dignitaries of church and state to suppress
this comic and replace it with the significative. Molière's comedies reflect this development, but they also reflect his stubborn
adherence to the carnivalesque and its perspective on life: hence
his quarrels over *L'Ecole des femmes, Tartuffe, Dom Juan,* and *Le
Malade imaginaire.* With their stress on individual dignity and
responsibility, Reformation and Counter-Reformation ushered
in an era that failed—though with some notable exceptions—to
appreciate the spirit of the absolute comic and farce and was
capable only of grasping the significative. Only in this century
have we slowly come to recognize that this failure of the past
resulted in neglect of those works of literature that partake of
the carnivalesque. Only recently have we come to see again
what Euripides understood centuries ago and made the central
idea of his *Bacchae,* namely, the harm that is done whenever
farcical laughter is suppressed—even if those responsible for its
suppression are inspired by the highest ideals.

In his *Bacchae* (EuB:10), Euripides shows the destruction of
all those who, precisely because of their purity of heart and insistence on rationality at the expense of all else, defy the powers
of nature and thereby, symbolically, those of Dionysus. God of
wine and all reproductive forces in nature, Dionysus was also

revered as the god of creative imagination and of theater in particular. In Euripides' tragedy, Dionysus, having come from Asia to Thebes, claims to be a son of Zeus, "changed in shape from God to man" (EuB: 227). The wild joy and orgiastic behavior associated with his worship is offensive to Pentheus, the young king of Thebes, who vows to destroy the stranger and corruptor of morals:

> "That wand shall cease its music, and that drift
> Of tossing curls lie still—when my rude sword
> Falls between neck and trunk! 'Tis all his word,
> This tale of Dionysus. . . ." (EuB: 235)

To the virtuous king, even Teiresias' plea to submit to the power of Dionysus and to acknowledge him is of no avail, so that Pentheus not only becomes the butt of laughter but actually perishes altogether:

> "King Pentheus! Dream not thou that force is power;
> Nor, if thou hast a thought, and that thought sour
> And sick, oh, dream not thought is wisdom!—Up,
> Receive this God to Thebes; pour forth the cup
> Of sacrifice, and pray, and wreath thy brow." (EuB: 237)

Pentheus cannot acknowledge that men are fools. He will never submit to the power of the vine, never see the wisdom and consolation that may be found in Dionysus's grape—as Rabelais was to do centuries later. He therefore cannot defend himself against the powers of nature once they flood in upon him, and he is destroyed by the very women—his sisters, his mother—now blinded by the passions from whose natural flow he had tried too hard to protect them. In condemning Rabelais' absolute comic, Voltaire assumed the role of Pentheus toward Dionysus, as it were, and the god might have seen fit to punish him with death. But Rabelais, in a comic rather than a tragic mode, would have called both Pentheus and Voltaire *agelasts,* worthy of destruction by laughter. This raises not only the question of crime and punishment in the realm of the carnivalesque—a question I shall discuss in chapter 2—but also that of the proximity of the tragic and the comic, so that we feel challenged once more to discover the "rules" that make us either laugh or cry.

It did not occur to Baudelaire to compare tragedy and comedy. Such comparisons seem the prerogative of our century, scientific, not so much in the earlier sense of careful classifications, but rather in searching for and recognizing underlying structures, revealing similarities and dissimilarities and, thereby, hidden meanings. Quite recently René Girard assumed the task of such a comparison in an essay exploring the precarious balance between tears and laughter. (GiPB). He was intrigued by the structural similarities between a scene in Sophocles' fifth-century B.C. *Oedipus Rex* and one in Molière's seventeenth-century comedy *Le Bourgeois gentilhomme*. Molière's wealthy old Would-be Gentleman, anxious to acquire the education and demeanor expected of a nobleman, surrounds himself with four teachers, paid to provide him with culture, instantaneously. But these teachers—each imbued with his importance—spend little time teaching and instead "argue heatedly about the merits of their respective disciplines. According to the dancing master, music would not be much without dancing. According to the music master, dancing without music would not exist at all. According to the fencing master, even musicians and dancers need good fencing occasionally, in order not to cease to exist. . . . A fourth man appears, the philosopher in residence. . . . With a learned reference to Seneca's treatise on anger, he steps into the midst of the quarrel to put an end to it" (GiPB:811). But since he tries to appease the others by telling them that philosophy is, after all, more important than all other disciplines, he only adds fuel to the ongoing quarrel.

Structurally, as Girard easily convinces us, the situation among the three male figures of *Oedipus Rex*—Oedipus, Creon, and Teiresias—at the beginning of that tragedy is al-

most identical to that of Molière's four teachers. They clash
with equal violence because each indulges in similar delusions
of personal grandeur as they all discuss the means of solving
the problem of the plague that ravages the city of Thebes. The
capacity of a situation to be either tragic or comic led Girard
first to ponder why the effects of tragedy are different from
those of comedy and, second, to study the physical properties
of these effects, namely, those of tears and laughter. On closer
scrutiny, crying and laughing both proved to be physiological
convulsions that differed only in degree and seemed to result in
a medical purification reminiscent of Aristotle's notion of catharsis—so mysterious and mystifying a concept that it has been
interpreted throughout the ages in physiological as well as numerous psychological ways. Girard's deliberations, although
they concern themselves mainly with tears and laughter as
physiological phenomena, take into consideration that tragedy
and comedy not only share a number of situations of the kind
already singled out but also may be based on identical myths
capable of moving us either to tears or laughter. And it is the
enigma of *what* brings about *which* reaction, as well as our interpretation of the signs provided, that is crucial to any reader
or spectator—not just the critic or theoretician—,because it af-
fects our acceptance or rejection of a work of literature and that
means ultimately our understanding of it. Our reaction to Nabokov's *Lolita* may depend on whether we view it as a realistic
narrative or a hilarious parody, or as both. When Rousseau
proclaimed Molière's *Misanthrope* to be a tragedy he apparently
imposed upon it meanings that differed from those its author
had in mind when he wrote it a century earlier and called it a
comedy.

Girard realized that the tragic plot of Racine's *Andromaque*
could easily be summarized in such a way as to make it appear
comic. All that is needed to achieve this feat is a certain distancing permitting us to recognize the relationships among the
main characters as a mechanism. Once we no longer view the
characters as individuals struggling between the passions of

love and jealousy, they appear to be puppets moving to a prescribed pattern that is comic in its repetitiveness: "Orestes loves
Hermione who does not love him. Hermione loves Pyrrhus
who does not love her. Pyrrhus loves Andromaque who does
not love him. Andromaque loves Hector who cannot love any-
more, being dead" (GiPB:817). One can easily agree with
Girard that, in the tragic mode, the individuality of the protagonist is of foremost importance, whereas, in the comic mode,
the sovereignty of the individual is minimized to an extent that
makes us aware of a hidden clockwork which controls him
(GiPB:816). Indeed, the validity of this observation becomes
strikingly apparent if we compare Ionesco's recent play *Macbett*
with Shakespeare's *Macbeth,* whose plot and characters the
French playwright appropriated without significant changes.
The contemporary play is a parody verging on the grotesque.
Shakespeare presents individuals and, with subtle psychology,
reveals their secret desires, their struggles between loyalty and
ambition, their drowning in the pools of blood they shed, and
their collapse under the burden of guilt they heap upon themselves. Ionesco shows these same characters as if they were
mere puppets pulled hither and thither by the machine they set
in motion by means of murder and which continues to engen-
der murder in geometric progression. The play's generals are
dressed alike and, in automaton-like movements and speech,
convey the impression of objects impersonal and interchangeable. The effect is as grotesque as that of Goethe's
Sorcerer's Apprentice, who, having learned the magic formula,
can turn the broom into a servant that carries water for him
from the well, but was never taught how to stop him: What
started out as a boon has turned into a nightmare. In its gro-
tesqueness and underlying seriousness, Ionesco's *Macbett* is
vivid proof of the subtle line that divides the tragic from the
comic and sometimes allows both to exist side by side, one
reflecting upon the other and altering it. Socrates' argument in
Plato's *Symposium* concerning the ability of a comic playwright

to compose tragedies may well be considered testimony to this proximity of the comic and the tragic.

In the eighteenth century, in the Preface to his *Mariamne,* Voltaire discussed the proximity of tragedy and comedy in the face of critics who maintained that this tragedy did not adhere to the Aristotelian tenets of the genre (VŒ). They found its subject matter lacking in the scope and universality required of tragedy and put it down as being no more than a conjugal quarrel between an amorous old husband and a young wife unwilling to submit to his embraces—as a subject for comedy, in other words (VŒ: 167). Defending the play, Voltaire—proving himself a structuralist before the invention of the term—argued that a number of tragedies by his great dramatic predecessor Racine, for instance, *Britannicus, Phèdre,* and *Mithridate,* had similar plots and also dealt with intimate human passions rather than with matters of state. Racine's *Mithridate* is, he claimed, fundamentally the story of an old father in love with a young woman who is also loved by his two sons, and it is through an ancient, not very elegant trick, that the father ascertains to whom her heart belongs. Phèdre is a stepmother, encouraged by an old go-between to reveal her passion for him to her stepson, who proves to be in love with another. Nero (in *Britannicus*) is an impetuous young man who, having fallen in love with the young Junie bethrothed to his rival Britannicus, not only decides to divorce his wife and marry Junie but also hides behind a curtain to eavesdrop on her conversation with her beloved.★

Once embarked on his quest for tragic plot structures that might also serve comedy, Voltaire discovered that in Molière's *L'Avare* (The Miser, whose plot the playwright derived from a comedy by Plautus) the same fundamental relationship among characters prevailed as in *Mithridate.* The Miser is an old man

★Voltaire might have referred also to a number of Greek tragedies, e.g., *Phèdre's* predecessor *Hippolytus* and, above all, Sophocles' *Trachiniae,* whose protagonist bids his son to kill him and marry his mistress.

wooing the young woman his son loves, though neither of
them realizes at first that he is the other's rival. In both tragedy
and comedy, it is the young man who ultimately marries
the woman. Yet Molière's comedy produces laughter, while
Racine's tragedy moves to tears. The situation is puzzling, but
as Voltaire tried to account for it, he began to play down the
importance of plot and to stress instead the social status of the
characters involved. He thought it appropriate that we laugh at
an old bourgeois miser and equally fitting that we should be
moved to tears by a weakness of the admirable old king. His
argument is in keeping with Aristotelian notions of the dif-
ference between the characters of tragedy and comedy. According to the *Poetics,* those in tragedy are elevated, usually kings
and princes, those in comedy of a more lowly status and often
ludicrous. For the sake of defending his tragedy, Voltaire also
used another argument to be found in Aristotle's *Poetics,*
namely, that the language of tragedy is elevated, that of comedy taken from ordinary life.

Yet in spite of Voltaire's defense, we cannot but realize
that the structural pattern of *Mariamne* was so much the property of comedy and had occurred so frequently and with such
infinite variations on its plot in scenarios of the commedia
dell'arte, that is, of Italian farce, that entire theatrical companies
were composed in conformity with it. Troupes usually consisted of two amorous young couples, three old men—the lecherous and rich Pantalone, his counterpart or double, the
doctor, often from Bologna, and the braggard captain
Spavento—and finally, servants—two or more *zanni,* one a
rogue, the other a glutton. The average company thus had
from ten to twelve actors, whose orchestration of characters
and masks lent itself to an endless number of constellations and
variations on the basic plot, which invariably concluded with
the victory of the young over the old men. The interest, however, was seldom provided by the young lovers but rather by
the grotesque old misers and lechers (usually wearing masks)
and the ingenious servants (also masked and often disguised for

the sake of the plot), who took upon themselves the roles of masterminding the defeat of the cleverly manipulating old men. Youth was destined to win out, against all the laws of society but quite in keeping with those of nature. The visible theatrical division between the young and the old corresponded, moreover, to another division that affected the human relationships among these groups. The old men were either fathers or potential fathers-in-law of the young men and, because they were frequently suitors of the young women, turned out to be their sons' rivals. The old represented the establishment; the young were dependent on them in every sense of the word, so that the often fierce and unequal struggle between old and young could end happily for the young only with the help of the clever servants or of fortunate coincidences.

This comic structure is so ancient and so pervasive and still so prevalent in Shakespearean comedy that Northrop Frye thinks of it as the paradigm for all comedy (Fry*AC*). He is undoubtedly correct when he believes this victory of youth over old age to have its origin partly in spring rites, but he is less convincing, it seems to me, when he defines comic plots in general as "a ritual moving toward a scapegoat rejection followed by a marriage" and the theme of comedy as "a dream pattern of irrational desire in conflict with reality" (Fry*AC*: 112). Northrop Frye speaks of the "mythoi or general plot" of comedy as one of "a young man who wants to marry a young woman" but whose "desire is resisted by some opposition, usually paternal" until "near the end of the play some twist in the plot enables the hero to have his will" and harmony reigns (Fry*AC*: 163). But it is difficult to ignore the fact that Frye's formulae fail to include either the farce found in modern literature or the very elements that, in times past, added comedy to the usually insipid romance of the young by provoking a comic of the kind Baudelaire designated as grotesque, absolute, or farcical. The old men were not simply—as Frye has it—father figures, father surrogates, or what he calls "heavy fathers," and "blocking characters" that delay the final harmony. By mini-

mizing their grotesque qualities and those of the ever present
servants, whom he doesn't even mention, the critic stresses
only the "significative" elements of such comedy. He thus ex-
cludes from the realm of the comic all that is absolute and, in
the case of Molière, for instance, arrives at a total misinterpre-
tation and underrating of his genius when he states that "in
Molière we have a simple but fully tested formula in which the
ethical interest is focused on a single blocking character, a
heavy father, a miser, a misanthrope, a hypocrite, or a hypo-
chondriac" (Fry*AC*:167). His stress on final harmony as the
end of comedy concerns only the lovers and overlooks the importance of what is most fundamental in the absolute comic,
the scapegoat who makes possible the lovers' union in many
comedies and farces. His erroneous view would deal a shatter-
ing blow to classic French notions of comedy and tragedy: it
would crush Voltaire's argument and declare Racine's *Mithridate* a comedy. One might say that Frye's definition of comedy
omits the comic, and therefore cannot satisfy us here.

That the father/son struggle, so prominent in comedies of
the commedia dell'arte type and present also in tragedy, came
to arouse the interest of psychoanalysts was to be expected. It
prompted them also to speculate on the proximity of the tragic
and the comic. The French psychocritic, Mauron (Mau*P*), who
rightly considered the youth/old-age pattern an essential in-
gredient of ancient as well as comedia dell'arte and mo-
lièresque comedy, defined it as oedipal. In Molière's *Ecole des
femmes* (*School for Wives*), for instance, he discerned the following schema:

> son (greenhorn)——woman : Horace——Agnès
> father (greybeard)   : Arnolphe

If we stress its oedipal aspects, the comedy's plot may be
summarized as follows:

> Arnolphe, the rich middle-aged bachelor, is about to marry his
> young ward Agnès, an orphan he has brought up in cloistered

isolation and totally untutored so as to assure for himself a wife too naive to cuckold him. Young Horace, the son of a long absent friend, has come to seek his advice and financial assistance while awaiting the arrival of his father. He is well received, and, by pure accident, notices Agnès seated on her balcony in a neighboring house. The two innocents fall instantly in love with each other, so that without knowing her identity or her relationship to his fatherly friend, Horace has become Arnolphe's rival. Of course, he ultimately wins Agnès, in spite of Arnolphe's desperate manipulations to keep her under lock and key.

If Arnolphe is seen as a father figure and Horace as the son (their relationship might warrant such a view), then their vying for the same young woman's heart might possibly be assumed to be oedipal rivalry. But this assumption still raises the question as to what makes this oedipal struggle the property of comedy when, in Racine's *Mithridate* or his *Phèdre,* an analogous situation is to be found in the realm of tragedy.

In an attempt to find an answer, Mauron refers us to a study by Jekels (Je*P*) that considers the question of guilt the crucial determinator. In tragedy, Jekels had observed, it is the son who is guilty; in comedy, it is the father. The son's guilt consists in his interference in his father's love relationship; that of the father, in vying with the son for the love of the young woman. But the punishment of the guilty son is usually death and the result tragedy, whereas the punishment of the guilty father is degradation and laughter—hence, comedy. By implication, Jekels touches on the interesting questions of tragic versus comic guilt and justice, questions that seem to me crucial in determining comic laughter, especially since they transcend any individual "father/son" rivalry and deal with relationships that, in comedy, are oedipal only in the widest, that is, the archetypal sense of the term in which it is compatible with spring rites. As anthropologists and psychoanalysts remind us, in societies that celebrate such nature rites, "the horizontal organization of age groups obviates personal conflict in the sense of a hostile father-son relationship, because the terms 'father' and 'son' connote group characteristics and not personal relations. The older men are 'fathers', the young men 'sons', and this collective group solidarity is paramount. Conflicts, so far as they exist at all, are between the age groups and have a collective and archetypal, rather than a personal and individual, character" (Ne*OC*: 141).

Such recent findings in anthropology and folklore infuse with new meaning those statements in Aristotle's *Poetics* (Ast*P*) that relate to the common origins of tragedy and comedy but for a long time have seemed irrelevant and insignificant. We are told by Aristotle that both genres started with improvisations during Dionysian rites. In each, a poet, imbued with the spirit of Dionysus, that is, one who imbibed wine, led a chorus in song and dance. The performance was tragic when inspired by the dithyrambs of satyrs, comic when consisting of Phallic rhythms and lyrics. The philosopher tells us that at the time of his writing (the fourth century B.C.) many Greek cities known to him still engaged in such improvisations in honor of Dionysus, while theaters staged the tragedies and comedies of the greatest Greek playwrights, whose work had grown out of such festivities. Though choruses were still a part of theatrical performances, the improvising poet-leader had long since been replaced by two or more actors. One poet's epic tale had become tragedy; another's lampooning—comedy. A few additional remarks in the *Poetics* inform us that comedy was written by poets with an inferior bent and dealt with lowly characters and the ludicrous, while the tragic action moved on elevated levels and involved kings and princes. In contrast to that of tragedy, the plot of comedy moved from unhappiness to happiness.

Even this scant outline of the common origin of the genres and their eventual differentiation into comedy—grotesque phallic revelry that ended happily—and tragedy, "an imitation of an action," shows comedy as belonging to the realm of fantasy and play rather than mimesis. Erich Neumann reminds us that in seasonal fertility rites

> the representative of the old year or year-cycle was just as young as the new king who succeeded him after his death. Only by virtue of his identification with the year was he symbolically old and therefore doomed to die. The lamentation which even in quite late times was followed, without any pause, by resurrection testifies to the ritual nature of this sacrifice. It also disproves the naturalistic explanation that the vegetation was killed by the summer heat and rose again in the spring. That would be to assume that between death and resurrection there lay a period of draught and wintertime—a spell of some duration, which is not at all the case. On the contrary the resurrection—originally that of the new king—followed immediately upon the death of the old. The conflict between the two kings was only symbolical and not a factual conflict between young and old. (N*OC*: 184–85).

The observation that the sacrifice in these rites was only symbolical, not real, throws significant light upon the part played by the scapegoat—in this case the king. Such make-believe is in sharp contrast to the reality of what René Girard believes to be the true origin of tragedy: a communal violence, occasioned by vague feelings of guilt, that must spend itself and succeeds in doing so if it finds a victim it can accuse and whose immolation seems to redeem the guilt of all (Gi*VS:*121, *passim*). Although there is never in evidence a logical link of cause and effect in such mass behavior, a group catharsis is magically effected.

It is Freud to whom we owe one of the most remarkable analyses of such tragic scapegoat rites:

> But why had the Hero of tragedy to suffer? and what was the meaning of his 'tragic guilt'? I will cut the discussion short and give a quick reply. He had to suffer because he was the primal father, the Hero of great primaeval tragedy which was being re-enacted with a tendentious twist; and the tragic guilt

was the guilt which he had to take on himself in order to relieve the Chorus from theirs. The scene upon the stage was derived from the historical scene through a process of systematic distortion—one might even say, as the product of a refined hypocrisy. In the remote reality it had actually been the members of the Chorus who caused the Hero's suffering; now, however, they exhausted themselves with sympathy and regret and it was the Hero himself who was responsible for his own sufferings. The crime which was thrown on to his shoulders, presumptuousness and rebelliousness against a great authority, was precisely the crime for which the members of the Chorus, the company of brothers, were responsible. Thus the tragic Hero became, though it might be against his will, the redeemer of the Chorus.

In Greek tragedy the special subject-matter of the performance was the sufferings of the divine goat, Dionysus, and the lamentation of the goats who were his followers and who identified themselves with him. That being so, it is easy to understand how drama, which had become extinct, was kindled into fresh life in the Middle Ages around the passion of Christ. (Fre*TT*:156)

What is important in this conception of tragedy is that the tragic scapegoat rites, if they were, indeed, reminiscent of that original murder of the father whose memory still weighs upon the conscience of mankind, assumed mimetic aspects: death was "real" within the framework of the play; whereas in comedy, the "killing" of the king was merely symbolical and, as make-believe, could induce laughter. Although such laughter was imbued with its own kind of violence, the spectator knew that the beatings administered to the scapegoat were not fatal, that its ejection was only simulated, and its death only apparent. Such awareness on the part of the spectator that what he sees is play creates a distance between him and the victim that prevents commiseration or pity and makes possible the detachment needed for laughter. The protagonist of comedy is killed by laughter rather than by a sword. But we must once more ask how we are to know whether a scapegoat ejection is tragic or comic, if, indeed, the game we are playing is one of discovering the rules.

Why do we not shed tears over the fate of the carpenter in Chaucer's *The Miller's Tale?* The carpenter is as upright and virtuous as Pentheus, whose death we find tragic. He loves his young wife, who cruelly deceives him and makes him the laughing stock of their town. And should we not condemn the widow of Ephesus who vowed to die beside her dead husband, but readily forgets her grief for the sake of a newfound lover, willing to allow her husband's corpse to be strung up on a gallows to conceal her lover's negligence and save him from death? Why did Baudelaire, in describing the English mime scene, record no moral indignation on the part of the audience, although a poor woman was not only robbed of her meager possessions but also of the tools of her trade—her broom, her mop, her bucket, even the water needed to do her work? Why do we laugh freely and without resentment at the Would-be Gentleman of Molière—made a scapegoat in spite of his many sterling qualities? Indeed, we even rejoice at the union of young Horace and Agnès in *The School For Wives,* although it shatters the dreams of a fine bourgeois who had envisioned honest marriage, free of its ordinary danger. Isn't Arnolphe, so crudely deceived by his ward and a young man he befriended, worthy rather of our sympathy? Is he not tragic? The answers to these questions are closely associated with those of crime and punishment in comedy, as we shall see later. They are also linked with our anticipation of "tragedy" as mimesis and "comedy" as play belonging to the field of nonreality and fantasy. If they can answer such questions, literary terms assume functions that go beyond nominalism and begin to serve as guideposts.

Gregory Bateson (Bat*P*), observing animals, gave a remarkable account of the complexities and paradox of play and fantasy. He witnessed two young monkeys "playing at " combat, that is, engaged in combat without being truly engaged in it. The monkeys went through all the customary motions of combat, but it was clear to Bateson that they were only pretending and that they knew that they were pretending: their biting was not dangerous; their threats were not meant to be believed. Bateson concluded that the monkeys had ways of communicating to each other that they were "playing." They were apparently exchanging messages to that effect. But the message "this is play" is always fraught with difficulty. It is as paradoxical as

> all statements made within this frame are untrue.
>
> I love you.
>
> I hate you.

The statement "this is play" implies that what is expressed is not to be taken to mean what it seems to express. It thereby introduces elements of irony and distancing into the relationship existing between the sender and the receiver of the message—whether they are animal or human. The possibility of playing depends, in fact, on the effectiveness of the signals that define certain activities as play and as a fantasy rather than the real thing. The activity is set off, "framed," as it were, and the frame helps us in our interpretation of it—even if its nature is paradoxical. Whether in religious rite or theater, the "frame" is a metacommunication telling us something about itself, namely, "this is play" (Bat*P*: 177–93). In literature, especially in works written for the theater, such terms as "tragedy" and "comedy" have helped us traditionally to establish frames. While to some extent all literature is play as compared to discursive writing, the term tragedy announces a work as mimetic, while the absolute comic usually conveys the message that it is an expression of the author's creative mind, a fantasy, and thus, doubly, play.

In our quest for the rules, it is imporant, however, to realize at what price participants in a game—whether animal or human—misinterpret such metacommunication. Bateson mentions a custom prevailing in the Adaman Islands where "peace is concluded after each side has been given ceremonial freedom to strike the other" (BatP:182). If the peacemaking blows are "mistaken for 'real' blows of combat . . . the peacemaking ceremony becomes a battle" (BatP:182). Johan Huizinga's mention of slanging matches comes to mind, a custom so prevalent in Greek culture that "the word *iambos* is held by some to have meant originally 'derision,' " but one also widespread in early Germanic literatures (HuHL:68). One of the slanging matches singled out by the Dutch scholar as typical not only reveals an enjoyment in playful abuse and taunts but also the danger inherent in such situations whenever the message "This is play" has not come across: "The Langobard chieftains have been invited to a royal banquet by Turisind, king of the Gapidae. When the king falls to lamenting his son Turismond, slain in battle against the Langobards, another of his sons stands up and begins to bait the Langobards with taunts (in the Latin original: iniuriis lacessere coepit) . . . whereupon one of the Langobards answers. . . . The king restrains the two from coming to blows, and 'then they bring the banquet to a merry end' (laetis animis convivium peragunt)" (HuHL:69). Huizinga is convinced that the last words leave no doubt about "the playful character of the altercation." But it is equally obvious that, without the king's intervention, the blows might have become "real" and that the nature of the king's intervention had to be understood by all as part of the game for them to be able to sit down afterwards to an amicable feast. As reality, the blows meant war; as play, they meant performance and farcical comedy.

The character of such slanging matches was clearly preserved in the lovers' quarrels of the commedia dell'arte, so much a standard fare of such theater that all the how-to books of the trade provided skeleton patterns upon which actors and

actresses could "improvise" according to need. The following
brief excerpt of a sample altercation between lovers may give
some notion of the customary playful abuse:

> WOMAN: You tied . . .
>
> MAN: You forged . . .
>
> W: Hatred . . .
>
> M: Contempt . . .
>
> W: You will destroy . . .
>
> M: You will reject . . .
>
> W: I say that I hate you . . .
>
> M: I say that I detest you . . .
>
> W: Our knot is untied . . .
>
> M: Our bond is destroyed . . . (PA:100–2)

In Shakespeare's comedies, abuse in the form of dazzling verbal
playfulness usually ends in reconciliation, and it is interesting to
realize that much of our contemporary theater has revived the
slanging match pattern of insult and reconciliation, though
putting it to use in less traditional ways. In Beckett's *Waiting
For Godot* (BeWG), the two bums Vladimir and Estragon, having nothing to do, nowhere to go, and doomed to waiting for
Godot, begin to quarrel, just to pass the time. When they are
about to get into a fist fight, Estragon suggests: "That's the
idea, let's abuse each other." Stage directions indicate that they
turn, move away from each other, turn again to face each
other, and begin to insult one another:

> VLADIMIR: Moron!
>
> ESTRAGON: Vermin!
>
> V: Abortion!
>
> E: Morpion!
>
> V: Sewer-rat!
>
> E: Curate!
>
> V: Cretin!

E: Crritic! (*with finality*)

V: Oh! (*He wilts, vanquished, and turns away.*)

E: Now let's make it up. (Be*WG:* 48)

It is all a game. They refer to it as playing ball. In Ionesco's *Macbett* (Io*M*) the slanging match pattern is utilized by Banco and Macbett to express their growing hatred for Duncan with snowballing intensity; Duncan becomes their scapegoat:

BANCO: This blood we have spilled for him . . .

MACBETT: The dangers he involves us in . . .

B: He owes us everything . . .

M: Even more.

B: [We demand] the right to increase our wealth.

M: Autonomy.

B: To be master of my own territory.

M: He must be driven from it. (Io*M:* 70; my translation)

We cannot deny Huizinga's observation, of course, that a conscious deviation from mimesis is essential to all literature, even that which calls itself realistic. But it is true also that playfulness has always been associated with theater and with comedy in particular, as indicated by the terms employed in Romance and Germanic languages to designate them—as the Dutch scholar has so abundantly shown. These languages often use the same words for presenting drama, for the drama itself, and for playing games or joking. This has such significant bearing on our discussion of comedy and the comic that we might well listen to Huizinga:

Attic comedy grew out of the licentious *komos* at the feast of Dionysus. Only at a later phase did it become a consciously literary exercise and even then, in the days of Aristophanes, it bears numerous traces of its Dionysian past. In the so-called *parabasis,* the chorus, divided into rows and moving backwards and forwards, faces the audience and points out the victims with taunts and derision. The phallic costume of the players, the disguising of the chorus in animal masks are traits of remote antiquity. It is not merely from caprice that Aristophanes makes wasps, birds, and frogs the subject of his comedies; the whole tradition of the theriomorphic personification is at the back of it. (Hu*HL:*144)

Huizinga likens Aristophanic comedies to "festive antiphonal songs" of an earlier period, and there can be no doubt but that they resembled slanging matches, were abusive and licentious, and, above all, nonmimetic, and that it was essential to grasp their playfulness so as not to be offended by them. For if we assume with Huizinga that all theater is essentially ludic, then we must conclude that the absolute comic, in particular, appeals to man as *homo ludens,* and it is by announcing itself as belonging to this realm of the imagination that it prepares us to accept its lewdness, its violence, and its immorality as well as its special notions of justice—so different from those prevailing in tragedy.

This is brought out, strikingly, in a scene in Aristophanes' *The Archanians* (Aph*A*). In any tragedy, the protagonist Dicaeopolis would clearly be doomed rather than be the playwright's "good citizen." He has, in the midst of war, made a separate peace with the enemy, and his fellow citizens are about to kill him. As they approach his house, he comes out, leading in procession his household—his wife, daughter, and servants—all in honor of Bacchus. The ceremony they engage in is believed to resemble ancient phallic processions:

> DICAEOPOLIS (*comes out with a pot in his hand; he is followed by his wife, his daughter, who carries a basket, and two slaves who carry the phallus*): Peace, profane men! Let the basket-bearer come forward, and thou, Xanthias, hold the phallus well upright. Daughter, set down the basket and let us begin the sacrifice.
>
> DAUGHTER OF D. (*putting down the basket and taking out the sacred cake*): Mother, hand me the ladle that I may spread the sauce on the cake. (Aph*A:*437–38)

Dicaeopolis's procession is a defiance of his persecutors as well as a glorification of a life of the pleasures of the body. In tragedy he would have been presented as the pacifist, braving those grasping citizens who want war for selfish reasons and defending his views even at the risk of death. In this comedy, he never becomes anything but a comic, that is, a make-believe scapegoat. As the Chorus threatens to stone him, he sings his lewd and immoral hymn to Bacchus:

> DICAEOPOLIS: It is well! Oh, mighty Bacchus, it is with joy that, freed from military duty, I and all mine perform this solemn rite and offer thee this sacrifice; grant that I may keep the rural Dionysia without hindrance and that this truce of thirty years may be propitious for me. Come, my child, carry the basket gracefully and with a grave, demure face. Happy he who shall be your possessor and embrace you so firmly at dawn, that you fart like a weasel. Go forward, and have a care they don't snatch your jewels in the crowd. Xanthias, walk behind the basket-bearer and hold the phallus well erect; I will follow, singing the Phallic hymn; thou, wife, look on from the top of the terrace. Forward!
>
> (*He sings*) Oh, Phalés, companion of the orgies of Bacchus, night reveller, god of adultery and of pederasty, these past six years I have not been able to invoke thee. With what joy I return to my farmstead, thanks to the truce I have concluded, freed from cares, from fighting and from Lamachuses! How much sweeter, oh Phalés, Phalés, is it to surprise Thratta, the pretty woodmaid, Strymodorus' slave, stealing wood from Mount Phelleus, to catch her under the arms, to throw her on the ground and lay her, Oh, Phalés, Phalés! If thou wilt drink and bemuse thyself with me, we shall tomorrow consume some good dish in honour of the peace, and I will hang up my buckler over the smoking hearth.
>
> (*The procession reaches the place where the* CHORUS *is hiding.*)
>
> LEADER OF THE CHORUS: That's the man himself. Stone him, stone him, stone him, strike the wretch. All, all of you, pelt him, pelt him! (AphA: 438)

Yet, unlike a tragic hero, Dicaeopolis offers no noble reasons in defense of his actions. All he wants is to live what was considered by Aristophanes, and later by Rabelais, "the good life." Though he is forced to put his head on the block, he is saved from certain death by his wit. Imagination triumphs over the brute forces of reality, of both social and political justice, that demanded his death. His is a triumph of fantasy and a fantasy triumph, not unlike those of Molière's *Would-Be Gentleman* and *Imaginary Invalid*. There is little that is mimetic about this scene of a religious rite, with its sense of festivity, its costumes, its masks, and its slanging dialogue. These are the signs rather that convey to us the metacommunications: "This is play"; "we are not dealing with realities"; "we are in the realm of the imagination and of fantasy, where everything is permitted"; "what you see, the abasement, the insults, the beatings, the threat of execution—is not what it is"; "it is something else"; "you are invited to accept this paradox"; "you may laugh about lewdness and immorality because they are not measured by ethical standards." If we grasp this metacommunication, this "frame" wherein all we see and hear is enclosed, we have entered the world of farce and the absolute comic. If we fail to do so, we may feel as offended by this absolute comic as were Pentheus of the *Bacchae;* some contemporaries of Molière; Voltaire; and many nineteenth- and early twentieth-century critics, among them Bergson and Freud.

Bergson was blind to and misunderstood all that was playfully carnivalesque in Molière's comedies and arrived at the erroneous conclusion that "laughter singles out and would fain *correct*" individual defects such as the "rigid, the ready-made, the mechanical, in contrast with the supple, the ever-changing and the living, absent-mindedness in contrast with attention, in a word, automatism in contrast with free activity" (BerL: 145). While his insight into the essence of laughter was extraordinary and his description of the comic as "something mechanical encrusted upon the living" highly ingenious, one regrets that he could conceive of laughter only in terms of social morality and as "narrowed down to individuals and individually typical phenomena of social life," to speak in Bakhtinian terms (BakR:67). He did not take into consideration the absolute comic with its different morality. Like Freud after him, Bergson could conceive of liberating laughter and the degradation of what it laughs at only in terms of specific social norms and, thereby, failed to establish that wider perspecitve of human experience wherein laughter and tears reveal their common origin and we become aware of those "rules" that unite and separate them. Yet is is only if we can conceive of justice also *sub specie aeternitatis* rather than exclusively within society and localized as to time and place, that we may be able to fathom the meaning of farcical laughter and its choice of scapegoats. For as Huizinga, appropriately, quotes Plato: "God alone is worthy of supreme seriousness, but man is made God's plaything, and that is the best part of him. Therefore every man and woman should live life accordingly, and play the noblest games, and be of another mind from what they are at present. . . . Life must be lived as play, playing certain games, making sacrifices, singing and dancing, and then a man will be able to propitiate the gods, and defend himself against his enemies, and win in the contest" (HuHL:212).

two
Carnivalesque
Justice

WHAT then are the stakes in the game of the absolute comic?
If we accept the notion shared by Aristotle and a few contemporary critics and anthropologists that comedy and tragedy
have a common origin in religious rites; if we assume, moreover, that both genres end with the ejection or death of a scapegoat whose death is mimetic in tragedy and make-believe in
comedy, our continued quest for the "rules" of the game cannot ignore the question of the nature of the scapegoat and his
relationship to the play's hero. With regard to tragedy, the answer comes easily to mind: scapegoat and hero are one and the
same person, for it is clearly he who is immolated or ejected at
the end—whether his guilt is poorly defined and even, as Freud
suggests, imposed upon him by a guilt-ridden community de-
sirous to rid itself of pent-up violence; whether his guilt and
punishment are preordained by the gods; or whether, in making his own existential choices, he has proved himself tainted
with a tragic flaw. But comedy presents us with infinitely
greater complexities. If we consider its hero to be the romantic
young man who gets the girl in the end, as Frye suggests, then
this hero is clearly differentiated from the scapegoat, Frye's
"heavy father" and "blocking character" who has to be elimi-
nated because he stands in the way of the desired union of
the young. And what about comedy's clever servant who
frequently brings about the union of the young lovers and is
just as frequently immolated? Additional complexity is added if

we consider the scapegoat's crime. Most critics, even those of the caliber of Bergson and Freud, have presumed that it is a flaw in character that comedy "would fain correct"—thus thinking exclusively in terms of a significative comic. In the psychocritical view of Mauron, on the other hand, the comic crime is that of a "father" engaged in rivalry for the same woman with his "son." Such assumptions, however, fail to assist us in our quest for the "rules" because they limit all comedy to the realm of romance, forgetting the importance of the *agelast* as a comic scapegoat and his manifold infringements on carnivalesque notions of life and death.

If we look closely at literature of the absolute comic and farce, we find surprisingly often that the comic scapegoat—far from being the "heavy father" blocking the union of the young—is a cuckolded husband who becomes the laughing stock of all concerned, while his adulterous wife triumphs and frequently is the object of tacit or open approval. How are we to explain this amazing fact? I believe that a clue for its understanding may well be gleaned from the story told by the Wife of Bath in Chaucer's *Canterbury Tales* (Ch*CT*). Her tale centers upon the question of what it is that women most desire. The hero of her story is a young and exceedingly handsome Knight at the Court of King Arthur who, having raped a young woman, is to be put to death by decree of the King, though temporarily saved through the intervention of the Queen and her women. Yet, upon the ladies' request, he must start out on a journey to find out what it is that women most desire; he will be truly pardoned only if his answer proves acceptable to them. The answers to his question vary from "richesse," "honor," "joliness," "rich array," "lust abedde," "to be widow and wedde," to "flatterye," "attendaunce . . . bisinesse." But, after having interrogated many ladies (a medieval poll), he is still mystified and fears for his life. It is only in an encounter with an old woman that he is given an answer he believes will be convincing to the Queen and her women. He is willing to reward the old hag generously and consents to grant her any wish she may have, once the answer has proved right. A day is set and the answer presented:

> "My liege lady, generally," quod he,
> "Women desire to have sovereigntee
> As well over hir husband as hir love,
> And for to been in maistry him above.
> This is your most desire, though ye me kille.
> Doth as you list: I am here at your wille."
>   In all the court ne was there wife ne maide
> Ne widow that contraried that he saide.
> But saiden he was worthy han his lif. (ChCT:ll.181–89)

The unanimity with which the Queen and her following accept the answer gains particular poignancy because of their previous display of a total lack of sovereignty: The decision over the Knight's life or death had been entirely in the hands of the King; the ladies could only use their charms to plead with him for mercy. Their wish for sovereignty over men is thus as divorced from reality as is an ugly duckling's dream of becoming a swan. It can come true only in the realm of fantasy. Nor is it immaterial in the story's context that the young Knight, once his life has been saved, is about to go back on his promise when the old hag tells him that she wants him to marry her. He finds her too old and too ugly, and it is again in the spirit of nonmimetic carnivalesque farce that she defeats him with clever arguments and gains sovereignty over him. Once this is established, however, she changes from old and ugly to young and beautiful. This is a fantasy triumph and a triumph of fantasy as wonderful as that of Molière's Imaginary Invalid who has defied death. Women's sovereignty clearly belongs to the world of the absolute comic. Bringing it about means turning the world upside down in the spirit of carnival.

We can more fully appreciate the part fantasy played in the telling of this tale if we juxtapose it with a report of a charivari staged in 1517 to punish an outrage committed by a woman against her husband. It is discussed by Natalie Davis in her *So-*

ciety and Culture in Early Modern France (DazSC), and though it was written long after Chaucer's tale and in a different country, we are justified in assuming that the status of women in society had neither worsened nor improved essentially during the interval. Davis' report speaks of a parade on the ass planned against a well-off tanner because it had come to the attention of the authorities that he had recently been beaten by his wife. The parade was organized "in order to repress the temerity and audacity of women who beat their husbands and of those who would like to do so; for according to the provision of divine and civil law, the wife is subject to the husband; and if husbands suffer themselves to be governed by their wives, they might as well be led out to pasture" (DazSC: 116). Whether or not we believe that the moral tone of this report was informed by the growing spirit of Calvinism, what cannot be contested is its severe attitude against women. It is one that in real life would totally preclude any superiority by woman over man. It was only in the spirit of carnival that women were listened to and that Erasmus' Stultitia or the carnivalesque Mère Folle could gain sovereignty. But even Mère Folle was, in fact, a man in disguise. In the city of Dijon, for instance, a highly respected male citizen was elected each year to the post. This was because, in assuming the role of a woman, a man could, as it were, play the fool and feel free to criticize society, since women were thought to be unruly by nature. (Transvestism was practiced during carnivalesque festivities by both sexes, having as little to do with homosexuality as that of Dona Flor's husband (see chapter 3). The phenomenon might well deserve—as Davis rightly suggests—more careful attention to its manifestations in seventeenth- and eighteenth-century life as well as literature.)

If the report of the early sixteenth century gives evidence of the real place of woman in society, its stress on morality concerning an event of a fundamentally carnivalesque nature and therefore belonging originally to the realm of fantasy is nevertheless startling and seems to be expressive of the spirit of

Calvinism that ultimately came to supress all carnivalesque festivities or to interpret them in a manner oblivious to the spirit of the absolute comic. What had been considered a game wherein everyone participated as both actor and spectator lost its character of make-believe. As the game came to be seen as "realistic," hurt pride took the place of laughter and, in the seventeenth century, often led to drawn-out lawsuits (Daz*SC passim*). It is curious to notice, moreover, that literature shows an analogous development. Amoral and carnivalesque tales known to the Middle Ages and the Renaissance become, under the aegis of Protestantism on the one hand, and the Counter-Reformation on the other, *novelas ejemplares,* exemplary tales—are even used as sermons by preachers. Collections of such tales show the modifications they have undergone throughout the sixteenth and seventeenth centuries, and the moral twists they were given during those later periods point up strongly their transition from the realm of the imaginary to the realm of "realism" (see, e.g., Mr*P*). It is interesting to observe that in this process women characters lose that superiority over men that the imaginary realm of carnivalesque literature and the absolute comic granted them.

Until the ludic quality of such tales, that is, the grammar of the absolute comic, was forgotten, however, woman's image represented the fantasy triumph of the suppressed over the mighty. Davis gleefully evokes it:

> First . . . a rich treatment of women . . . happily given over to the sway of their bodily senses or who are using every ruse they can to prevail over men. There is the wife of Bath, of course, who celebrates her sexual instrument and outlives her five husbands. And Rabelais' Gargamelle—a giant of a woman, joyously and frequently coupling, eating bushels of tripe, quaffing wine, joking obscenely, giving birth in a grotesque fecal explosion from which her son Gargantua somersaults shouting "Drink, drink." Then the clever and powerful wife of the *Quinze joies de mariage*—cuckolding her husband, foiling his every effort to find her out, wheedling fancy clothes out of him, beating him up,

and finally locking him in his room. Also Grimmelshausen's Libuschka, alias Courage, one of a series of picaresque heroines—fighting in the army in soldier's clothes; ruling her many husbands and lovers; paying them back a hundredfold when they take revenge or betray her; whoring, tricking, and trading to survive or get rich. Husband-dominators are everywhere in popular literature, nicknamed among the Germans St. Cudgelman (Sankt Kolbmann) or Doktor Siemann (she-man). The point about such portraits is that they are funny and amoral: the women are full of life and energy, and they win much of the time; they stay on top of their fortune with as much success as Machiavelli might have expected for the Prince of his political tract. (DazSC: 134)

As this array indicates, the literature of "Women on Top" (this is the title Davis has given to her chapter) is, indeed, stupendous, but I prefer to think of it not as that of "unruly women"—as Davis suggests—but rather as that of the absolute comic and, hence, as nonmimetic and belonging to the realm of fantasy. For the women presented in this literature are not judged by moral or social standards and, therefore, cannot be called unruly. The justice meted out to them and those with whom they associate is that of carnival. Their triumph is fleeting and nonmimetic. It is the fantasy triumph of the meek and powerless over those in authority. The morality prevailing in these tales and farces is that of the oppressed, not the rulers, and their liberating laughter belongs to the realm of the imaginary.

A closer look at carnivalesque literature will bear this out and we may well choose at random from its riches. Keeping our purpose firmly in mind, we may present the structure of Chaucer's *Merchant Tale* (ChCT) as follows:

Old January, "sixty yeer a wifeless man was he/ And followed ay his bodily delit/ On women, there as was his appetit" (ll. 4–10), wants to marry "a young wife and a fair" (l. 27). At his age, marriage seems to him the most desirable thing in the world, although he discusses the matter with a number of people, all of whom give him different advice. Up to this point, the story's pattern is so familiar and must have been so popular that we encounter it in Rabelais, whose Panurge contemplates marriage, and in one of Molière's musical farces, *Le Mariage forcé* (The Forced Marriage). It lends itself to raucous abuse and subtle praise of woman and marriage. Rabelais' Panurge never does marry. Molière's Sganarelle, suddenly convinced that his betrothed will cuckold him, wants to give up the whole idea, but is farcically beaten into submission, knowing that, together with a wife, he will be burdened with her lover. Yet January does encounter May and, being "ravished in a traunce/ At every time he looked on hir face!" (ll. 506–7), he decides to marry her. But January had not reckoned with his young Squire Damian, who at once becomes enamored of Lady May and, languishing for her love, falls ill. Innocently, January commends him to the care of Lady May and her ladies, and the result is inevitable: the young lovers hear the voice of the turtle. It is here that the tale becomes cruel. The old man, having lost his eyesight and become more jealous as a consequence, walks with his wife in the garden. Pretending that she cannot reach a pear that is too high up on the tree, she requests his aid and, as "He stoupeth down, and on his back she stood" (ll. 1104), Damian, perched in the tree, makes love to her. For the lovers this is indeed a fantasy triumph; the old jealous husband unwittingly serves them as go-between. When, unexpectedly, January regains his sight and is outraged at what he has seen, Lady May cleverly convinces him that what he *believed* he saw was a delusion because he had not yet regained his "parfit sighte," and that, indeed, delusion is something we all fall prey to. Thus neither Damian nor Lady May is found out, although they have had their pleasure of each other. The jealous old husband has been cheated rather cruelly and, in the eyes of those who listen to the tale, made the butt of laughter. But no moral censure is meted out to Lady May for her adultery and treachery. What counts is her fantasy triumph. In the world of the absolute comic and farce, it seems essential and right that the young and pretty woman find love in the arms of one who is able to give it to her.

A similar notion prevails in Chaucer's *Miller's Tale* (Ch*CT*). Here, too, the basic pattern is that of a pretty woman, Alison, "wild and young," married to a well-to-do, jealous old man, Carpenter John. Living in the guesthouse they keep is the poor but sly and clever scholar Nicholas. On a day when her husband is away on business, Nicholas begins with the young wife "to rage and playe" and asks her to grant him her favors. Alison is equally attractive to the prim, neatly dressed clerk Absolon who courts her with much gentility, but she prefers her clever scholar. Again the story pattern is rather ordinary, but it becomes unique when Nicholas tries to figure out how to make possible his not-so-romantic union with Alison. This is where John's stupidity helps. Nicholas convinces him that the stars he has consulted indicate the coming of a terrible flood. For the three of them to escape it, three boats must be built and hidden under the rafters of the barn. John swallows the tale and himself hides out in his boat while the two lovers make sport in his bed. In this story the deceit is more cruel, the old man's suffering more lasting, since not only is he injured as his boat is cut from its high mooring, but he is also made a lasting fool of before the townspeople, who believe him mad.

We would be totally amiss, however, were we to judge the tale's characters by any standards of what *we* consider moral and socially acceptable behavior or fair play. In a recent issue of the *CEA Forum,* published by the College English Association, Nathaniel B. Atwater in his essay entitled "Poetic Justice and the *Miller's Tale*" (Atw*J*), notes two different interpretations of the tale. The first, by E. Talbot Donaldson, finds the Miller's world

> distinguished by its even-handed justice. . . . The senile lover gets his just deserts when he is cuckolded, injured, and ridiculed. Hende (clever) Nicholas, who glories in the physical reality of life, is, despite all his cleverness, punished in an appropriate manner. The effeminate Absolon, whose fastidiousness must

appear to the gross Miller as a kind of mania, receives equally appropriate retribution. Justice is, however, chivalrous: to the heroine of a courtly romance no ultimate evil ever comes, and Alison escapes scot free. (quoted from *Chaucer's Poetry: An Anthology for the Modern Reader*. New York: Ronald Press, 1975)

Atwater agrees by and large with this interpretation but, rightly maintaining that this tale is not a courtly romance and Alison not a courtly heroine, adds his own:

> What we do have is a fabliau told by the drunken Miller ostensibly to match the *Knight's Tale*. The rules are different by virtue of propriety alone, but I have noticed that my students unfailingly argue as Donaldson does. They are convinced that John, Nicholas, and Absolon get their due, whereas Alison gets off free. I argue differently because the *Miller's Tale* is a comedy with a return to normality [Atwater uses Frye's terminology] at the end. Consequently Alison quietly gets what might be the longest and most harrowing sentence of them all. That is, she is stuck for the duration with Old John, a fate she might well deserve. . . .

In the spirit of the absolute comic to which this tale belongs, neither interpretation is quite acceptable, however, because each is informed by the philosophy of life that pertains to the significative comic rather than to farce. It is true that Alison is not a "heroine of courtly romance [to whom] no ultimate evil ever comes." But neither is harmony restored at the end of all comedy, nor does she get her right deserts in any moral sense of the word, because no one in the realm of fantasy ever considers what may happen after the tale ends. Lovers and others, as we know, always live happily ever after. What matters and what the story emphasizes is that Alison—like many a young, pretty woman in the literature of the Middle Ages and the Renaissance—outwits her jealous old husband in a manner totally unrealistic and wholly in the spirit of a momentary carnivalesque fantasy triumph. In that sense she succeeds and deserves no punishment. Her immorality and cruelty are not condemned in that world of the imagination. If the carpenter John is made the scapegoat, this is but part of the idiom of that tradition, and it is equally fitting to that idiom that Absolon cannot become her lover, because he could never "rage and playe" with "wild young" Alison. What is intriguing is that Absolon's vengeance, meant for Alison, is unwittingly meted out to Nicholas. Accident and, we might say, fate play a part in this, and the fact that the *hende* scholar was "scalded in the toute," that part of his anatomy that procured him so much enjoyment, belongs to the carnivalesque tradition of the trickster that I will discuss in the last chapter. For Nicholas is, indeed, a trickster figure, sharing its ambivalence as both devil and savior.

The extent to which such patterns of carnivalesque justice prevail becomes still clearer if we look at Boccacio's *Decameron* (BoD). The eighth tale of the Seventh Day is, for instance, described as follows: "A husband grows suspicious of his wife, and discovers that her lover comes to her at night, forewarning her of his arrival by means of a string attached to her toe. Whilst the husband is giving chase to the lover, his wife gets out of bed and puts another woman in her place, who receives a beating from the husband and has her tresses cut off. The husband then goes to fetch his wife's brothers, who, on discovering that his story is untrue, subject him to a torrent of abuse" (BoD: 15). Another tale, the fourth, told on that same day, displays the same ruthless cleverness on the part of the wife, who gets away scot free, while her long-suffering husband is being ridiculed, until she attains "sovereignty" over him. This tale is that of wealthy Tofano, unjustly jealous of his beautiful wife Ghita. We are told that "on perceiving how jealous he was, the lady took offense and repeatedly asked him to explain the reason, but since he could only reply in vague and illogical terms, she resolved to make him suffer in good earnest from the ill which hitherto he had feared without cause" (BoD: 538). Thus Ghita accepts the favors of a young man and, encouraging her husband's growing fondness for wine, slips away from him every evening as soon as he is sufficiently drunk in order to join her lover. Tofano finally becomes suspicious and, noticing her gone one night, locks the door of the house. Upon her return, she thus finds herself locked out, and as he mocks her vain attempts to open the door, she pleads with him to let her come in. But to no avail. It is only when she threatens to drown herself in the well and Tofano hears her fall into the water (not knowing that she has only thrown a rock into it), that he rushes out of the house to rescue her. But Ghita cleverly seizes the opportunity to run into the house and lock Tofano out. In answer to his more and more anxious pleas, she now ridicules him as a drunkard before neighbors and kinfolk who have come, attracted by the noise. Tofano has become the comic scapegoat. In this tale, husband and wife are finally reconciled, as he realizes that his jealousy has been excessive. But what is essential is that the woman's conduct is never questioned either on moral or social terms of justice. She has, as it were, beaten her husband. She is "on top," and she remains blameless in spite of her adultery. It is not her "unruliness" that matters (for unruliness assumes certain social rules) but rather the fact that, in the realm of fantasy, she has achieved that sovereignty that women dream of, according to the tale of the Wife of Bath.

The *Decameron* tale seems to have enjoyed immense popularity. It belongs to the treasure house of farce, and its variants may be found in Western European as well as Indian lore (LahH:710). Molière used it twice: once in a farce that is one of his earliest extant and again later in a comedy. The title of the farce is *La Jalousie du Barbouillé* (The Jealous Clown; (*barbouillé*, simply meaning that the actor's face was daubed white, which in farce identified him as an old man) (MoJ). The Barbouillé is married to a young woman, Angélique, who blatantly carries on an affair with a young lover. But in spite of her husband's just complaints, he is, like Tofano, made the butt of laughter before her parents and neighbors, as he is locked out of his own house. To compound the elements of farce, Molière added another character, Le Docteur, a pedant, to whom the Barbouillé turns in vain for advice in his various predicaments. While it lacks the verbal dexterity of the Boccaccio tale, from which it may or may not have been directly derived, the farce translates into clever visual stage business the upside-down world that is suggested by the narrative. This translation is made possible because of the Italianate stage setting, namely, that of the commedia dell'arte with its two streets meeting at right angles and lined with houses.

When husband and wife first quarrel, both do so at street level. When Angélique finds herself locked out and begs for forgiveness, her husband looks down upon her from the height of his window. When she succeeds in tricking him and locking him out in his turn, it is she who appears at the window, whereas he is pleading with her on the street below. The farcial husband–wife struggle is dramatically orchestrated, with the wife, though weaker and younger, triumphant and "on top" at the end. Stage displacements thus translate into visual terms the carnivalesque quality of a world turned upside down.

In this farce, the husband–wife relationship with its ups and downs has as a farcial counterpoint that of the Barbouillé and the Docteur. Here it is the haughty, absentminded pedant who is degraded by the Barbouillé when, filled with rage at his incapacity to understand his concrete human problems of infidelity and jealousy, the Barbouillé drags the pedant across the stage, feet first. But the Docteur has his own fantasy triumphs as he degrades language, turning Latin into a monstrous conglomerate of various tongues and, in the manner of the festive exercises of medieval and Renaissance clergymen, indulges in eroticized discussions of grammar and abstruse etymologies. Flirting with Angélique, who claims that she, too, could be a docteur if she wanted to, he agrees with her, in language grotesquely concealing rather than revealing what it is he wants to say:

"You can be a doctor whenever you wish, but I believe that you are a pleasant doctor. You look as if you followed your whims;

of the parts of speech you like only the conjunction; of genders only the masculine; of declensions only the possessive [the genitive]; of syntax only the *mobile cum fixo* [the combination of what is fixed with what is moving]; and, finally, of metrics only the dactyl, because it consists of one long and two short syllables." (Mo*J*:27; my translation)

Many examples could be cited of such parodies in the Middle Ages that degrade grammar by making its terms concrete and allude to the body and to sex. Since it was mainly the clergy that indulged in such spicy double-talk, most texts that are preserved are in medieval Latin, and I shall quote from at least one of them for the pleasure of those who can read it and the challenge to those curious enough to follow its rhythms and recognize enough of its vocabulary to understand the implications:

> Et prima coniugatio
> cum sit presentis temporis,
> hec: amo, amas, amat
> sit nobis frequent lectio,
> Scola sit umbra nemoris,
> liber puelle facies,
> quam primitiva species
> legendam esse clamat.
> Dum ad choream tenditur
> gradu pluralis numeri;
> dum cantu conclamatur;
> dum sonus sono redditur,
> iungatur latus lateri
> quod fixum sit vel mobile,
> quod Veneri flexibile,
> dum cantu conclamatur. (Le*P*:224, ll. 33–48)

We must remember, of course, that Latin was the language of the Church and that such profanations were felt to be a fantasy triumph, temporarily debasing that which was held high and sacred. Such was the spirit of the absolute comic.

Yet it is indicative of the waning of that spirit that in the

comedy *George Dandin ou le mari confondu* (MoGD), which Molière wrote more than ten years later—by then he was no
longer a peripatetic actor but a success in Paris and Versailles—
the playwright omitted the figure of the pedant and his Latin
altogether, although the plot of that comedy is identical with
that of the *Jealous Clown*. The playwright replaced this carnivalesque figure—in terms of its farcical value—with the
parents of Angélique, now very much visible as grasping, con-
ceited, and desperately poor nobility, determined to detest their
son-in-law for his lack of nobility and to exploit him merci-
lessly because of his wealth. A social motif begins to assert itself as against the absolute comic of the farce, making the comedy more significative, even if the general spirit of the
carnivalesque is maintained. The two versions of the same plot
illustrate that transition of the comic from the absolute or farce
to the significative that was taking place in the seventeenth century. The Angélique of *Dandin*—a lady rather than the simple
woman that was her predecessor and namesake in the farce—is
an accomplished hypocrite, indulging in polite double entendre. Her lover, invisible in the early farce, appears onstage,
and there ensues between them amorous dialogue. Here, too,
the woman's immorality triumphs, but George Dandin is no
longer the nameless, clownish scapegoat of the farce. Unre-
fined though his feelings may be, they have become those of an
individual, intensely unhappy and suffering, as he decides at the
play's conclusion to leave Angélique to her devices, since there
is no solution to his predicament: "When one has married an
evil woman, the best thing to do is to go throw oneself, head
first, into the water (MoGD:328; my translation). If Dandin's
plight remains comical, nevertheless, if it does not become
mimetic and realistic, this is because of the character's inherent
absurdity, stressed even more strongly through interludes of
music and dance. Molière proves a master in keeping a balance
between the significative and the absolute comic. Like the characters of farce that resemble him, Dandin is too rigid, too jealous, too severe in his demands upon his wife, in short, an

agelast incapable of laughing at himself. His punishment is thus deserved according to the justice prevailing in the realm of the carnivalesque. The woman on top is, in the idiom of farce, the logical complement to his degradation, regardless of her own merits or lack thereof.

It is quite obvious, however, that subsequent centuries no longer understood this idiom. Molière's comedy had been, at first, greeted as *archicomique* (supercomical). By 1736, Riccoboni, himself a famous man of the theater, thought it deserved to be called a "comedy" rather than a "farce" (MoŒ 6:479*n*1). But about twenty years later, the same man rejected it as being inadmissible in a theater that respected the *bienséances* (good manners and morals). He found it, in fact, scandalous, as did Rousseau in a letter written in 1758 to his friend D'Alembert, deploring the fact that a woman was being applauded who was unfaithful to her husband, deceiving and dishonoring a man foolish enough to have married her for her nobility (MoŒ6:492). D'Alembert, agreeing with Rousseau, ascribed this deplorable situation to a marriage totally ill-assorted and prompted, on the part of Dandin, by the vanity that made him dream of nobility, although such dreams proved unattainable. Even more revealing, with regard to a growing lack of understanding for the woman on top, is Voltaire's comment, in 1764, that a number of spectators were scandalized by the comedy's heroine who, though a married woman, gave a rendezvous to a lover. Something so shocking could be justified only by the fact that Dandin had, in his stupidity, married the daughter of a ridiculous nobleman (MoŒ6:504). Quite evidently, eighteenth-century France applied to comedy standards of morality and justice that differed from those of the absolute comic.

But the idiom of the absolute comic is clearly linked with that of the woman on top. Her sovereignty over a stupid old husband incapable of loving her is not personal; it remains independent of her own sense of responsibility toward society or adherence to that society's morals. It is a part rather of powers and laws that transcend social mores, those of Love and Nature. Within the realm of the carnivalesque, Angélique's behavior, though ruthless and stupid if looked at from a moral and social point of view, is justified. There is implicit in tales of such carnivalesque character and origin that deeper philosophy of life and death that conceives of man not so much as the individual but as a mere link in the never ending chain of life and its corresponding dance of death. But as the seventeenth and eighteenth centuries were shifting the emphasis toward the individual and the social, they could not but come to misinterpret and therefore ill receive all that was carnivalesque in this sense. (We shall see later that the postwar twentieth century, while trying to preserve the importance of the individual, has again come to see man in that larger perspective and can, therefore, appreciate anew the spirit of the absolute comic.) To Molière, though he was writing at a time when emphasis began to shift rapidly, medieval and Renaissance traditions of farce were still the sources of inspiration. Whether consciously or as an outgrowth of the comic spirit that had nourished him, he subscribed fully to the concept that Love exerts sovereignty over social customs to the extent that it can not only disregard but even alter social justice. To grasp the strength of such concepts in the tradition of the absolute comic, it is important to recall the curious story told by Filostrato on the Sixth Day of the *Decameron*. The tale's title announces it as follows: "Madonna Filippa is discovered by her husband with a lover and called before the magistrate, but by a prompt and ingenious answer she secures her acquittal and causes the statute to be amended" (BoD: 498).

Madonna Filippa is not presented as a young girl who falls for the first young man that comes her way because her husband is too old to satisfy her. She is described rather as a very beautiful and well-bred woman of great intelligence who is deeply in love with a handsome young noble of her city. Her husband, having discovered her one evening in her own bedchamber in the arms of her lover, is determined to invoke a city statute decreeing that "every woman taken in adultery by her husband should be burned alive, whether she was with a lover or simply doing it for money" (BoD: 498). To the magistrate's question whether her husband's accusation is true, she gives an answer so remarkable that it must be quoted here in full:

> "Sir, it is true that Rinaldo is my husband, and that he found me last night in Lazzarino's arms, wherein, on account of the deep and perfect love I bear towards him, I have lain many times before; nor shall I ever deny it. However, as I am sure you will know, every man and woman should be equal before the law, and laws must have the consent of those who are affected by them. These conditions are not fulfilled in the present instance, because this law only applies to us poor women, who are much better able than men to bestow our favors liberally. Moreover, when this law was made, no woman gave her consent to it, nor was any woman even so much as consulted. It can therefore justly be described as a very bad law.
>
> "If, however, to the detriment of my body and your soul, you wish to give effect to this law, that is your own affair. But before you proceed to pass any judgment, I beseech you to grant me a small favour, this being that you should ask my husband whether or not I have refused to concede my entire body to him, whenever and as often as he pleased." Without waiting for the *podestà* to put the question, Rinaldo promptly replied that beyond any doubt she had granted him whatever he required in the way of bodily gratification.
>
> "Well then," the lady promptly continued, "if he has always taken as much as he chose to take, I ask you, Messer Podestà, what am I to do with the surplus? Throw it to the dogs? Is it not far better that I should present it to a gentleman who loves me more dearly than himself, rather than allow it to turn bad or go to waste?" (BoD: 500)

The lady is freed, and the podestà asks the court to amend the statute. Rinaldo is quite mortified, after having made such "a fool of himself," but his wife, "having, so to speak, been resur-

rected from the flames, returned to her house in triumph"
(BoD: 501).

The story reminds us of the Wife of Bath's Prologue to her
tale. Having been widowed five times, she would be quite
willing to add a sixth to the number of her husbands, if God
should thus decree. She even speaks with approval and admiration of such holy men as Abraham and Jacob, who were each
married to more than one wife at one and the same time. Hers
is the sentiment that prevails in the realm of the absolute comic:
she sees no virtue in virginity and challenges everyone to find a
passage in the Bible indicating that God recommended it and
forbade marriage. What Boccaccio's tale suggests even more
strongly is Andreas Capellanus' *Art of Courtly Love,* wherein
this thirteenth-century clerk describes a Paradise of Love destined only for those women who had been good lovers. All
others are excluded from it (KeGD: 509). Because loving well
was imposed upon women by Nature herself, the Widow of
Ephesus was fully approved of within the framework of such
thinking. Had she not loved her husband enough to be willing
to remain in his tomb after his death? Was she not heartbroken
about her loss of him? What was wrong, then, if she let herself
be comforted by the soldier who entered the tomb and found
her so disconsolate? And did she not have to comfort him in
her turn when he needed help because the body of the hanged
man he had been assigned to guard was stolen? What greater
homage could have been paid to Love and Nature than her sur-
render of her husband's corpse to replace that of the hanged
man on the gallows and thereby save her lover's life? Only
agelasts would have found her actions shocking.

Rabelais' Panurge, in fact, cruelly punishes a woman because she refuses her love to him. In telling of his attempts to
conquer that great Parisian lady, he boasts of his brusque manner of approaching her, coming directly to the point and
"omitting the mass of long prologues and protestations habi-
tually made by doleful and contemplative lent-lovers who
never tamper with the flesh" (RG: 239). When, upon his re-

peated attempts, she refuses to be compliant, he plans his revenge. Seating himself beside her in church, he sprinkles a certain powder upon her sleeves that proves irresistible to dogs. They approach from all directions, and Panurge watches with great glee as, on leaving the church, she leads a procession "in which more than six hundred thousand and fourteen dogs were seen all around her, bothering her greatly, and everywhere she passed fresh hosts of dogs followed her trail" (RG: 244). Her failure to love well has made her the butt of laughter. She has sinned against Love and Nature and has been degraded because of it and made a scapegoat.

If hers is a negative reaction to these two great powers, Boccaccio's *Decameron* in its entirety pays homage to them and venerates them. It is by no means accidental that the young people who tell the tales are moving further and further away from the city of Florence with its ugly reality of the plague and that, before returning to it, they have moved from garden to garden, the third and last of which is called the "Valley of the Ladies." Although, like the two previous gardens which served them as an abode, it is an earthly paradise and seems a sanctuary to Venus, it is even more secluded than the others and can be reached only by a narrow path. It is round, as if drawn by human hands with a compass, so that Nature and human order seem to combine in it in perfect harmony. The young man presiding on the day the group arrives in the valley is Dioneo, a name evoking that of the goddess Dione, the Venus Genetrix of Nature and Love. As he is crowned king for the day, Dioneo asserts that, due to the special circumstances to which they have been prey (their departure from the tainted city with its dead and dying), "divine as well as human laws" should be suspended. But if the laws of society and religion recede into the background, those of Nature become all powerful, as they do in carnival, and the *Decameron's* story tellers have equal license to turn the world upside down, for a period equally circumscribed.

It is the sovereignty of Love that asserts itself in the *De-*

cameron's Introduction to the Fourth Day. The tale told here is that of Filippo who, having lost his beloved wife, withdrew with his young son to the slopes of Mount Asinaio, where he lived like a hermit, fasting, praying, collecting alms. He kept his son in complete seclusion and when he had to go to the city, always went alone. On one occasion, however—now being an old man and his son eighteen—he took him along, thinking that the boy was concerned only with the glories of life eternal and would not be corrupted by what he might see. The son, quite to the contrary, was profoundly impressed by what he saw and above all by a party of elegantly dressed and beautiful young ladies. He showed such eagerness to know what they were, that his father told him they were evil and that they were called "goslings." But words and designations not-withstanding, the son was as strongly attracted to them as any young man would be and begged his father for one of the "goslings," so that the old man "realized that his wits were no match for Nature" (BoD: 328).

The same admission that Love and Nature are sovereign was made by the author himself in that very Introduction, when he claimed that "to oppose the laws of nature, one has to possess exceptional powers, which often turn out to have been used, not only in vain, but to the serious harm of those who employ them" (BoD: 331). Messer Lizio, the father of beautiful young Caterina was to testify to the truth of this statement. Because of her very innocence, his young daughter spontane-ously confessed her love to Ricciardo, a sprightly youth who frequented her father's house, as soon as he told her of his. In spite of the fact that she is watched so closely by her parents, the young lovers manage to spend the night together and are discovered in the morning by Caterina's father. In its mixture of touching innocence and the cunning of desire, the tale attests as strongly to the power of Venus Genetrix as does that of young Masetto who, pretending to be a deaf mute, had been hired to tend the garden in a nunnery "renowned for its holi-ness." The young man has "all the nuns vie with one another to take him off to bed with them—last not least the Mother Superior" (BoD:234). The story's ending is an ironic fantasy triumph of Nature and Love over established religion, as it describes Masetto as being "now an elderly and prosperous father who was spared the bother of feeding his children and the expense of their upbringing" and who could proudly proclaim that this "was the way that Christ treated anybody who placed a pair of horns upon His crown" (BoD:241).

As previous discussions suggested and subsequent ones will confirm, degrading of the sacred and elevation of the profane is an essential element of this realm of the absolute comic. In his first great comedy, *L'Ecole des femmes* (School For Wives) (MoSW), for instance, Molière presented his audience with a similar admixture of the two, celebrating the power of Love over all that seemed socially just and justified. His success was overwhelming, but so was the opposition he encountered from seventeenth-century spectators and readers who were beginning to look with contempt upon the absolute comic. While many of his critics may have been moved by personal envy, as has frequently been maintained, others who professed themselves unable to stomach the absolute comic of Rabelais may have been truly shocked by its vestiges in Molière's *L'Ecole des femmes*. Agnès, the comedy's young woman, is not married but proves to be both the innocent, moved and educated by the great powers of Love and Nature, and the "woman on top." Not being Arnolphe's wife and not even having consented to such a marriage, she is neither adulterous nor treacherous to an old husband. But neither does she merely sail into the arms of her young lover Horace in the manner of Boccaccio's Caterina, who is found by her father in bed with her lover. Still better guarded by Arnolphe than Caterina was by her parents, she must use cunning to break down her prison walls when she suddenly recognizes them as such and realizes that Arnolphe has been her jailer. Her fantasy triumph consists of the fact that in spite of her naiveté she outwits her clever guardian, so well versed in the prevailing mores of his day that he is able to lecture her on the behavior expected of a good wife and to deliver a sermon on the punishment awaiting women who fail to conform to such rules. Arnolphe is, of course, the comedy's *agelast* and becomes its scapegoat, ridiculed and quietly slinking away at its conclusion when all others are gathered in happiness. To him applies the statement Boccaccio made in the Introduction of the *Decameron*'s Fourth Day, namely, that "in order to oppose the laws of nature, one has to possess exceptional powers, which often turn out to have been used, not only in vain, but to the serious harm of those who employ them" (BoD: 331). For in depriving Agnès of her right to give and receive love freely, Arnolphe did oppose the laws of Nature. He would have been, moreover, the first to admit this—as indicated by his amusement at Horace's tale of his lover and the old dragon who guards her, neither of whom he identifies with himself and Agnès. But what he recognizes as grotesque in "another," he is not aware of in himself, blinded as he is by jealousy and fear of cuckoldry.

To explain the relationship between Arnolphe, Agnès, and Horace merely as oedipal because the two men desire the same woman bypasses the very core of the absolute comic, which shows old age vying with youth but youth helped by the power of Love, regardless of social rules and established authority. The struggle is one of age groups rather than individuals, and it is not so much as an individual but as the representative of a group that Arnolphe is doomed. Yet the triumph of the penniless, powerless young lovers over the wealthy and well-established old man is a fantasy triumph and does not belong to the real world. It is not mimetic but carnivalesque. It is ultimately achieved only because of sudden reversals in the life of Agnès and certain discoveries concerning her identity. It is true that Molière conferred upon Arnolphe qualities of character that lift him above the jealous old men of the carnivalesque, so that we are not totally impervious to his final defeat and suffering. As has been pointed out by critics, Arnolphe's mania to learn whether Agnès is "faithful" to him is not unlike Oedipus' quest for a truth whose knowledge will destroy him. Molière's protagonist expresses his suffering in ways bordering on the tragic. If René Girard, describing Oedipus, said of him that he made himself the scapegoat, Arnolphe says the same of himself:

> Oh, cruel probing of a mysterious evil,
> Wherein the surgeon suffers all the pain! (Mo*SW:* 53)

Yet the playwright managed to keep him a character in the realm of the absolute comic and did not individualize him to an extent that would lift him to the level of a significative comic which would "fain correct." How well Molière achieved this becomes apparent if we compare Arnolphe with a similar character created by Cervantes in his exemplary *novela* "The Jealous Extremaduran" (Ce*JE*).

An old Extremaduran gentleman, having made a fortune in the colonies, returns home and thinks of marrying but is also frightened by the thought. "By nature he was the most jealous man in the world, even without being married; the mere thought of marrying was enough to arouse his jealousy, weary him with suspicions and startle him with imaginary evils, so much so that he resolved at all costs not to marry" (Ce*JE:* 149). Nevertheless, when he chances upon a poor but beautiful young girl, he decides that "this is the girl that heaven wishes me to have" (Ce*JE:* 149). But "he had scarcely taken his marriage vow when he was suddenly attacked by a raging jealousy, and without any reason began to tremble and to be more worried than he had ever been in all his life" (Ce*JE:* 150). His jealousy expresses itself in extraordinary ways. He is unwilling to let any tailor measure her and has to find another young woman of her size to have dresses made for her. "He shut up all the windows facing on to the street, and opened up skylights all over the house. At the street entrance which is called the 'house door' in Seville, he had a stable built for a mule, and above it a straw loft and a room for the man who was to be in charge of it, who was an old Negro eunuch; he raised the walls above the level of the roofs" (CeJE: 150). Yet this prison was beautifully furnished indoors, and the young bride, still playing with dolls, moved into it, saying "that she had no will but that of her husband and master, to whom she would always be obedient" (CeJE: 151).

Not even a male animal was permitted in the house, and yet the young woman, in her great innocence, believed that this was the way it should be. Nevertheless, this closely guarded fortress is conquered by a totally worthless young man-about-town who considers it a challenge to win the girl over and shrewdly succeeds in doing so by plying the servants with money, music, and wine and having them put the old man to sleep with a "magic" powder. It all ends in tragedy, however, because the old man wakes up, sees his wife in the young man's arms, although she had never submitted to his advances, and dies either of the effect of the "magic" powder or of sorrow, not without blaming himself for what had happened: "I was like the silkworm, making the house in which I was to die" (CeJE: 178). He realizes that he should have considered the discrepancy in age between himself and his young wife as well as the impossibility of youth to withstand the call of love and the cleverness of go-betweens. He does not blame his wife and wishes her to marry the young man after his own death, leaving her his entire fortune. She, however, "went off to be a nun in one of the most enclosed convents in the city" (CeJE: 180). (It must be remembered, however, that this short story is *exemplary* and was meant to have moral overtones. In a brief farce, Cervantes used the same material to comic effect.)

The resemblance between Arnolphe and the Extremaduran is obviously striking, yet the two "stories" affect us quite differently. Cervantes' *novela* is mimetic. His jealous Man sees the error of his ways and tries to mend them. His death is noble, his sentiments of the highest morality—except for his fatal flaw, his jealousy. His death, though based on misunderstanding, is "real" and tragic. His young wife Leonora never feels passionate toward the young intruder, never deceives her husband, and never is a "woman on top," nor do Love and Nature assert their sovereignty. She remains submissive till the end, so that she experiences no fantasy triumph over the old husband. He is, therefore, never made a comic scapegoat. He is seen as an individual throughout the *novela,* and we cannot but be moved by his realization that he "was like the silkworm, making the house in which [he] was to die" (Ce*JE:*178). His error in opposing the laws of Nature—considered a crime in the realm of the absolute comic—is so ennobled by his understanding and generous attitude toward Leonora whom he wrongly suspects, though she can never prove her innocence—that the reader comes to dwell on serious thoughts of appearance versus reality and the intricacies of human behavior and relationships.

While Cervantes' *novela* thus moves into the realm of tragedy, Molière's play provides us with the sort of "frame" that declares it to belong to the realm of the absolute comic, and it is this very "frame" that was attacked by those who criticized the comedy. There is Agnès' naive account to Arnolphe of the pleasure she derived from being greeted by a young man, her guardian's friend Horace, who passed by her balcony and whom she joyously greeted in return each of the many times he repeated the exercise. In her innocence, she takes romantic metaphor literally and then regales Arnolphe with her halting tale of the visit Horace paid her because her eyes had "wounded" him and only she could "cure" him; of "something" he took away from her and which, upon anxious questioning by Arnolphe, turns out to be nothing more than a ribbon. There is the grotesque presence of the peasant couple appointed by Arnolphe to guard her; their *patois;* and their slapstick stage business that make the blows they intend for each other hail upon Arnolphe; the definition of jealousy the peasant gives to his wife, using references to food and comparing a woman to a "soup" into which her husband would not want other famished men to dip their fingers.

But it is above all Arnolphe who is a figure of the absolute comic when true passion and jealousy take the place of those feelings he had merely imagined, as soon as he recognizes his careful precautions as being threatened by the young lover. The effect is heightened by his previous certainty that he could mould Agnès at will by reading her his grotesque marriage code, a carnivalesque parody of rules, compiled from ancient philosophers and known to the humanists of the late sixteenth and seventeenth centuries. His preaching to Agnès, moreover, his evocation of Hell's boiling cauldrons awaiting coquettish and unfaithful wives who disregard their husbands' honor, is couched in the form of a carnivalesque *sermon joyeux,* although Molière, when reproached for this, claimed it to be but a "moral discourse." The *sermon joyeux,* we are told by Petit de Juleville (Pe*T*), "originated with the Feast of Fools: it was started by whosoever in the noisy drunkenness of the feast, first thought of getting on the Christian pulpit to parody there the preacher in bacchic improvisation. Later such farcical preachers—chased from the church at last—found refuge in the theater and could continue there the parody of Christian discourse: the genre was expanded and regularized; it adopted verse form; its texts, extracts from the Holy Scriptures the meaning of which was distorted, were preserved" (Pe*T*: 259–260; my translation). In creating the figure of Arnolphe, Molière therefore not only prepared us for carnivalesque laughter by giving him the name of the patron saint of cuckolds (St. Arnolphe) but also by making him, unwittingly, the bearer of carnivalesque traditions that parodied marriage and religion.

There can be no doubt that Arnolphe, infinitely more than a "blocking character" preventing the union of the young, is rather the *agelast,* rigid and unable to accept the fact that life means perpetual change, that it cannot adhere to outmoded established order. In the realm of the absolute comic and carnivalesque festivities, Bakhtin assures us, those were also subject to mockery and uncrowning who were men of prominence but did not wish or were unable to laugh at themselves:

They strut majestically, consider their foes the enemies of eternal truth, and threaten them with eternal punishment. They do not see themselves in the mirror of time, do not perceive their own origin, limitations and end. They do not recognize their own ridiculous faces or the comic nature of their pretensions to eternity and immutability. And thus these personages come to the end of their role still serious, although their spectators have been laughing for a long time. They continue to talk with the majestic tones of kings and heralds announcing eternal truths, unaware that time has turned their speeches into ridicule. Time has transformed old truth and authority into a Mardi Gras dummy, a comic monster that the laughing crowd rends to pieces in the market-place. (BakR: 212–13)

Arnolphe, trying to outwit young love, deserves to be a comic scapegoat. However, in the realm of the absolute comic, it is not only Love but also Death, that other great force of Nature, that demands supremacy. No one can truly outwit Death: when he seems most compliant, he proves most triumphant. This fact is comically exploited in a Swiss-German folksong, wherein a young man regrets his marriage to an old though gentle woman and pleads with Death to take her away so that he may marry a young one, only to realize soon thereafter that it would have been better had Death not been so "kind" to him. Chaucer's *Pardoner's Tale* (ChCT: 370–90) is one of the most striking examples of Death's triumphing in a way that makes us indulge in the liberating laughter of the absolute comic and banishes those fears of the end that dog man. Although the tale is so well known, I must briefly recount here its salient features: Three young revelers who have been drinking heavily decide to go out and kill treacherous Death because he has taken away one of their friends. On their way to carry out their decision, they encounter an old man who—though alledgedly tired of his life—is afraid of their threats and tells them where Death may be found. Ironically, not a person but a pot of gold awaits them, so that they forget about killing and begin to think of how best to appropriate this treasure. They decide to guard it until darkness falls and to send the youngest to town for provisions. In the meanwhile, the two who remain—forgetting that all three have sworn eternal brotherhood to one another—decide to kill the third as soon as he returns. He, on the other hand, convinces himself that there is no reason why he should share the treasure with the other two and fills two of the three bottles he buys not only with wine but also with a deadly poison. Those for whom it is destined drink it after having killed him, so that Death remains victorious in a cruel though comic way.

It is as if Death were laughing at those who try to defy him. Images come to mind of Thomas Mann's *Death in Venice,* where revelers with their daubed faces appear to mock but are truly mocked by the death that rides the city. It is the same irony that prevails in the last Diapsalmata of Kierkegaard's *Either/Or.* The narrator tells there of the wonderful thing that happened to him as he was "caught up into the seventh heaven. There sat all the gods in assembly. By special grace I was granted the privilege of making a wish. 'Wilt thou,' said Mercury, 'have youth or beauty or power or a long life or the most beautiful maiden or any of the other glories we have in the chest? Choose, but only one thing.' For a moment I was at a loss. Then I addressed myself to the gods as follows: 'Most honorable contemporaries, I choose this one thing, that I may always have the laugh on my side.' Not one of the gods said a word; on the contrary, they all began to laugh. From that I concluded that my wish was granted, and found that the gods knew how to express themselves with taste; for it would hardly have been suitable for them to have answered gravely: 'Thy wish is granted' " (Ki*EO:* 42). Kierkegaard's conclusion conforms, of course, to his spirit of irony: The gods' laughter, rather than signifying that his wish is granted, is as hollow as that of Death vis-à-vis the three revelers of the *Pardoner's Tale* who had set out to defy him. Man is as incapable of having the last laugh as he is of outwitting Nature.

Such hollow laughter echoes equally through the Don Juan legend wherein—though this may seem surprising to those who think of Don Juan exclusively as the seducer—death had, to begin with, a most decisive part, as demonstrated by Oscar Mandel in the Introduction to his *The Theatre of Don Juan* (Ma*DJ*). The *comedia* of the Spanish priest Tirso de Molina, the source of all subsequent theatrical creations with Don Juan at their center, was originally inspired by folk tales and ballads dealing with the sovereignty of Death. Of the many variants of legends extant, Mandel quotes a *romance,* a Spanish ballad, told by a simple woman of the people to the Spanish scholar Juan Menéndez Pidal and which reads as follows:

> A spark (un galán) was on his way to church to attend Mass. He didn't go for the sake of Mass, but to look at the young and pretty girls. In the middle of the road he saw a skull. He looked at it long and gave it a great kick. The skull bared its teeth as though laughing. "Skull, I invite you to my feast tonight." "Don't jest, good knight, for I pledge you my word." The spark went home astounded. All day he was melancholy. When the night arrived he ordered supper. He had not eaten a mouthful when somebody knocked at the door. He sent one of his pages to see who it might be. "Servant ask your master whether he remembers his promise." "Servant tell him I do; let him come in and be welcome." He gave him a golden chair for his body, and gave him many dishes, but he refused to eat. "I did not come to see you or to eat your supper. I came to bid you to walk with me to church at midnight." At midnight the cocks were singing; at midnight they went to the church. In the middle of the church there was an open grave. "Knight, go in, go in, go fearless to the grave. There you'll sleep with me, and eat my supper too." "I will not go in; God has not allowed it." "Were it not there is a God, were it not you called on God, were it not these relics hang on your chest, you'd enter here alive whether you wanted to or not. Go home now, low-born villain, and if you meet another skull, bow to it and say for it a *pater noster,* and throw it into the charnel-house. You will want this done to you when you leave this world."(7)

The legend's many variants show the precarious balance between seriousness and laughter and how easily one may turn into the other, depending on emphasis, "frame," and reading.

The protagonist of this ballad is obviously a prankster whose kicking of the skull shows his irreverence for Death and the dead. While Tirso's Don Juan never kicks a skull, he shows similar irreverence to and defiance of Death when he kills the Commander and, in a number of the legend's variants, insults the Commander's Statue by pulling its beard and inviting it to dine with him. His own punishment and death are not so much a result of his ruthless seduction of women but rather of that invitation, and it is upon the Statue's arrival at his house that comic tradition has seized. Outstanding commedia dell'arte actors vied to play the part of Don Juan's servant who must open the door for the stone guest, and we have the proud description of the eighteenth-century Biancollelli, most famous among them, of how he acted the scene:

> "Someone knocks at the door. A servant goes to open and returns very frightened, knocking me down; I get up . . . and go to the door. I come back horrified, knocking down three or four other servants, and I say to Don Juan that the one who made this sign to me [he refers to the Statue's nodding in assent to the dinner invitation] is at the door. He takes a candle to go and receive him. In the meanwhile I hide under the table, and as I stick my head out in order to see the Statue, Don Juan calls me and threatens to kill me if I do not come back and sit down at table. I tell him that I am fasting, then, obeying his repeated orders, I sit down at the table and cover my head and face with the napkin. My master tells me to eat. I take a bite and, the moment I try to eat it, the Statue looks at me and moves its head in a manner that frightens me. . . . I tumble down head over heels, the glass in my hand." (Ke*CM:*123; my translation).

In this scene fear has been translated into farcical stage business. Biancollelli's acting is interlaced with *lazzi* that show his acrobatic skill and arouse laughter somewhat in the manner of the pantomimes of the English company of actors Baudelaire so greatly admired. Biancollelli's performance belongs totally to the realm of the imagination and is lacking in all verisimilitude. It does not wish to be mimetic and sends out all possible signals to make us understand this.

Molière's *Dom Juan* must be counted among the most brilliant recreations of the Tirso de Molina *comedia*. But I shall discuss it in the last chapter because his Dom Juan is above all a trickster figure. Death, though it occurs at the end, plays only a minor part in this work. It is rather in his *Malade imaginaire* that the playwright juggles Death in the way Chaplin juggled the globe in the *Great Dictator*. Argan, the Imaginary Invalid, indulges in fantasy that seems capable of overcoming Death until at last it crushes him—and so does the author himself, although both are immortalized by his art. In this comedy, which, in spite of all its gaiety, perpetually deals with sickness and its inevitable culmination in death, three scenes project extraordinary farcical power. In one the actor-playwright pretends to have died—a ruse suggested to him by the servant Toinette as a way of finding out how much Béline, his second wife, "loves" him. As he reluctantly agrees to play the part, he asks whether "there's no risk in pretending to be dead?" (Mo*II:* 270) Molière put to use the age-old farce that appears in Petronius' *Satyricon,* a work well known in seventeenth-century France, wherein Trimalchio, the freed slave, bulging with fat, overindulging in food and drink, arrogant, newly rich and surrounded by all that is vulgar, has invited guests to his own "wake." It is a sumptuous feast and, upon having gorged himself with exquisite food and drink, he stretches out upon his couch, asking all to pretend that he is dead and to say something nice about him. The novel's tone clearly suggests that nothing nice will be said about Trimalchio. But variants of this farce are more explicit and make the pretended dead man hear all that he would not wish to hear. In the *Malade imaginaire* Argan is made to suffer in similar manner: his wife's relief at being rid of him and her eagerness to get hold of all he has willed her make him more receptive to the love of his children whom he had disinherited for her sake. In this case, farce did not so much turn the world upside down as right it.

In another scene, his brother Béralde tries to convince Argan not to put too much trust in medicine and doctors and regrets that he cannot take him "both for your amusement and to convince you of the error of your ways, to one of Molière's plays on this subject," only to hear Argan (the part was acted by Molière) retort: "I've no patience with your Molière and his plays. It's all very amusing I must say to be holding up worthy people like doctors to ridicule" (Mo*II*: 259). And when Béralde continues to defend the playwright, he is told: "The devil! If I were a doctor I'd have my own back on him for his impertinence. If he were ill I wouldn't help him though he were at death's door. He wouldn't get the slightest bleeding or the smallest injection however much he begged and prayed for 'em. 'Die and be damned,' I'd say, 'and that'll teach you to make fun of the doctors!' . . . He's a very foolish fellow and if the physicians are wise they'll do what I've told you" (Mo*II*: 260).

In a third scene, Argan's physician M. Purgon curses him for having neglected to take a medicine he prescribed, while the Invalid's attitude is a parody of that of a penitent before his Maker:

> PURGON: I declare that I abandon you to your evil constitution, to the disorder of your bowels, the corruption of your blood, the bitterness of your own gall, and the feculence of your humours.
>
> . . . .
>
> ARGAN: Oh Lord!
>
> P: I foretell that within four days you'll be in an incurable condition.
>
> A: Oh mercy!
>
> P: You'll fall into a state of bradypepsia . . . dyspepsia . . .

apepsia . . . diarrhoea and lientery . . . dysentery . . .
dropsy . . . autopsy that your own folly will have brought
you to. (MoII:263)

Purgon's curse, this crescendo of illnesses culminating in death,
is at last happily resolved in the spirit of carnival. Argan's ultimate admission to the Faculty of Medicine, burlesque
though it is, was based, we are told by the editor of the Grands
Ecrivains edition of the playwright's *Oeuvres,* on what was
customary during such inductions in seventeenth-century
France, including the use of music (MoŒ9:259–72). It appears
that details were furnished Molière by one of his physician
friends, later reprimanded for his indiscretion. With great skill
and imagination the playwright thus welded farce into reality
and reality into farce. But this may well be one of the reasons
for the strong opposition he encountered among his contemporaries. His infusion of actual situations into the realm of the
absolute comic, together with the growing dislike for that
realm, blurred the vision of his critics, who mistook the carnivalesque for the significative. Argan's mention of his ail-
ments, his lengthy discussion of the various parts of his phy-
sique and references to excrement, on the one hand, and food,
on the other; his insistence that his daughter marry the fool he
has chosen for her; the doctor's learned nonsense; Argan's pretended death; the kitchen Latin of the final ceremony—all these
should have signaled to the audience that the comedy belonged
to the realm of the absolute comic. But as men in medicine and
dignitaries of the Church found themselves more and more
confronted by a world of individuals, capable of criticism, they
misinterpreted these signals and winced under what they
began to consider real irreverence. Like the charivari victims of
Geneva and Lyon, they were ready to avenge themselves. In
his argument with Béralde, Argan seems to have expressed
their very feelings when he fulminated against "Molière."
They were unable to understand Argan's triumph over death as

the metaphysical consolation it represented within the idiom of farce and rather conceived of it as blasphemy, transferring it from the realm of fantasy into that of mimetic reality.

One is reminded once more of that precarious balance that exists between tragedy and comedy. In the realm of the absolute comic, even violence and death may evoke laughter, whereas they will make us weep when presented in the idiom of the tragic. Nothing illustrates this more clearly than a juxtaposition of the Rabelaisian tale of Friar Fliptail with the story of Pentheus in Euripides' *Bacchae*. Stephen Fliptail becomes the victim of the poet François Villon, who had planned to regale his town with a passion play. As the sacristan of the town, the Friar had rejected Villon's request "to lend him a cope and stole, to dress up an old peasant who was playing God the Father" (*RG*:478). Fliptail refused on pompously bureaucratic grounds, maintaining that "by their provincial statutes they were strictly forbidden to give or lend any article to an actor." To punish such rigidity, Villon and his actors, dressed up in their costumes as devils "in wolves-, calves-, and ram-skins, surmounted by sheeps' heads, bulls' horns, and great kitchen hooks, with stout leather belts round their waists, hung with large cow-bells and mule-bells, which made a horrible din," and lay in wait for Fliptail, whom they knew to be returning from collecting alms and to be riding a young mare who had not yet been covered. When the devils, "carrying black sticks full of squibs" saw Fliptail in the distance, they "waved long lighted firebrands, on to which . . . they threw great handfuls of powdered resin which produced terrible flames and smoke" and cried: 'As God's my life that's the man who wouldn't lend God the Father so much as a cope. Let's give him a good fright.' 'That's a grand idea,' " said Villon, and

> When Fliptail came up, they all rushed tumultuously into the road to meet him, throwing fire from all directions at him and his mare, clanging their bells and howling like real devils: "Hho, hho, hho, hho. brrourrrourrrrs, rrrourrrs, rrrourrrs! Hou, hou,

hou. Hho, hho, hho! Don't we make fine devils, Brother Stephen?"

The mare, thoroughly scared, began to trot, broke into a gallop, reared and plunged, and broke away, all the time dealing her rider double kicks, and farting with terror. This was too much for Friar Stephen, who was flung from his seat although he clung to the pommel of the pack-saddle with all his might. But his stirrup straps being of rope, the leather thongs of his right sandal became so entangled in them that he could not get it free of his stirrup. So he was dragged along on his arse by the mare, who kept on kicking out at him and dashing over hedge, bush, and ditch, wild with terror. In the end she broke his skull open, so that his brains fell out near the Hosanna Cross. Then his arms and his legs snapped off, one after another, and his trailing bowels were left to feed the crows. In the end his mare returned to the monastery, bringing nothing of him back except his right foot and shoe, which were still entangled in the stirrup. (RG:479–80)

Fliptail is clearly an *agelast*. He is the stiff-necked representative of law and order, incapable of seeing the duties assigned him in the perspective of man's fundamental foolishness and the ultimate futility of his endeavors. This makes him guilty in the realm of the absolute comic. He has not sinned against the gods or any standards of ethics. Nor has he done any wrong from the point of view of society or the order to which he belongs. He has, in fact, upheld their laws. But he is guilty of that rigidity that denies life itself for the sake of the letter of the law. Because of that he becomes the comic scapegoat, driven out of town and even killed. But this death is a make-believe death of carnival. If we were to think of it as real, it would seem to us too severe a punishment—even in the perspective of the severity of his "comic" crime. In purely ethical terms, we might, indeed, find the rowdy behavior of Villon and his friends out of order and altogether wrong. But we can feel no pangs of guilt or shed tears over Fliptail's death, because it does not belong to the realm of the mimetic but rather to that of the creative imagination and, thereby, to the world of the absolute comic. Rabelais' storyteller, Lord Basché, has availed himself of all signals that convey it to us as something to be laughed about: the disguise of the actors as devils—concealing, in the manner of carnival, their true identity rather than revealing it through their clothes; the weird noises they make; the frightened and indecent behavior of the mare that carries Fliptail; the comic dissection of his body—as detailed as that experienced by Homeric heroes, though less heroic; the whole improbable account of Fliptail's demise. If our laughter at Fliptail's death is liberating, however, it is so also because we cannot identify with his "suffering." He is not an individual. He is rather the representative of clerical authority that, in his person, has been pulled down from its mighty seat. It has been abased by ordinary people who are triumphing over it. In the real world, the clergy holds the power, as Fliptail's denial of a simple request indicates. But in the carnivalesque world of fantasy, the powerless win out over established authority. Their triumph is a fantasy triumph and a triumph of fantasy, and it is this aspect that seems to permeate all laughter in the realm of the absolute comic, whether we think of Boccaccio, Chaucer, or even Molière, whose genius imbued it occasionally with new meaning, as we shall see.

Pentheus in the *Bacchae* (Eu*B*) was equally punished for being what might be called an *agelast*. Pentheus was also physically torn to pieces, and all that was left of his body was his bloody head. As we have seen, he was made the butt of laughter by Dionysus and, as a punishment for his denial of the powers of sex and regeneration Dionysus stood for, was made to dress in women's clothes and to act clownishly the part of a woman. But Pentheus' death is tragic. The play becomes a tragedy, because Pentheus' *ethics* are pitted against those of the god and the god is shown to win and assert his power. It was the god who chose Pentheus as the scapegoat, and the scapegoat was duly immolated—by his mother, whom the god had so blinded with passion that she mistook her own son for the wild animal she intended to hunt and kill. We easily understand the logic of such justice. It follows the logic of the real world: opposition to divine power will, ultimately, bring about tragedy. Justice is administered by the powerful to the weak. There is no room here for fantasy to triumph. All is mimetic, and death is real, as all is decreed from above.

But the justice of the absolute comic and of farce is seldom on the side of what is ethical or what is decreed from above. Its most salient feature is usually the triumph of the meek over those in power, though not in the spirit of rebellion but rather in that of a momentary turning upside down of the world as it is known. It is in that spirit that the lower clergy may triumph over the higher, though the defeat may not be as fatal as that of Fliptail. The fourth story told on the First Day of Boccaccio's *Decameron* is in that spirit and described thus: "A Monk, Having Committed a Sin Deserving of Very Severe Punishment, Escapes the Consequences By Politely Reproaching His Abbot With the Very Same Fault" (Bo*D*:89). We are told that "In Lunigiana . . . there is a monastery that once had a greater supply of monks and of saintliness than it nowadays has, and in it there was a young monk whose freshness and vitality neither fasts nor vigils could impair" (Bo*D*:89). As he strolled about the monastery one day, he encountered a very beautiful girl and, feeling assailed by "carnal desire," he invited her into his cell. The Abbot, walking by the door of the monk's cell, heard the woman's voice and waited for the monk to leave his cell in order to take him to task. But the monk, having some suspicion of what might have happened, left the cell but asked the girl to stay. The Abbot seeing him leave alone, decided to surprise the girl, but, on entering the cell, was also attracted by her and made love to her. He nevertheless tried to chide the monk for the sin he had committed. But the monk who had observed all that had happened between the Abbot and the girl shrewdly promised "never again to commit the same error" and always to follow the Abbot's good example.

The tale is not concerned with the fact that both monks have broken their vows of chastity, but clearly with the relationship between higher and lower clerical authority. It indicates by implication the degrading of the Abbot, both because he has been trapped and caught by the monk and because the young cleric's ironic statement shows him up as the hypocrite he is and provides the monk with unlimited freedom. The young monk has triumphed over authority, and what comes to mind is the Feast of Fools and the singing of the inferior clergy "He hath put down the mighty from their seats, and exalted them of low degree." Against the backdrop of the monastery famous for its great saintliness, the young monk's sin is forgivable, but the Abbot's behavior and his hypocrisy in rebuking him must be triumphed over in the realm of the absolute comic. It is important, however, to realize that there is neither outright censure nor rebellion involved in this triumph. It has the quality of play. It is fantasy.

A quite similar tale is told about a convent, "widely renowned for its sanctity and religious fervour, which housed a certain number of nuns, one of them being a girl of gentle birth, endowed with wondrous beauty" (BoD: 688). The girl, Isabetta, falls in love with a young man who is no less passionately in love with her. They find some way of meeting, but one night the young man is seen by another nun as he leaves Isabetta's cell. All the nuns learn about it and are determined to report the scandal to the Abbess, a lady "whose goodness and piety were a byword among all the nuns and everyone else who knew her" (BoD: 680). But they decide to wait until they know that the young man is in Isabetta's cell and then call the Abbess. However, "the Abbess was keeping company that night with a priest, whom she frequently smuggled into her room in a chest, and . . . fearing lest the nuns, in their undue haste and excess of zeal, should burst down the door of her chamber, . . . leapt out of bed as quick as lightning and dressed as best as she could in the dark" (BoD: 689). So it happens that instead of her veils, she picks up the priest's breeches and puts them on her head.

No one notices her mistake, because the nuns have eyes only for the "damnable sinner," and the guilty girl is so embarrassed that she does not dare look up, while the Abbess administers "the most terrible scolding that any woman was ever given" and the other nuns begin to feel sorry for her. But suddenly the girl realizes what the Abbess has on her head and understands what she has been up to. Taking heart, she asks the Abbess to "tie up her bonnet," a remark that prompts all the nuns to look up and makes everyone aware that there is no way in which the Abbess can conceal her own guilt. This made her change her tune, and she started to argue that "it was impossible to defend oneself against the goadings of the flesh" (BoD:691). As a result of this event "they were all at liberty to enjoy themselves whenever they pleased. Isabetta was then set at liberty, and she and the Abbess returned to their beds" (BoD:691).

Again a representative of the higher clergy, in this case a woman, is made the butt of laughter as compared to the simple nun. Only when carnivalesque laughter turned into satire, as during the Reformation, or was taken as criticism, as was the case during the Counter-Reformation, was such laughter considered offensive. Before this time, the telling of such tales in itself presented a fantasy triumph of the oppressed over the mighty, as the following parody of an Abbott (SchS), one of the most popular of its kind, clearly indicates. The fact that it was written in Latin indicates that it originated among the clergy.

The Abbot's belly had become for him literally an object of adulation and adoration. "Plus meditator de eo quam de deo, plus de salamantis quam de sacramentis, plus de salmone quam de salomone," we are told in a strange sort of Latin that we might translate as: He meditated more about it (his belly) than about God, was more concerned about meats than the sacraments, more about salmon than Solomon. The Abbot's world is a world upside down. Since his deified belly is part of his body, this, too, has to be taken care of. To protect it from the hair shirt, when the Abbot makes his rounds in the monastery in the demeanor of a somber ascetic a shirt of the finest linen had to cover it first. At table, strictly obeying the rules that prohibit the eating of quadrupeds, he eats fish—but prepared in infinite variety: fish broiled, fried, poached, stuffed, dipped in egg, and followed by a variety of fowl: swans, cranes, geese, chickens, turkeys, pigeons, phaesants, etc. He devoutly circumvents the rules that forbid him to eat more than five eggs at a time by having them dished up in eleven different ways, each containing no more than five. Wine must, of course, accompany his meal and, forced to select the most suitable, he has to sample many. Having decided upon the right wine, he is obligated to drink a toast to peace and to the Holy Church, to mankind, the ocean, and the weather, anxious to omit nothing of importance. To top it all off, he dreams of finding a woman to whom he will whisper: Tu mihi sola places, tu mecum nocte iacebus" (you alone please me very much, you will lie with me tonight) (SchS:399).

Established religion was, obviously, one of the powers that carnivalesque laughter temporarily brought to grief. The absolute comic, whether in tales or plays, offers astonishing examples of the sacred abased through juxtaposition with the profane. *Joyeux sermons* (Joyous Sermons), that were, in France and elsewhere, part of festivities, and theatrical performances frequently travestied sacred texts by treating of matters of sex and food with the pompousness usually associated with sermons. While they sometimes aimed at satire, they usually were expressions of sheer joy in verbal fantasies, employing the form of the coq-à-l'âne, a discourse defined as disjointed in that it passed from one subject to another without logical transition: "Sauter du coq-à-l'âne" meant literally "to leap from the rooster to the donkey" and was probably reminiscent of medieval animal debates (LiD). According to Picot, such sermons, often starting with the Latin invocation "In nomine Patris, et Filii et Spiritus Sanctu. Amen" (in the name of the Father and the Son and the Holy Spirit. Amen), jumbled together all sorts of languages and notions and did not hesitate to address themselves in one and the same phrase to Bacchus, Venus, and the Christian God (PiS1:6). Crammed with debasing references and verbal play, they represented a carnivalesque fantasy triumph over what was usually considered sacred. Because of their irreverent mixture of Latin, latinized French, and gallicized Latin, it is impossible to translate them, but their very sound—and it was mainly sound they relied on—conveys their mingling of the sacred with the profane, as this brief sample from Picot's collection may indicate:

Sancta Bufecta, reculés de nobis. (Sancta Bufecta, spare us.)

Sancta Sadineta, aprochés de nobis. (Sancta Sadineta, come to us.)

Sancta Fachossa, ne faschés point nobis. (Sancta Fachossa, take no offense at us.)

Sancta Grondina, ne touchés nobis. (Sancta Grondina, do not touch us.)

Sancta Fumeta, ne meprissés nobis. (Sancta Fumeta, do not scorn us.)

Sancta Gloriosa, allés loing de nobis. (Sancta Gloriosa, go away from us.)

Sancta Mignarissa, reculés de nobis. (Sancta Mignarissa, spare us.)

Sancta Bouffecta, aprochés de nobis. (Sancta Bouffecta, come to us.)

Sancta Jalousia, reculés de nobis. . . . (Sancta Jalousia, spare us.)

Omnes Sancti Prenastises, libera nos Domine. (All Saints Prenastises, liberate us, Oh Lord.)

De femme pleine de tempeste. (From woman full of fury).

Qui a une mauvaise teste. (Whose state of mind is bad.)

Et le cerveau contaminé.—Libera nos Domine. (And whose brain corrupt. Deliver us, Oh Lord.) ("Le Pèlerinage de mariage," (PiS3:314–20)

Scholars have discovered innumerable examples of such travesties, permissible within the framework of the absolute comic
but seemingly sacrilegious to later ages and, even today, perhaps too daring in their juxtaposition of the sacred and the
profane. We are told, for instance, that, in the Martyr play of
Saint Didier, the Fool taunts the Bishop of Longres for having
the Saint's bones exhumed, asking him whether he intends to
become a mason and whether he truly believes that, in this
world, God will abase the mighty and exalt the meek.

Paul Lehmann assures us that one of the best-known parodies in this tradition—condemned later as sacrilegious—was a
dialogue between King Solomon and the legendary Marcolf,
wherein Solomon cites mainly passages of biblical wisdom but
is answered by Marcolf in the most obscene manner with Latin
words twisted in such a way that they become coarse sexual
references or evoke such connotations in the vernacular. The
same scholar refers to a sermon or *Historia de Nemine* (Story of
Nobody) whose author, Radulf, had carefully scanned the
Bible and the liturgy, as well as the work of such writers as
Cicero, Horace, and Maximian, etc., and—mistaking *nemo* (nobody) for a proper name—had decided to extract from these
works the story of Nemo (L*eP*: 237–45). While some scholars
believe that Radulf's intentions were serious—an assumption so
absurd that it seems unlikely—subsequent parodies based on his
work were certainly not meant to be anything but parodies.
Nemo became St. Nemo, and Lehmann mentions a picture of
Nemo printed about 1500, an empty square with the caption
"Figura Neminis, quia nemo in ea depictus." (The picture of
Nemo, because no one is depicted here.) In Brueghel's well-
known canvas, "Elk" (Dutch translation of *Nemo*) seeks himself. The popularity of the "legend" of Nemo may have been
inspired by the fact that clerics, in after-dinner conversations,
sometimes discussed philosophical questions of Being and
Nothingness.

The "legend" vied in popularity with the *Coena Cypriani*
(The Cyprian Supper), known at least since the ninth century.

It begins with words reminiscent of the biblical description of the Wedding of Cana, where Christ turned water into wine: "There was a King in the east by the name of Johel, who, at Cana in Galilee, wanted to give a great banquet." The entire story is sprinkled with biblical (both Old and New Testament) references and echoes, and the effect aimed at is utterly grotesque. All sorts of biblical figures are assembled. Adam is at the center, Eve sits on a fig leaf, Cain on a plough, Abel on a reversed milk pail, Noah on the ark. As the banquet starts, food and drink are grotesquely administered according to the character of each biblical personality: Christ drinks champagne, since the wine made of dried grapes was called *Passus* and he suffered the *Passio*. The guests take their after-dinner naps in manners appropriate to their occupations in the Bible and bring food to the married couple in whose honor the banquet is given in the same droll fashion: Petrus offers a cock, Abraham a ram, Christ a lamb, etc. Whatever the original intent of this work, Lehmann asserts that it was turned into a lively versified parody in the latter part of the ninth century and enjoyed great popularity until the seventeenth century (L*eP*: 25–29; 245), when one of the censors of Molière's *Dom Juan* referred to the tradition disapprovingly, and the great Jesuit preacher Bossuet vowed that parodies of the sacred would be banned from the stage of the Italians and from that of Molière (Mo*Œc* 5:333–34).

Molière's century was forgetting that such parody was not concerned with negativity and that, even for Rabelais and Montaigne, carnivalesque laughter had been as universal as seriousness. "It was," according to Bakhtin, "directed at the whole world, at history, at all societies, at ideology. It was the world's second truth extended to everything. . . . It was, as it were, the festive aspect of the whole world in all its elements, the second revelation of the world in play and laughter" (Bak*R*: 84). Molière found himself undoubtedly at a cultural watershed, and the problems encountered by his *Tartuffe* must, in part, be explained by the clash of the carnivalesque with the classical spirit that wished to suppress and deny it and, ultimately, succeeded in doing so. Yet Bossuet's angry censure proves that this laughter was still as alive as were, Jung reminds us (Ju*TF*), "the strange ecclesiastical customs based on memories of the ancient Saturnalia" that were celebrated on the days immediately following the birth of Christ—that is, in the New Year—with singing and dancing:

> The dances were originally harmless *tripudia* of the priests, lower clergy, children, and subdeacons, and took place in church. An *episcopus puerorum* (children's bishop) was elected on Innocents' Day and dressed in pontifical robes. Amid uproarious rejoicings he paid an official visit to the palace of the archbishop and bestowed the episcopal blessing from one of the windows. The same thing happened at the *tripudium hypodiaconorum,* and at the dances for other priestly grades. By the end of the twelfth century, the subdeacons' dance had degenerated into a real *festum stultorum* (fools' feast). A report from the year 1198 says that at the Feast of the Circumcision in Notre Dame, Paris, "so many abominations and shameful deeds" were committed that the holy place was desecrated "not only by smutty jokes, but even by the shedding of blood." In vain did Pope Innocent III inveigh against the "jests and madness that make the clergy a mockery," and the "shameless frenzy of their play-acting." Two hundred and fifty years later (March 12, 1444), a letter from the Theological Faculty of Paris to all the French bishops was still fulminating against these festivals, at which "even the priests and clerics elected an archbishop or a bishop or pope and named him the Fools' Pope" (*fatuorum papam*). "In the very midst of divine service masqueraders with grotesque faces, disguised as women, lions, and mummers, performed their dances, sang indecent songs in the choir, ate their greasy food from a corner of the altar near the priest celebrating mass, got out their games of dice, burnt a stinking incense made of old shoeleather, and ran and hopped about all over the church." . . . In certain localities even the priests seem to have adhered to the *"libertas decembria,"* as the Fools' Holiday was called, in spite (or perhaps because?) of the fact that the older level of consciousness could let itself rip

on this happy occasion with all the wildness, wantonness, and irresponsibility of paganism.* (Ju*TF*:257–58)

Jung, who based his remarks mainly on information gleaned from Du Cange's *Glossarium* of Middle and Low Latin Latinity, also alludes in this respect to the traditional *festum asinorum,* the Feast of the Ass, which was celebrated in France in memory of Mary's flight to Egypt and which displayed some of the salient aspects of grotesque celebration and staging. Like most carnivalesque celebrations, this feast combined praise and abuse, as it degraded the sacred and exalted the profane, providing the spectacle of a world upside down—as Brueghel presented it on his canvas entitled *Proverbs.* We are told by Jung:

> In Beauvais the ass procession went right into the church. At the conclusion of each part (Introit, Kyrie, Gloria, etc.) of the high mass that followed, the whole congregation *brayed,* that is, they all went "Y-a" like a donkey (*"hac modulatione hinham concludeba-tur"*). A codex dating apparently from the eleventh century says: "At the end of the mass, instead of the words 'Ite missa est,' the priest shall bray three times (*ter hinhamabit*), and instead of the words 'Deo gratias,' the congregation shall answer 'Y-a' (*hin-ham*) three times." (Ju*TF*:258)

As we shall see, Nietzsche's evocation of an Ass Festival in *Thus Spake Zarathustra* clearly parodies such parodies.

Tendencies to bring the ass into symbolic relationship with Christ existed, Jung maintains, from ancient times, and there is much evidence that "the god of the Jews was vulgarly conceived to be an ass—a prejudice which extended to Christ himself—as is shown by the mock crucifixion scratched on the wall of the Imperial Cadet School on the Palatine" (Ju*TF*:259). Such

---

* The quotes in Jung's book are extracted from Du Cange's *Glossarium,* "Kalendae."

delight in abasing the sacred by playfully linking it with the profane is, in fact, of so universal and pervasive a nature that it was observed likewise among the Pueblo Indians and described by Adolf Bandelier in his *Delight Makers* (BanD). During Indian religious festivals clowns offered slapstick entertainment, Bandelier tells us; nothing was sacred to them, everything was permitted, as long as it contributed to the delight of the tribe (BanD: 127–37) and its comic sense of justice.

It would seem, then, that the idiom of the absolute comic—unless forcefully suppressed—is timeless and universal. In contemporary literature, it has clearly been put to use again after a long period of such repression. Having familiarized ourselves with its grammar, we can easily recognize it in its modern garb as we become aware of what it is we share with, and what makes us different from, those who came before us.

three
Tears and Laughter in Modern Farce

THE haunting ambivalence of farcical laughter is decidedly of our time. It is somewhat surprising, therefore, that its literary manifestations were either totally ignored or rejected as too gross for their considerations by the two most outstanding thinkers of this century who attempted to define the essence of laughter and the comic. Bergson (Ber*L*), in his seminal study on laughter, never took farce seriously into account, although his basic notion that we laugh whenever something mechanical is imposed on something living might well have been extended to include it. Neither did Freud (Fre*J*), in his brilliant essay on wit—admittedly inspired by Bergson's observations—assign to farce the place it might have deserved in such a work. Yet Freud, perhaps more than any other modern figure, has again made such laughter palatable to modern taste, as he made us see man once more *sub specie aeternitatis*. Himself the product of "pre-Freudian" upbringing, he seems—not unlike the Moses of the Old Testament—to have led his people out of captivity to a promised land without being able to enter it himself. His compatriot Kafka, however, was permitted such entrance, so that his work abounds in farce.

In Kafka's novel *The Castle,* (Ka*C*), for instance, the protagonist K. is entrapped in a "Catch-22" situation: He has come to a village to work as land surveyor, believing that he

has been engaged by the authorities of the Castle that domi-
nates the place. But he cannot go about his vocation, his work,
until he is recognized by the Castle—something for which he
strives in vain. Nor can he leave the Castle village because of
his desire for recognition. His entrapment would appear to be
more tragic than comic were it not for the fact that farce plays
counterpoint to his frustration, culminating in a dream scene
that we might consider the central episode of the narrative.
Having spent an entire day in vain attempts to speak to any
Castle official who might help him, K. finds himself at night in
the inn reserved for officials of highest rank. Inadvertently, he
stumbles into a room where one of them, Bürgel, is bedded
down. Bürgel proves most willing to give friendly advice to
the unexpected intruder, but K., dead tired, collapses on the official's bed, his head drowsily drooping on the bureaucrat's
naked and hairy chest.

Occurring as it does after various characters of the novel
have described the utter remoteness and robotlike functioning
of a bureaucracy that all nonofficials are dependent on, this
sudden physical intimacy between pompous, impersonal of-
ficialdom and humble petitioner is strikingly grotesque. In a
lengthy conversation with Olga, a village girl who befriends
him, K. has learned of the total hopelessness of her own family's
efforts to communicate with the Castle—her father's attempts,
for instance, to intercept any Castle official on his way to or
from the village in order to admit to a crime he had not committed and of which he had not been accused, but which he
believed to be secretly held against him by the Castle. K. has
been told by her of the many roads leading from the Castle to
the village, of the uncertainty as to which of these a given official might travel, of the extraordinary speed of the officials'
movements, and above all of the fact that "no official can settle
anything without the necessary documents, and certainly not
on the main road; he can't pardon anything, he can only settle
it officially, and he would simply refer to the official proce-
dure, which had already been a complete failure for father"

(KaC: 279). Moreover, none other than the village mayor described to K. that "peculiar characteristic of our administrative apparatus" (KaC: 88). Any decision concerning a case, he maintained, might be long in the making or unexpectedly made somewhere but never discovered, since government agencies found it difficult to communicate with one another (KaC: 88). Because of this, some officials might be "still passionately canvassing things that were decided long ago" (KaC: 89), their desks piled high, their coaches filled with countless files multiplying on their own, as it were, less and less related to the original request that brought them into existence.

K. himself has, of course, tried to move heaven and earth to obtain an audience with the highly placed official Klamm, who has remained, however, totally elusive. The few friends K. has managed to make in the village were all cultivated by him for a selfish purpose: to help him gain access to the Castle and its officials. Were we able to think of the Castle as a seat of divinity, a symbol of purity and a depository of faith, as some critics have, K.'s struggle might strike us as admirable and even saintly. He would then appear to be a seeker after truth and salvation. But it would be impossible to confer upon the Castle, that absurd bureaucratic maze with its utter whimsicality, the sort of sanctity that would imply that K. is striving for saintliness. He is, moreover, much too ruthless and self-seeking, obviously out to exploit friend and foe alike for his purposes. Any doubts we might harbor concerning this should vanish in view of the farcical way in which K.'s behavior is mimicked by his two assistants, who are more of a hindrance to him than a help.

K's assistants suffer from the same rejection the Castle metes out to him and, like his, their stubborn refusal to accept their lot turns their perpetual clamor for recognition into farce. Having been ejected by K. from the room they had occupied in his apartment, they engage in desperate antics in the hope of being readmitted: climb fences so that he will notice them through the window, rap on window panes, and frantically and beseechingly stretch out their clasped hands toward him. It is as if they were miming and translating into the concrete language of the body what K. had been doing all along vis-à-vis the Castle; their echoing of his striving on a lower and more farcical scale makes *his* appear ludicrous. It is therefore doubly farcical that K.'s restless clamor for recognition is replaced by helpless drowsiness at the very moment when he should have been shouting with joy at the opportunity of being face to face with a Castle official well disposed, moreover, to concern himself with the problems of petitioners and not the least bit startled by K.'s intrusion into the privacy of his bedchamber or K.'s informality of falling asleep on his naked chest.

But during that miraculous moment of opportunity K. has so fervently wished for and that should have been the crown of his quest, all he feels is profound annoyance at Bürgel's voice droning on in an endless monologue. All he wants is sleep, until he dozes off into a dream that provides him with the inner satisfaction he had vainly sought on the outside and the laughter that should have been his all along. His dream seems the very essence of farce:

> K. was asleep, it was not real sleep, he could hear Bürgel's words perhaps better than during his former dead-tired state of waking, word after word struck his ear, but the tiresome consciousness had gone, he felt free, it was no longer Bürgel who held him, only he still sometimes groped toward Bürgel, he was not yet in the depths of sleep, but immersed in it he certainly was. No one should deprive him of that now. And it seemed to him as though with this he had achieved a great victory and already there was a party of people there to celebrate it, and he or perhaps someone else raised the champagne glass in honor of this victory. (KaC:342)

In K.'s dream, this victory is repeated over and over again:

> There was no leaving off celebrating it, because fortunately the outcome was certain. A secretary, naked, very like the statue of a Greek god, was hard pressed by K. in the fight. It was very

funny and K. in his sleep smiled gently about how the secretary was time and again startled out of his proud attitude by K.'s assaults and would hastily have to use his raised arm and clenched fist to cover unguarded parts of his body and yet was always too slow in doing so. The fight did not last long; step for step, and they were big steps, K. advanced. Was it a fight at all? There was no serious obstacle, only now and then a squeak from the secretary. This Greek god squeaked like a girl being tickled. And finally he was gone, K. was alone in a large room: ready for battle he turned round, looking for his opponent; but there was no longer anyone there, the company had also scattered, only the champagne glass lay broken on the floor. K. trampled it to smithereens. (KaC:342–43)

As the broken glass pricks him and interrupts his dream, K. finds himself looking at Bürgel's bare chest and wondering whether it is that of the Greek god he has just defeated and whether he should not haul him out of bed for the ticklish fool he is. But K. merely drops off into a still deeper sleep, while Bürgel's voice drones on, revealing to him all the secrets that, had he heard them, would have led to the fulfillment of his striving.

However, it is just then that those secrets lose any and all importance to K. because, during the brief space spent in dream and in the realm of the imaginary, his world has been turned upside down for him: he, the meek petitioner, has won a victory over the powerful and proud Greek god, the representative of authority, Bürgel. Farcically, authority has been toppled from its pedestal and made doubly laughable because of its naked vulnerability and ticklishness, its girlish giggling, and its inability to keep up its appearance of superiority. Without clothes, without insignia of authority, its bearer has become not only an ordinary human being but even a silly one, whose recognition of K. is no longer significant to him. Thus K.'s victory becomes for him an existential one, in a Kierkegaardian sense of the word, in that it reveals to him his own human dignity as grounded in his own self and independent of the approval of others. This deflation of worldly authority and reversal of power can but arouse the merriment of the crowd that is part of the dream, and, at the same time, that of the reader—although it is equally essential that K. is ultimately left alone. Obviously, there is nothing prurient about the official's nakedness. Nor must K.'s aggressiveness be seen in sexual terms: nakedness merely helps to create the farce of the situation as it deflates pomposity and thereby turns the world upside down.

Nakedness conjures up a similar mood in Günter Grass' delightful excursion into adolescent fiction, *Cat and Mouse* (Gr*CM*), although the events surrounding it are of a totally different nature. The time during which they occur is that of the Second World War and the place a boys' school in northeastern Germany. The occasion is the visit to the institution of one of its recent graduates, now a war hero, a lieutenant commander and much decorated U-boat captain. He has come to address the student body and, in his honor, the girls of a neighboring school have been invited to sit in the first rows of the auditorium. The mood among the adolescent boys is a mixture of admiring awe and cynicism toward the war hero, and they are more absorbed in passing notes to the visiting girls than in listening to the high-flown speech of the lieutenant commander, introduced pompously and with learned eloquence by the principal. He has been sitting on the platform, a picture of arrogant smugness, "cap perched with dignity on his parallel knees. Under the cap his gloves. Dress uniform. The hardware on his neck plainly discernible against an inconceivably white shirt" (Gr*CM*:60), and as such he has been closely observed by one of the most recalcitrant and critical students in the audience, "the great Mahlke," as Pilenz the narrator calls him. During the entire session Mahlke gives barely concealed evidence of excitement at the orator's display of stupidity and conceit. Mahlke is the maverick of his class, an adolescent of such integrity and intelligence that his schoolmates admire his superiority, while keeping a safe distance from him. Pilenz is the exception. He would have sacrificed much for the sake of his friendship with Mahlke and it is significant that Mahlke rather than the visiting lieutenant is the hero of his tale, although it was the lieutenant's visit that made of Mahlke a perpetrator of farce and ultimately a tragic hero.

Having exchanged his uniform for the school's gym clothes so as to regale the upper class with his presence during their gym period following the lecture, the lieutenant commander is to discover with dismay that his proudest decoration, a huge medal, has disappeared by the time he puts on his uniform again. No appeal to honesty and honor, no threat of punishment by principal or visitor results in its retrieval. No one can be accused, although some of the students seem to have their own ideas about the matter. Those of Pilenz are oddly confirmed when, after school, he rejoins Mahlke on their favorite "playground," a barge partly sunk at such distance from the seashore that only good swimmers can negotiate it. There he finds the great Mahlke, listening to the phonograph he has ingeniously hidden in the sunken barge and wearing a ribbon with "it" on his neck. The situation is one of farce, as the narrator describes it:

> It was very funny-looking, because he had nothing else on. He sat huddled, naked and bony in the shade with his eternal sunburn. Only the knees glared. His long, semi-relaxed pecker and his testicles lay flat on the rust. His hands clutching his knees. His hair plastered in strands over his ears. . . . And that face, that Redeemer's countenance! And below it, motionless, his one and only article of clothing, the large, the enormous medal a hand's breadth below his collarbone. (GrCM:74–75)

The encounter of the two friends is exuberant:

> "Hey, Pilenz! What do you think of my trinket? Not bad eh?"
> "Terrific! Let me touch it."
> "You'll admit I earned it."

"I knew right away that you'd pulled the job."

"Job nothing. It was conferred on me only yesterday for sinking five ships on the Murmansk run plus a cruiser of the *Southampton* class . . ."

Both of us determined to make a show of lightheartedness; we grew very silly, bawled out every single verse of "We're sailing against England," made up new verses . . . ; forming megaphones of our hands, we blared out special communiqués, announcing our sinkings in terms both high-flown and obscene, and drummed on the deck with our fists and heels. . . . Wild with glee, he removed the article from his neck and held the ends of the ribbon over his hip bones with a mincing little gesture. While with his legs, shoulders, and twisted head he performed a fairly comical imitation of a girl, but no particular girl, the great iron cookie dangled in front of his parts, concealed no more than a third of his pecker. (Gr*CM:* 75–76)

Here again nakedness is part of the farce that evokes our laughter. While suggesting no prurience, it seems to debase the medal dangling in front of Mahlke's private parts and thereby to deflate all the false rhetoric and pomposity of the young war hero and the school principal. What adds to the power of this farce is not only the fact that a young and vulnerable schoolboy has outwitted pompous and powerful authority—as represented by the school principal and the chauvinistic war hero—but also that his joke is played out against the threat of severe punishment. In the story such punishment is ultimately meted out because moral consideration makes Mahlke voluntarily confess his "crime." Punishment would have been impossible had he merely enjoyed his victory and hidden or sunk his treasure. But even Mahlke's moral considerations could spoil only in retrospect that moment of laughter when imagination had turned the world upside down.

Like Kafka's, Grass' fiction is replete with moments of farcical laughter. In *The Tin Drum* (Gr*TD*)—the novel that first gained him international fame—Oskar, the monstrous dwarfish protagonist with a child's body and an adult's cynicism, uses his voice, a powerful instrument capable of cutting glass, to give strength to the poor and deflate the strong. Hiding in dark doorways during the weeks before Christmas, he cuts holes into shop windows with his voice. The poor, hypnotized by those articles on display that they want but cannot afford, can thus reach out and take what unexpectedly and joyfully has been made available to them. The rich, often pillars of society who would openly condemn stealing, are abased as they, too, submit to temptation and thereby realize that they are but human. As an adult writing about that phase of his childhood, Oskar weighs the morality of his act:

> Was it evil that commanded Oskar to enhance the already considerable temptation offered by a well-polished plateglass window by opening a passage through it?—— I must reply: Yes, it was evil. . . . On the other hand, without wishing to minimize the wickedness of my acts, I am compelled now that I have lost all opportunity or inclination to tempt anyone, to say to myself . . . : Oskar, you not only contented the small and medium-sized desires of all those silent walkers in the snow, those men and women in love with some object of their dreams; no, you helped them to know themselves. Many a respectably well-dressed lady, many a fine old gentleman, many an elderly spinster whose religion had kept her young would never have come to know the thief in their hearts if your voice had not tempted them to steal, not to mention the changes it wrought in self-righteous citizens who until that hour had looked upon the pettiest and most incompetent of pickpockets as a dangerous criminal. (GrTD:130)

As readers, we may well repeat Oskar's question concerning the morality of his enterprise, but we might also realize that farcical laughter disappears and gives way to sobriety and dullness if we look at it in strictly moral terms.

Ambivalence seems equally essential in preserving the laughter of farce. This becomes more obvious yet when we look at Oskar's most cherished toy, the tin drum, from which the novel derives its title. The childish cynic or cynical child employs it as yet another tool to turn the world of the grown-ups upside down. With his murderous drumming, he changes the victory rallies of the Nazi party into chaotic mass flight, and with his immature persistence in having his last drum fixed, he transforms his uncle's complacent and cowardly existence into something approaching heroism and martyrdom. Uncle Jan, who had so carefully avoided all political involvement and who was possibly Oskar's father, being the lover of his mother, returns with Oskar and his broken drum, to the very heart of conflict, the Polish post office, in quest of the janitor who can fix Oskar's drum, and is trapped there when the Nazis attack it. Jan, the antithesis of a hero, the elegant and refined young post office employee who had opted for Poland when Danzig ceased to be a free city, spends a night of siege and horror, a horror as ambiguously farcical as that which Lina Wertmueller presents in her film *Seven Beauties*. While the post office is being shelled, Oskar and Jan take shelter in the storeroom for undeliverable mail, where they are soon joined by a dead man and the janitor Kobyella, who is seriously wounded. To lessen pain and nervous strain, the three play cards by the light of a candle; the game soon becomes a game against death itself, a refusal by little Oskar to let Kobyella die by seeing to it that the cards are in movement all the time and by sticking a fresh cigarette between the janitor's lips as soon as the previous one has been finished. Ironically, for the first time in his life Jan seems to be winning at cards, at the very moment that he loses the game of life, as death invades the post office on all sides:

> Jan slammed down the ace of hearts and was absolutely unwilling and unable to understand, the truth is he had never fully understood, he had never been anything but a blue-eyed boy, smelling of cologne and incapable of understanding certain things, and so he simply could not understand why Kobyella suddenly dropped all his cards, tugged at a laundry basket with the letters in it and the dead man on top of the letters, until first the dead man, then a layer of letters, and finally the whole ex-

> cellently plaited basket toppled over, sending us a wave of let-
> ters as though we were the addressees, as though the thing for us
> to do now was to put aside our playing cards and take to read-
> ing our correspondence. . . . But Jan didn't feel like reading
> . . . , he wanted to play out his grand hand, he wanted to win,
> Jan did, to triumph. He lifted Kobyella up, set the basket back
> on its wheels, but let the dead man lie and also neglected to put
> the letters back in the basket. (Gr*TD:241*–42)

Jan, crazed by the night's experiences, cannot understand why
Kobyella "just wouldn't sit still but sagged lower and lower"
and, addressing him as Alfred, Oskar's father with whom he
had played many a game of cards, begs him not to be a spoil-
sport, but to finish the game. When all fails, Jan explodes into
hysterical laughter and starts building a house of cards that
collapses at the same time the siege ends and all are taken prisoners. They are shot the next morning, and only the child survives. The episode is as stark in its farcical elements as is that of
Seven Beauties, who—once the proud and swaggering Don
Juan of his village—is ordered to make love to his Nazi prison
guard, a repulsive and gigantic woman, and realizes that his life
depends on her satisfaction with his performance.

Laughter and death are fused to create almost equally
frightening farce in Joseph Heller's *Catch-22* (HeC). The novel's protagonist Yossarian, through whose consciousness
events are filtered, conveys to us his experiences in a World
War II hospital and tells the story of the "soldier in white."
Though his arrival is at first dreaded by the hospital inmates,
because being severely wounded, he may moan day and night,
the soldier in white turns out to be incapable of emitting any
sign of life, feeling, or thought. He appears to be a silent, mo-
tionless object, a construct made "entirely of gauze, plaster and
a thermometer, and the thermometer was merely an adorn-
ment left balanced in the empty dark hole in the bandages over
his mouth early each morning and late each afternoon by Nurse
Cramer and Nurse Duckett right up to the afternoon Nurse
Cramer read the thermometer and discovered he was dead"

(He*C*: 171). To Yossarian, it seems as if the soldier in white might have continued to exist forever in his state of motion-lessness and speechlessness, had it not been for this discovery of Nurse Cramer's.

Bergson's conception of the comic as something mechani-cal imposed upon something we expect to act like a living or-ganism proves to be an essential element in the mood of farce Heller has conjured up here in the presence of death. For we are made to see the soldier as an object: his bandages are brushed off daily by the two nurses who also, with wet dish towels, wipe the dust several times a day from "the slim black rubber tubes leading in and out of him to the two large stoppered jars, one of them hanging on a post beside his bed, dripping fluid into his arm constantly through a slit in the bandage while the other, almost out of sight on the floor, drained the fluid away through the zinc pipe rising from his groin" (He*C*: 173). Al-though he is seemingly cleansed and fed, the soldier, dead or alive, seems detached from all that might be called individ-uality. He has no name, no identity. He is no more, and proba-bly less, than a robot, and totally controlled by others. The rubber tube supplying his body with liquid, and the other draining it, suggest carnivalesque notions of man as the tempo-rary depository of material and spiritual nourishment. This far-cical effect is strengthened when we are told that "changing the jars for the soldier in white was no trouble at all, since the same clear fluid was dripped back inside him over and over again with no apparent loss . . . the two (jars) were simply un-coupled from their respective hoses and reversed quickly" (He*C*: 174). Death seen in this impersonal light is both frighten-ing and farcical; laughter seems to lessen our fear of it. Both moods are reflected in the remarks of the other patients. One man wonders whether a living being had ever been inside the bandages at all or whether "they sent the bandages here for a joke" (He*C*: 173–74). Another suggests that they "hook the two jars up to each other and eliminate the middleman" (He*C*: 174). Notions of heroism traditionally associated with war are thoroughly deflated by this episode, as they are by the novel in its entirety. Death, on the other hand, seems somewhat less formidable if it can be made impersonal and laughed about in the spirit of defiance we traditionally associate with carnival.

Against a totally different background, Nabokov succeeded in creating a comparably ambivalent mood of farce in his novel *Lolita* (NaL), which he so lovingly refers to as having afforded him "aesthetic bliss" and the occasion to express his exhilaration at "philistine vulgarity." The novel's farcical high point is the encounter of the irate protagonist Humbert Humbert with Quilty, the successful playwright, Lolita's abductor and, it turns out, also her initiator into debauchery when she was still a school girl. Humbert Humbert has come to Quilty's residence early in the morning to avenge himself, as her lover, for the loss of his nymphet and, as her "father," for the nymphet's original loss of innocence. He has come as the knight in shining armor to mete out the punishment of death to a man he knows to be guilty of what he and society consider a crime. But the duel the two engage in is painted with strokes so broadly farcical and even grotesque that we find it hilarious without feeling anguish for the villain or admiration for the victor. While violent death and dying conjure up the tradition of the Western, our awareness of farce turns it into parody. What might have been a moment of tragic dimensions and implications, the punishment and final destruction of a villain by a jealous lover and avenging father, has become exhilarating because of its "philistine vulgarity."

When, after years of unsettling and anguished search, Humbert—his gun Chum safely tucked away in his pocket—finally locates Quilty, he finds him alone in his huge house, sleeping off the drugs of the previous night. Having entered his house in the early morning hours, Humbert watches his quarry come out of the bathroom "leaving a brief waterfall behind him" (NaL: 296), and sees him "gray-faced, baggy-eyed, fluffily disheveled in a scanty balding way" sweeping by him "in a purple bathrobe" (Na*L:* 296). "He either did not notice me," he muses, "or else dismissed me as some familiar and innocuous hallucination—and, showing me his hairy calves, he proceeded sleepwalker-wise, downstairs" (Na*L:* 296). When Quilty and his visitor finally come face to face, however, in the Oriental parlor of the house, events and the dialogue that ensue run the entire gamut of farce:

> "Now who are you?" he asked in a high hoarse voice, his hands thrust into his dressing-gown pockets, his eyes fixing a point to the northeast of my head. "Are you by any chance Brewster?"
>
> By now it was evident . . . that he was in a fog and completely at my so-called mercy. I could enjoy myself. "That's right," I answered suavely. 'Je suis Monsieur Brustère.' Let us chat for a moment before we start."
>
> He looked pleased. His smudgy mustache twitched. I removed my raincoat. I was wearing a black suit, a black shirt, no tie. We sat down in two easy chairs. (Na*L:* 297)

It is obvious that Quilty believes the intruder to be from the telephone company and, in his drugged state, is even pleased when he learns that he is mistaken after all; Humbert is gloating at the helplessness of the criminal he is planning to do in and who has to admit to him his guilt. However, once aware of the danger he is in, Quilty looks for escape and protection, only to be forced back into his seat each time by Humbert's threats. Even the cigarettes he is trying to grab are denied him:

> "Quilty," I said. "I want you to concentrate. You are going to die in a moment. The hereafter for all we know may be an eternal state of excruciating insanity. You smoked your last cigarette yesterday. Concentrate. Try to understand what is happening to you. . . . I pointed Chum at his slippered foot and crushed the trigger. It clicked. He looked at his foot, at the pistol, again at his foot. I made another effort, and, with a ridiculously feeble and juvenile sound, it went off. The bullet entered

> the thick pink rug, and I had the paralyzing impression that it
> had merely trickled in and might come out again. . . . He
> reached for it (Chum). I pushed him back into the chair. . . . It
> was high time I destroyed him, but he must understand why he
> was being destroyed. (NaL:299)

Noticing an opportunity to get hold of Chum during the battle
of words that ensues, Quilty finally sends Chum "hurtling
under a chest of drawers" but is again violently shoved back
into his chair as he rises to grab it.

> Fussily, busybodily, cunningly, he had risen again while he
> talked. I groped under the chest trying at the same time to keep
> an eye on him. All of a sudden I noticed that he had noticed that
> I did not seem to have noticed Chum protruding from beneath
> the corner of the chest. We fell to wrestling again. We rolled all
> over the floor, in each other's arms, like two huge helpless chil-
> dren. He was naked and goatish under his robe, and I felt suffo-
> cated as he rolled over me. I rolled over him. We rolled over
> me. They rolled over him. We rolled over us. (NaL:300–1)

Narrator Humbert himself here compares the scene to
those obligatory in Westerns but has to admit:

> Our tussle, however, lacked the ox-stunning fisticuffs, the fly-
> ing furniture. He and I were two large dummies, stuffed with
> dirty cotton and rags. It was a silent, soft, formless tussle on the
> part of two literati, one of whom was utterly disorganized by a
> drug while the other was handicapped by a heart condition and
> too much gin. When at last I had possessed myself of my pre-
> cious weapon, and the scenario writer had been reinstalled in his
> low chair, both of us were panting as the cowman and the
> sheepman never do after their battle. (NaL:301)

But as soon as Humbert has regained his breath and recov-
ered his weapon, he asks Quilty again whether he wishes to say
anything before his death. Quilty's pleading to be reasonable
and postpone the matter is met by Humbert's "Feu."

> This time I hit something hard. I hit the back of a black rocking
> chair . . . my bullet hit the inside surface of its back whereupon
> it immediately went into a rocking act, so fast and with such
> zest that anyone coming into the room might have been flab-
> bergasted by the double miracle: that chair rocking in a panic all
> by itself, and the armchair, where my purple target had just
> been, now void of all live content. Wiggling his fingers in the
> air, with a rapid heave of his rump, he flashed into the music
> room and the next second we were tugging and gasping on both
> sides of the door. (NaL: 304)

Once more it is Humbert who wins, with the result that
Quilty, in despair, sits down at the piano, wildly playing and
snorting with fear, while attempting to open with one foot a
chest apparently containing a gun. But, as Humbert's next bul-
let catches him somewhere in the side, he rises higher and
higher from his chair, "as he rent the air—still shaking with the
rich black music—head thrown back in a howl, hand pressed to
his brow, and with his other hand clutching his armpit as if
stung by a hornet." (NaL: 304–5). Quilty rushes from the room
and is followed by Humbert, so that the two men dance a hor-
rid dance, one trying to escape through the front door, the
other preventing his escape, until Quilty, with strange dignity,
starts to mount the broad staircase again. There Humbert
shoots at him several times, while Quilty's face twitches absurdly and his voice, in "a detached and even amiable manner"
trails off assuring his adversary and the world at large "Ah,
that hurts atrociously, my dear fellow. I pray you desist . . ."
(NaL: 305). When Quilty finally succeeds in getting back into
his bedroom and rolling himself into his blankets, he is followed by Humbert who pumps more bullets into him until he
appears to be dead, and "a big pink bubble with juvenile connotations formed on his lips, grew to the size of a toy balloon,
and vanished," to the hum of "two flies beside themselves with
a dawning sense of unbelievable luck" (NaL: 306). Farce in the
face of death is still further heightened by the fact that Humbert, upon descending into the living room, finds there as-

sembled a group of Quilty's friends who have come to take him along to a game and are whiling away the time by drinking his gin. When he announces to them: "I have just killed Quilty," someone drunkenly exclaims "Good for you," and someone else asks him whether he wants a beer. Only after Quilty has managed to crawl out onto the landing once more and has finally subsided in a purple heap, does Humbert leave the house, realizing that this "was the end of the ingenious play staged for me by Quilty" (NaL:307). Killing has been reduced to a scenario or a game of chess, and death is as impersonal as it is unreal.

In this drawn-out fight, which the narrator tells us lasted about an hour, Quilty proves as immune to bullets as did earlier literary heroes to the swords and arrows of their opponents. Instead of the battlefield of epic heroes or the towns of the Westerns, the suburban house of a playwright supplies in *Lolita* the background for the battle of virtue against vice. What escapes from Quilty's lips at the moment of death or near death is appropriately not the immortal soul of Homeric heroes dying in battle but rather a bloody bubble resembling chewing gum.

We may well believe Nabokov when he assures us that the novel was not written by him to convey a moral message. For were we to accept Humbert as the moralistic avenger he believes himself to be, the author would hardly have presented him as wearing a dirty raincoat over a black suit and shirt, or with hands covered with blood. Far from being a hero in shining armor, a man of nobility, strength, and skill, Humbert is clumsy and drunk, a poor shot, and totally lacking in the chivalrous respect he might owe his opponent and in obedience to any code of honor. He is, moreover, a dubious defender of virtue, his own morals being as questionable as those of his nymphet. In assuming the role of a bourgeois father (stepfather) defending the honor of his nymphet daughter, he therefore turns into farce "philistine vulgarity," even if the occasion is a bloody one. We are again confronted with that ambiguity that not only permeates much of the laughter of modern literature but also informs its protagonists: "the great Mahlke" with his face of a savior, Oskar, the deformed hunchback who magically opens shop-windows for the needy, Humbert the avenger.

In their disregard for accepted morality, such characters resemble figures that were central in the tradition of carnivalesque festivities and were sometimes referred to as Lords of Misrule or tricksters. I shall discuss them later. While contriving and setting in motion the gaiety that permits the world to be turned upside down, these characters are often made to suffer in the end: Oskar ends up in a mental institution; Mahlke disappears at the height of his achievements and may well have committed suicide, Humbert ends up in prison. Nabokov admittedly set out to create in Humbert Humbert a farcical hero of similar ambiguity, maintaining that he wanted him both to win and to lose at one and the same time. Treating him as if he were a figure in a game of chess (the author's game), he also makes him the player of that game, who shoots his adversary and explains to him that he does so in the terminology of the chess player "because you took advantage of my disadvantage" (NaL:301). If Humbert Humbert, the clever player, earns for himself the reward of prison, he shares this lot with Felix Krull, Thomas Mann's shrewd confidence man who, even as a tender youth, had cheated hordes of vacationers in the summer spa his parents frequented and earned their admiring applause by pretending to play the violin (ManCK). Thomas Mann was clearly intrigued by such trickster figures, for he presented us with another, who ended his life in glory and became nothing less than Pope Gregorius. Basing his tale, appropriately entitled *The Holy Sinner* (ManHS), on the legend of the sixth-century pope, Mann created the unforgettably farcical episode, wherein Gregory (who has spent years in penitent isolation), once he has assumed his high office, receives an old woman in audience whom he recognizes, upon hearing her confession, as the woman he had once married, unaware of the fact that he was also her son and the fruit of her incest with her brother. He now greets her as "Mother" whereas she properly addresses him, the Pope, as "Father," although in reality he is both her son and her husband. God has forgiven, and joy reigns supreme.

A similarly immoral ambivalence of relationships, fusing death and laughter in joyful farce, occurs in the Brazilian novel by Jorge Amado, *Dona Flor and Her Two Husbands* (Am*DF*). Its initial episode centers around the sudden death of Dona Flor's first husband. But since she is the proud owner and sole teacher of the Cooking School of Savor and Art, the death scene is preceded by advice the heroine has given in answer to one of her students as to "When and What to Serve at a Wake." Her mouth-watering recipes are an essential part of her existence, and she herself is described by the author through imagery taken from food.

Yet when we first encounter her, it is as if life and joy had left her body as it has that of Vadinho her husband—though even his death had been in a certain way an affirmation of life. For it had taken place in the midst of carnival laughter, playful make-believe, and over-indulgence in food, drink, and sex. When Vadinho died, he was dressed up as a Bahian woman and enthusiastically danced a samba with a mulatta in the costume of a Hungarian peasant: "He whirled in the middle of the group, stomped in front of the mulatta, approached her in flourishes and belly-bumps, then suddenly gave a kind of hoarse moan, wobbled, listed to one side, and fell to the ground, a yellow slobber drooling from his mouth on which the grimace of death could not wholly extinguish the fatuous smile of the complete faker he had always been" (Am*DF*:5–6).

Lest the scene be misleading, it must be accompanied, however, with Amado's reassurance to the reader that Vadinho's wearing of women's clothes should not be seen as any lack of masculinity but rather as a carnival custom often adhered to by men "to enjoy themselves and have fun, not because of any deviant inclinations" (Am*DF:* 7). The author tells us, moreover, that "Vadinho had even tied under his white starched petticoat a huge cassava tuber, and at every step he raised his skirts and displayed the outsized, pornographic trophy, causing the women to cover their faces with their hands and let out malicious giggles" (Am*DF:* 7). It is against the backdrop of such exuberance that he collapses, and it is only then that the tuber assumes an aspect of obscenity, as it lies upon his lifeless body and no longer evokes laughter.

According to the notions prevalent in the bourgeois society of which Dona Flor's mother and some of her friends are the outspoken representatives, the young woman should have felt relieved by her husband's demise. He had been dissolute, a drunkard, a Don Juan; good-for-nothing, lazy, earning little, and gambling away not only his own money but also the meager and hard-earned savings of his wife. He went out every night, leaving her a prey to loneliness and bitter jealousy. He had flirted even with her students in the cooking school. But instead of considering his death as the beginning of something better and a new lease on life, the pretty young widow thought of it as an irreparable loss and Vadinho remained to her as unforgettable as he was to his numerous friends. The reason for this was that his dissoluteness was more than matched by unlimited kindness and generosity and that he had joyfully embraced life as if it were a beloved woman and women—Dona Flor in particular—as if they were the very essence of life:

> Vadinho knew her (Dona Flor's) weaknesses, brought them out in the open: that banked-down desire of the timid person, that restraint which turned violent and positively unbounded when given free rein in bed. When Vadinho was in the mood, there was no one more charming, nor could any woman resist him. Dona Flor was never able to hold out against his fascination, not even when she had made up her mind to do so, boiling with indignation and recent affronts. Time and again she had even come to hate him and to curse the day when she had linked her fate to that wastrel. (Am*DF:* 8)

So it was not only his death that had absolved him of all his shortcomings. Vadinho's seductiveness to women consisted in his innate ability to pay homage to love as a power of nature and to make it reign supreme by turning the world upside down and deflating bourgeois values.

It is due to this ability that even years later, when Dona Flor is married to a man endowed with all the bourgeois virtues Vadinho lacked, and who offers her all the respectability and security she had longed for—material comfort and a life so well regulated that even lovemaking is assigned its proper place and time—she still dreams of Vadinho's mad and unpredictable caresses. Her longing for him is so strong, in fact, that it calls him back to life, where, invisible to anyone but herself, he surrounds her with his tenderly teasing, caressing, and shameless presence. A chapter entitled "Of the Terrible Battle Between the Spirit and Matter, With Unique Happenings and Astounding Circumstances, Which Can Happen Only in the City of Bahia, and Let Him Who Will Believe the Tale," is not only a farcical account of Dona Flor's life divided between her two husbands—the attraction to the first, the fear of hurting the second to whom she feels great loyalty—but also one that belongs to the realm of the imaginary. For her first husband is but a ghost, even if in unghostly fashion he feasts on the delights of her body from which her second husband discreetly diverts his eyes. If sex is glorified in this novel, this is done in a manner almost impersonal, totally without prurience, and only in concert with those characters of the tale that are made most attractive and that accept sex as a force of nature.

The novel ends with a subtle irony that is at the same time a farcical hymn to love, as neighbors, observing the happiness of Dona Flor and her second husband passing them arm in arm on the street, comment to one another: "Just get a load of her. What a handsome, beautiful woman! A knockout, and you can see that she lacks for nothing at board or in bed. She even looks like a woman with a new lover, putting horns on her husband. . . . That doctor, with his dopey face, is a sly customer"

(Am*DF:* 518). While the interlocutor is assured that she is the most virtuous woman in Bahia, the author confides in us that "on the arm of that lucky dog of a husband, Dona Flor smiled gently. Oh, that mania of Vadinho's for feeling her breasts and buttocks on the street, fluttering about her like the morning breeze. That clear, rain-washed Sunday morning with Dona Flor strolling along, happy with her life, satisfied with her two loves" (Am*DF:* 518). Does Amado laugh—even if ever so gently and in spite of Dona Flor's certainty that she admires and loves her second husband—at this straitlaced bourgeois who fails, in spite of his intelligence, to understand those joys of the flesh that transcend materialism? Does he not turn the world upside down by instilling in us admiration for the irreverent Vadinho and deflating Dona Flor's respectable second husband? Is Dona Flor, indeed, the most decent woman in Bahia? To assure our laughter, the answer must remain ambivalent, as all depends on the values we invoke.

This becomes more evident yet when modern farce assumes the form of a fusion between the ludicrous, the scatalogical even, and the sacred. Toward the middle of Beckett's novel *Watt* (Be*Wt*), the narrator is identified as Sam (Samuel Beckett?) who, one day in the garden of his pavillion (part of an asylum it seems), espies the protagonist Watt (whom he had previously known in another asylum) walking toward him backward. As Watt grotesquely advances—perpetually falling into the shrubbery and painfully raising himself again—and turns his face toward Sam, the narrator recognizes in him both Christ and his own mirror image:

> And I saw his face, and the rest of his front. His face was bloody, his hands also, and thorns were in his scalp. (His resemblance, at that moment to the Christ believed by Bosch, then hanging in Trafalgar Square, was so striking, that I remarked it.) And at the same instant suddenly I felt as though I were standing before a great mirror, in which my garden was reflected, and my fence, and I, and the very birds tossing in the wind, so that I looked at my hands, and felt my face, and glossy

skull, with an anxiety as real as unfounded. (For if anyone, at that time could be truly said not to resemble the Christ supposed by Bosch, then hanging in Trafalgar Square, I flatter myself it was I.) (Be*Wt:*159)

But Beckett's denial of the resemblance between suffering man and Christ only strengthens his own earlier suggestion. And the association is still further developed in *Malone Dies* (Be*MD*), the second novel of the author's trilogy, wherein Macmann (Son of Man) is farcically caught in the rain in an open field, far from shelter and, in his absurd get-up, lies down on the ground in the posture of one crucified, as "the rain pelted down on his back with the sound . . . of a drum. . . . The idea of punishment came to his mind, addicted it is true to that chimera and probably impressed by the posture of the body and the fingers clenched as though in torment. And without knowing exactly what his sin was he felt well that living was not a sufficient atonement for it" (Be*MD:* 66–67).

This juxtaposition of the farcical and the tragic, the sacred and the profane, is even more pronounced in Beckett's play *Waiting For Godot* (Be*WG*), whose title itself is a bilingual pun on the English word *god* and the French suffix *ot,* which makes laughable whatever it is attached to, such as Pierre (Pierrot), Charles (Charlot), etc. (In a similar attempt at deflating authority, another Beckett character had called his old mother Mag because, as he explained, before saying Mag you had to say Ma and had the illusion of having a mother, while at the same time, the letter *g* spat on it.) From the very beginning of the play, Didi and Gogo, its protagonists, engage in farcical stage play and conversations that concern the nature of God. They wonder why, at the crucifixion of Christ, only one of the two thieves was saved and why only one of the Evangelists reported this event. In the midst of clowning, they discuss the question whether man is free or, as they put it, whether they are tied to God or Godot. As if in farcical answer to this serious question, the play's master-servant couple, Pozzo and Lucky, appears onstage tied together by a rope, suggesting by contrast that the friends Didi and Gogo need no tangible tie, while leaving unanswered the questions whether belief in God does need concrete evidence, or whether, indeed, God feels himself tied to man.

But it is above all the speech Lucky gives, upon being prompted by his master, that farcically raises the question of God's relationship to man. We hear him grotesquely juxtapose the sacred with the profane and the scatalogical, when his demented mind turns the pattern of reasoned discourse into farce. His stutter seemingly accounts for such words as "acacacacademy" and "anthropopopometry," and yet, the seriousness of his concerns becomes apparent when his speech is stripped of its elements of farce and travesty. He then seems to suggest simply that "given the existence . . . of a personal God . . . with white beard . . . outside time . . . who from the heights of divine . . . aphasia loves us dearly with some exceptions for reasons unknown . . . and suffers . . . with those who . . . are plunged in torment . . . it is established beyond all doubt . . . that man . . . fades away" (Be*WG:* 28–29). This kind of half-serious, half-playful travesty, which abases dogma, naive belief, and theological authority, is also to be found in the fiction of James Joyce. James S. Atherton has shown that Joyce travestied the litany, the liturgy, and even the "Our Father." The Lord's Prayer appears on one occasion in *Finnegan's Wake* as "haloed be her eve, her singtime sung, her rill be run, unhemmed as it is uneven." On another it echoes Germanic languages: "Oura Vatars that arred in Himmel" or "Ouhr Former who erred," to mention just a few of the farcical variations (Ath*W:* 187).

Our ears are not too well accustomed to this irreverent proximity of the sacred to the profane. But their juxtaposition not only enables modern authors to speak of serious matters playfully. It also represents a revival of an ancient tradition of which Joyce and Beckett—both scholars of medieval French literature—could not but be fully aware. As suggested above, in the Middle Ages, clergymen clearly enjoyed punning of the kind found in *Waiting for Godot,* and Lucky's speech might well be labeled a *sermon joyeux,* a joyous sermon often delivered by laymen in churches during medieval and Renaissance carnivalesque festivities and grotesquely travestying what was normally considered sacred. In *Thus Spake Zarathustra* (NiZ), Nietzsche re-created, in fact, a church service as it was said to have been celebrated during the Feast of the Ass. The philosopher utilizes the farce to register Zarathustra's dismay at the ease with which the masses, to whom he had been preaching, fell back into error. But, though the tale claims to be ancient, Nietzsche's concerns are modern and yet presented in medieval guise:

> All of a sudden however, Zarathustra's ear was frightened: for the cave which had hitherto been full of noise and laughter, became all at once still as death. . . . "What had happened? What are they about?" he asked himself. . . . "They have all of them become *pious* again, they *pray,* they are mad!" said he. . . . "They all lay on their knees like children and credulous old women, and worshipped the ass. And just then began the ugliest man to gurgle and snort, as if something unutterable in him tried to find expression; when, however, he had actually found words, behold! it was a pious, strange litany in praise of the adored and censed ass. And the litany sounded thus:
>
> 'Amen! And glory and honour and wisdom and thanks and praise and strength be to our God, from everlasting to everlasting!'
>
> —The ass, however, here brayed Ye-a.
>
> 'He carried our burdens, he hath taken upon him the form of a servant, he is patient of heart and never saith Nay; and he who loveth his God chastiseth him.'
>
> —The ass, however, here brayed Ye-a.
>
> 'He speaketh not: except that he ever saith Yea to the world which he created: thus doth he extol his world. It is his artfulness that speaketh not: thus is he rarely found wrong.'
>
> —The ass, however, here brayed Ye-a.
>
> 'Uncomely goeth he through the world. Grey is the fa-

vourite colour in which he wrappeth his virtue. Hath he spirit, then doth he conceal it; every one, however, believeth in his long ears.'

—The ass, however, here brayed Ye-a.

'What hidden wisdom it is to wear long ears, and only to say Yea and never Nay! Hath he not created the world in his own image, namely, as stupid as possible?'

—The ass, however, here brayed Ye-a.

'Thou goest straight and crooked ways; it concerneth thee little what seemeth straight or crooked unto us men. Beyond good and evil is thy domain. It is thine innocence not to know what innocence is.'

—The ass, however, here brayed Ye-a.

'Lo! how thou spurnest none from thee, neither beggars nor kings. Thou sufferest little children to come unto thee, and when the bad boys decoy thee, then sayest thou simply, Ye-a.'

—The ass, however, here brayed Ye-a.

'Thou lovest she-asses and fresh figs, thou art no food-despiser. A thistle tickleth thy heart when thou chancest to be hungry. There is the wisdom of a God therein.'

—The ass, however, here brayed Ye-a.'' (NiZ:350–51)

Zarathustra upbraids the worshiping crowd as blasphemers and receives diverse responses.

"And thou thyself, finally," said Zarathustra, and turned towards the ugliest man, who still lay on the ground stretching up his arm to the ass (for he gave it wine to drink). "Say, thou non-descript, what hast thou been about!"

. . . .

"O Zarathustra," answered the ugliest man, "thou art a rogue!

"Whether *he* yet liveth, or again liveth, or is thoroughly dead—which of us both knowest that best? I ask thee.

"One thing however do I know,—from thyself did I learn it once, O Zarathustra: he who wanteth to kill most thoroughly, *laugheth*." (NiZ:352–54)

If Joycean, Beckettian, and Nietzschean fusions of the sacred and the profane are reminiscent of popular medieval and Renaissance festivities, so are the allusions to food and feasting in Amado's *Dona Flor,* as well as the stuttering evocations of excrement by Beckett's Lucky, and the farcical intake and elimination of nourishment via rubber tubes of Heller's soldier in white. Günter Grass has dwelt elaborately on the more Rabelaisian aspects of these activities. His latest novel, *The Flounder* (GrF), abounds in cooks and their recipes as well as in eaters relishing their food. Under the author's pen, a semi-historical meeting between two seventeenth-century German poets, the learned Opitz and the young Gryphius, becomes a symphony of the sounds that accompany eating:

> At first only the smacking lips of the poet, who would soon be famous for his eloquent death-yearning and renunciation of all earthly joys, could be heard, then other sounds, the bubbling, gurgling, belching of Opitz's nervous and acid stomach, upset no doubt by the guest's presence. (GrF: 246)

The Flounder, protagonist and narrator, omnipresent and omniscient as well as ageless admirer of all female cooks he has known throughout the ages, also remembers the Neolithic, when his primordial cook ruled and

> "the inspection of feces was a feature of the cult. We neolithic folk had entirely different customs, and not just in regard to eating. Each of us ate singly, with his back to the horde, not shamed but silent and introverted, immersed in mastication, eyeless. But we shat together, squatting in a circle and exchanging shouts of encouragement.
>
> After the horde shit-together we felt collectively relieved and chatted happily, showing one another our finished products, drawing pithy comparisons with past performances. . . . Needless to say, the farting incidental to the rite was also a social affair." (GrF: 237)

He declares that earlier ages maintained toward fecal matter a religious and even playful attitude, similar to that still assumed by children.

But if Grass's narrator is aware of changing attitudes and assumptions, so is the reader. We may find it difficult to enjoy such reminiscences, and yet our first reaction is to laugh at them and think of them as farcical. Yet laughter is made easier because we think of the characters evoked by Grass as mythical rather than individual existents. Flounder, the protagonist and narrator of the novel by that name who is sometimes a fish and sometimes a man and Ilsebill's husband, is an equally mythical being in that his memory reaches from a distant past to the present. Thus he remembers a time when relationships between men and women, though passionate, affectionate, and playful, were not thought of as "grandiose emotions." Standing accused before a tribunal of women, the Flounder develops, in fact, what he calls "his theory of love as a means of putting an end to the domination of women" because it undermines what seems to him their natural supremacy by making them humble themselves before the males whom they wish to adore them. The Flounder plays as farcically and cunningly with logic as does Beckett's Lucky, though without using the madman's distortion of speech:

> "Love would unleash feelings. It would set a standard that no one could live up to. It would suckle but never appease a lasting dissatisfaction. It would invent a language of sighs, the poetry which at once illuminates and obscures. . . . It would give rise to supernaturally colorful dreams . . . paint the world in rosy colors. It would beguile women into compensating for their lost power by voraciously escalating their demands. It would become the everlasting plaint of every Ilsebill." GrF:262)

His disquisition, which was bolstered by quotations of poetry from the troubadours to the Beatles and anticipated the latest in pop songs and advertising slogans, concluded with the programmatic sentence:

> "Only if we succeed in persuading woman by subtle suggestion that love is a saving power and the certainty of being loved the supreme happiness and if concomitantly man, even though loved to the point of adulation, steadfastly refuses to love or to guarantee the longevity of his little love affairs, so that (woman depends) on the never-attained certainty that he loves her, still loves her, loves her and nobody else . . . —then alone will matriarchy be defeated, will the conquering phallic symbol overturn all vulvar idols, will man illuminate the prehistoric darkness of the womb and perpetuate himself forever and ever as father and as master." (GrF: 263)

With the help of such mythical perspectives we come to see our own world in a different light and are enabled to accept more easily the Flounder's totally aromantic attitude toward the relationship between men and women that we ordinarily call love. Because of such mythical distancing, the Flounder succeeds in elevating Agnes—kitchenmaid and bedfellow to two famous men whose needs for nourishment she fulfills with total impartiality—to the level of muse. In so doing, he also moves in the realm of the imaginary rather than the mimetic—in the manner of Cervantes' Don Quixote, who declares a garlic-scented peasant girl to be his princess Dulcinea. In both works—though for different reasons—romantic love is farcically dethroned, while another truth is glimpsed. In a similar manner, Ionesco pulled from their pedestal all heroic notions associated with war when he presented us with his own farcical version of Shakespeare's *Macbeth,* his *Macbett,* wherein generals mechanically vie for power and, far from living out heroic destinies, are mere robots, farcical puppets set in motion by empty ambition, who set in motion, in their turn, machines of war and murder they can no longer control and whose relentless march they are unable to stop. In his play *Man Is Man,* Brecht has portrayed, from the point of view of the simple soldier, the relentlessness of this mechanism that deprives man of his individuality, making all interchangeable in a manner both tragic and comic.

Even this brief sampling of modern farce, representing only a fraction of the riches available, gives proof of an enjoyment in degradation linguistic and otherwise of what society generally holds high—similar to that indulged in by antiquity and the Middle Ages and objectionable only during periods when bourgeois individualism asserted itself. Our own age, vehemently anti-authoritarian, has regained, it would seem, not only a healthy tolerance for comic outrage at all that is pompous and overbearing and a joy in toppling what is too high and mighty, but also a sense of the therapeutic value of such outrage and joy in a world in danger of losing all sense of proportion vis-à-vis individual life and death. If Beckett's redeemer never comes and instead all mankind is made the scapegoat—the very fate from which he was to save mankind—one needs to derive compensating and liberating laughter at least through carnivalesque (and that means imaginative, festive, and momentary) degradation of all that imposes itself as accusing and punishing authority. For such writers as Kafka and Heller, authority assumes the guise of civilian or military bureaucracy and of a society closed to any and all it cannot understand and therefore considers outside itself. For Beckett, it has religious dimensions. Grass and Amado direct their laughter frequently at what is considered, within a certain society, to be moral and exemplary in the relationship between the sexes. In Nabokov's and Heller's farce, even death loses some of its frightening aspects, as these writers surround it with rosy bubblegum or an absurd medical apparatus.

But whether in ancient or modern garb, the laughter of farce seems always ambivalent. Its degradation and deflation of all rigid authority—worldly bureaucracy, clerical and social pedantry and hypocrisy, and scholarly pomposity—is playful rather than sternly rebellious. If its comic defiance of Death and even God diminishes man's awe and fears, the laughter of the absolute comic—because of its origins in carnivalesque festivities—but briefly turns the world upside down instead of aiming at any permanent improvement. It remains as ephemeral as it believes man's very existence to be. Its manifestations are, therefore, neither mimetic nor realistic but rather belong to the realm of the imagination. Its butts—its scapegoats—playfully killed by laughter rather than mimetically by the sword, not only fail to arouse our compassion but are also instantly resurrected.

The laughter of farce is based on notions of justice quite different from bourgeois standards of morality and ethics. Compared to those standards, such notions often appear immoral, harsh, and cruel. For the justice of the absolute comic is informed by the laws of Nature, not those of society. It is this discrepancy that may well account for the fact that farcical laughter has met with rejection and repression for almost three centuries, that is, since the growth of bourgeois societies. For to misunderstand the tenets of such comic justice and its essential ambivalence means to misread the literature that embodies it and to condemn as gross and immoral what is meant to be largely a playful exercise, capable of turning the world upside down through the power of imagination. Readers and critics who apply mimetic standards to literature written in the vein of the absolute comic and remain innocent of the grammar of this particular idiom are bound to fail in their appreciation of it. Their false premises doom them to misreading. As one consequence, many texts pertaining to the absolute comic have been neglected for centuries and are only now being rediscovered. Another result has been the reduction to insignificance of what had originally been sources of rich and liberating farcical laughter. Chaucer's *Miller's Tale,* when seen in the light of twentieth-century American morals, is torn out of its tradition of farce that put women on top in a world whose realities deprived them of all rights. Molière's *Tartuffe*—if believed mainly to be a psychological study of a hypocrite to whom, by none other than the French King, well-deserved punishment is ultimately meted out—proves equally diminished as it is transported from the realm of imagination into one of "realism." It was as a result of a similar misreading that Rousseau considered Molière's *Misanthrope*—a work its author had clearly designated and meant to be a comedy—the tragedy of an honest man finding himself in the midst of the hypocrisy of seventeenth-century French salons and rejecting them. Like most eighteenth-century critics, Rousseau was impervious to the spirit of the absolute comic and of farce and merely conferred his own standards upon the work of a playwright that had been mainly nourished by the idiom of the carnivalesque and its notions of justice.

Rousseau's misreading, however, should alert us to the fact that it is not enough to be aware of the absolute comic's universal grammar and that we must also pay heed to modulations in taste, depending on time and place, to which this grammar is subject. These modulations determine to some extent the kind of comic scapegoat whose defeat literature celebrates and whom it selects to triumph over, even if only in fantasy. During the European Middle Ages and Renaissance, it was above all the clergy that was chosen as comic scapegoat: ordinary people triumphed over monks, monks over the higher clergy, and at the top of the ladder were the abbots. In a different context, wives triumphed over husbands who exerted too rigid an authority over them; young and beautiful lovers, with the help of clever servants, outwitted those who had the power to keep them apart—the wealthy and stingy fathers on whom they depended and who wanted to give their daughters in marriage to other wealthy old men. Alongside, and sometimes interwoven with these triumphs, were those of the naive and simple-minded over the pompously learned. Molière managed, in addition, to have imagination win out—if only briefly—over death and social prejudice. As we have seen, however, the scapegoats of modern writers are frequently bureaucracy and militarism, although bourgeois respectability also gets its due. At its most gripping, however, the absolute comic is played out today against a backdrop of fear and death, and it is there that it most strongly asserts its ambivalence, centered above all in the figure of a trickster as ancient as it is modern. I shall discuss this figure in the next chapter.

four
The Absolute Comic and the Trickster Figure

TRICKSTERS are the instigators of carnivalesque activities, whether Lords of Misrule, jesters, clowns, devils, or saintly prophets of the nature of Nietzsche's Zarathustra. They usually display saint-sinner qualities not unlike those evident in Thomas Mann's *Holy Sinner*. The comic justice meted out to them conforms in its ambivalence to their entire fictional existence, so that they are heroes both triumphant and suffering—none less than the Falstaffs and Tartuffes, none more than the servants of commedia dell'arte origin, Rabelais' Panurge, or Chaucer's Nicolas, who gets the girl in the *Miller's Tale* but is also "scalded in the toute." Tricksters therefore represent scapegoats of a special nature and deserve special consideration.

Trickster

Originally, Trickster was the name given to a clownish figure of mercurial unpredictability and changeability, a mythical hero of North American Indians, whose cycle of episodes was first recorded by Paul Radin (Ra*T*). He behaves at times as if he were an animal, at others like a human being. As Radin describes him, he is "at one and the same time creator and destroyer, giver and negator, he who dupes others and is always duped himself. He wills nothing consciously. . . . He knows neither good nor evil yet he is responsible for both. He possesses no value, moral or social" (Ra*T:*xxiii). I believe that his character is sufficiently illustrated by the following episodes chosen somewhat at random from the cycle. The first shows Trickster wandering about and chancing upon a lake:

> And there in the lake he saw numerous ducks. Immediately he ran back quietly before they could see him and sought out a spot where there was a swamp. From it he gathered a large quantity of reedgrass and made himself a big pack. This he put on his back and carried it to the lake. He walked along the shore of the lake carrying it ostentatiously. Soon the ducks saw him and said, "Look that is Trickster walking over there. I wonder what he is doing? Let us call and ask him." So they called to him "Trickster what are you carrying?" Thus they shouted at him, but he did not answer. Then again they called to him. But it was only after the fourth call that he replied and said, "Well, you are calling me?" "What are you carrying on your back?" they asked (Ra*T:*15).

When he finally tells them that he is carrying tunes but has met no one who will dance to them and therefore he has not been able to sing for a long time, the ducks consent to dance if he will make the music. But he requests that they close their eyes while doing so, and as they dance to his songs, a strange flapping of wings is heard every so often and a loud "quack." Each time Trickster asks the ducks to dance faster, and they obey, until one little duck opens its eyes and sees him wringing the necks of ducks, each wildly flapping and saying "quack" before it dies. The young duck shouts alarm, and it is now Trickster who has to close his eyes as the ducks pursue him and try to attack him, until they finally fly away. It is then that he cooks his loot. But, while dreaming of a wonderful meal, he falls asleep, and at once his dinner is stolen by small foxes (RaT: 15–16). Thus his labors have been in vain. He has successfully tricked others but has also provided them with enjoyment. He has triumphed over them but has also been persecuted by them, and he finally goes away empty-handed.

The second episode I have chosen presents the Trickster in all his naiveté that borders on stupidity but is nonetheless coupled with shrewd ruthlessness. Having fallen into his own excrement, he is engaged in cleaning himself and:

> [happening] to look in the water . . . much to his surprise he saw many plums there. He surveyed them very carefully and then he dived down into the water to get some. But only small stones did he bring back in his hands. Again he dived into the water. But this time he knocked himself unconscious against a rock at the bottom. After a while he floated up and gradually came to. He was lying on the water, flat on his back, when he came to and, as he opened his eyes, there on the top of the bank he saw many plums. What he had seen in the water was only reflection. Then he realized what he had done. "Oh, my what a stupid fellow I must be! I should have recognized this. Here I have caused myself a great deal of pain."
>
> Then he went on to the shore and ate as many plums as possible, and putting a belt around his racoon-skin blanket he filled it likewise with plums and proceeded downstream.
>
> Much to his surprise as he travelled along he came upon an oval lodge. He peeped in and saw two women with many children. He took one of the plums and threw it through the top of the lodge. It made a great noise. The women grabbed it. This he repeated and soon one of the women came out and saw, unexpectedly, a man standing there (RaT: 28–29).

The woman believes him to be her older brother and invites him into the lodge. The two women want to know where he got the plums and, promising to take care of their children if they wish to go and pick some, he gives them vague directions as to how to find the trees. But as soon as the women are out of sight, he kills their children, singes and cooks them. This would seem to be cannibalistic, were it not that the meat is now referred to as racoon meat, so that we seem to deal with a story regarding animals rather than human beings (Ra*T*: 28–29).

According to Radin, the greed and selfishness Trickster displays here—whether human or animal—are something he eventually outgrows in this story cycle. He is shown to become sexually mature and at the same time more social-minded. In the process of his sexual maturing, he even assumes the form of a woman, marries, and becomes a mother; and he finally reaches true selfhood, that of a man both benevolent and cunning (Ra*T*: 135–39). Indeed, his initial egocentricity ultimately gives way to total unselfishness: "He suddenly recollects the purpose for which he had been sent to earth by Earthmaker." And it is this realization that makes him remove all obstacles along the Mississippi so that his people will be able to settle there: "As he went along he killed and ate all those beings that were molesting the people" (Ra*T*:52). Having done these deeds, he ate a meal, then went into the ocean "and then up to the heavens" (Ra*T*:52). Trickster thus has become a hero, a savior, and a saint.

What is fascinating concerning this hero of North American Indian mythology is not only his ambivalence, his fantasy triumphs, and his moments of degradation when others triumph over him, but above all his universality. According to Radin, the Trickster myth is "found in clearly recognizable form among the simplest aboriginal tribes and among the complex. We encounter it among the ancient Greeks, the Chinese, the Japanese, and in the Semitic world. Many of the Trickster's traits are perpetuated in the figure of the medieval jester and have survived right up to the present day in the Punch-and-Judy plays and in the clown. Although repeatedly combined with other myths and frequently drastically reorganized and reinterpreted, its basic plot seems always to have asserted itself" (Ra*T*:xxiii). The anthropologist concludes from the universality and omnipresence of the myth that "we are here in the presence of a figure and a theme or themes which have had special and permanent appeal and unusual attraction for mankind from the very beginnings of civilization" (Ra*T:* xxiii). The figure seems to him to be an "archaic speculum mentis," so that it is difficult to decide whether those who listen to the stories laugh at the pranks Trickster plays on others, at those played on him, or at the implications his activities and behavior have for them (Ra*T:* xxiv). But laughter always accompanies the myth.

Two outstanding scholars were asked by Radin's publishers to add their commentaries to his observations, and Carl Jung's and Karl Kerényi's remarks provide us with precious additional insights. Jung thought of the figure as a " 'psychologem,' an archetypal psychic structure of extreme antiquity," that, in its clearest manifestations, is "a faithful reflection of an absolutely undifferentiated human consciousness, corresponding to a psyche that hardly left the animal level" (Ra*T:* 260). But the figure also made him aware of European analogies—an awareness bolstered by his knowledge of Bandelier's earlier study of North American Indian clown folklore in his *Delight Makers.* Jung was reminded especially of "Carnival in the medieval Church with its reversal of the hierarchic order, which is still continued in the carnivals held by student societies today" (Ra*T:* 255). What intrigued him above all in the Trickster was his contradictoriness, his inherent ambivalence that is equally present in "medieval descriptions of the devil as *simia dei* (the ape of God), and in his [the devil's] characterization in folklore as the 'simpleton' who is 'fooled' or 'cheated'." Turning to Greek mythology, the psychoanalyst believed he recognized the forerunner of European trickster figures in Mercurius, "a daemonic being resurrected from primitive times, older even than the Greek Hermes," but a being that also shared with the Trickster of American Indians "a fondness for sly jokes and malicious pranks, his power as a shape-lifter, his dual nature, half animal, half divine, his exposure to all kinds of tortures, and—last but not least—his approximation to the figure of a savior," a being, in fact, that like most saints and the Yahweh of the Old Testament inflicts suffering and suffers (RaT: 255–56).

Kerényi, also turning to Greek mythology, differentiated above all between two principal kinds of trickster figures: those who are utterly self-contained and self-seeking, and those that employ tricks not for their own selfish ends. He illustrated his point with references to Prometheus and Hermes: "Prometheus, the benefactor of mankind, lacks self-interest and playfulness. Hermes has both, when he discovers fire and sacrifice before Prometheus did—without, however, bothering about mankind. In the playful cruelties which the little god practised . . . and which conferred no benefit on mankind (at least for a long time to come), we see the sly face of the trickster grinning at us" (RaT: 181). But, according to Kerényi, Prometheus must be seen as a being whose inseparable and complementing double is his brother Epimetheus, and he explains that

> Every invention of Prometheus brings new misery upon mankind. No sooner has he succeeded in offering sacrifice than Zeus deprives mankind of the fire. And when, after stealing the fire, Prometheus himself is snatched away from mortals to suffer punishment, Epimetheus is left behind as their representative: craftiness is replaced by stupidity. The profound affinity between these two figures is expressed in the fact that they are brothers. One might almost say that in them a single primitive being, sly and stupid at once, has been split into a duality: Prometheus the Forethinker, Epimetheus the belated Afterthinker. It is he who, in his thoughtlessness, brings mankind, as a gift from the gods, the final inexhaustible source of misery: Pandora." (RaT: 181)

Hermes

To understand the trickster figure in a more European context, it is appropriate to turn, first of all, to the Greek god Hermes, who may well be considered its Western prototype, though Jung believes that this honor should go to Mercurius, who preceded him in antiquity. Hermes is, above all, known as the thief. The so-called *Homeric Hymn to Hermes* is of unknown authorship and, dating back to the sixth century B.C., represents "the canonical document for all subsequent descriptions and discussions of Hermes the Thief," as Norman O. Brown tells us (Br*H:*69). In the *Hymn,* the god is presented as having issued from Zeus's illicit love affair with Maia, "whom Zeus used to visit while his lawful wife Hera was sleeping" (Br*H:*69). It seems that the trickery at play when Hermes was conceived determined the very essence of his being. He turned out to be "an unusual child who was shifty, cunning, and thievish, and highly precocious. On the very day of his birth, he stole the cattle of Apollo," his older brother.

However, more remarkable than his thievery is the reaction to it. Neither his father Zeus nor the author of the *Hymn* greet it with moral indignation or disapproval of any kind. On the contrary, the poet hails Hermes, and Zeus's spontaneous reaction to his young son's dishonest behavior is laughter. One seems to discover in such laughter that admiration for the clever outlaw that we find in the stories of Robin Hood, for instance, or in such national "anthems" as Australia's "Waltzing Matilda" or Holland's "Piet Hein who stole the silver fleet." And one cannot but recognize a trace of it in the attitudes of administrators in higher education who laugh at the "cleverness" of students who beat the system, prompting the *Chronicle of Higher Education* (July 17, 1978) to suggest in a recent headline that "some campuses treat student tampering with computers as a prank, but one expert says they are producing a 'new generation' of crooks." Our sense of justice is determined, of course, by the "frame" for such activities. Hermes' thievery is a tale that belongs to the absolute comic and is the property of *homo ludens:* it is outside the realm of "reality" and the mimetic. The students' "pranks," on the other hand, are part of the real world and should be judged differently, were it not for that liberating moment of laughter to which mankind

so easily submits whenever established rules are made to topple
and the world is turned upside down.

In the Apollo–Hermes relationship the laughter is the
merrier because, Kerényi informs us, it is the older brother
who is tricked by the younger—in this case a mere baby. The
younger brother's tricking of his older sibling was so much a
part of trickster lore, in fact, that vase paintings portray "Hera-
cles in the guise of a trickster . . . trying to lure his brother,
who has taken refuge on the roof of a temple, down to him
with a basket of fruit or some other kind of delicacy. The club
is all too visible in his other hand" (Ra*T:*179). The analogy
with the Old Testament story of Jacob and his older brother
Esau comes at once to mind, where Jacob's trickery, which
deprives Esau of his rights of the first born, meets the same
parental indulgence as does that of Hermes. We learn from
Norman O. Brown that the popularity of the Hermes episode
is attested by its frequently being the object, not only of song
but also of numerous vase paintings that represent Hermes as a
small baby in his cradle—a "marvelous child" (Br*H:*77).

Now it is interesting that many saints and biblical figures,
such as Abraham, are thus depicted as "marvelous children"
whose very survival depends on their trickery and superhuman
strength that make them, in a sense, characters of the absolute
comic. According to Joseph Campbell, legend has it that
Nimrod, having read in the stars of Abraham's coming birth,
was filled with fear and trembling because the child was to give
the lie to his religion (Ca*H:*323). To prevent this from happen-
ing, Nimrod had a tower built wherein every pregnant woman
was to be imprisoned during the weeks preceding the birth of
her child. If the baby was a girl she was to be given costly gifts;
if a boy, he was to be killed. "It was about this time," the story
reads, "that Terah espoused the mother of Abraham and she
was with child. . . . When her time approached, she left the
city in great terror and wandered toward the desert." There, in
a cave, she gave birth to a son. "The whole cave was filled
with the light of the child's countenance as with the splendour

of the sun, and the mother rejoiced exceedingly. The babe she bore was . . . Abraham (Ca*H:* 324). Convinced that Nimrod would kill him, she abandoned her baby in the desert rather than see him die before her eyes. "She took the garment in which she was clothed, and wrapped it about the boy. Then she abandoned him in the cave. . . . God sent Gabriel down to give him milk to drink, and the angel made it to flow from the little finger of the baby's right hand, and he sucked it until he was ten days old. Then he arose and walked about, and he left the cave" (Ca*H:* 325). Abraham's very survival is a fantasy triumph, and similar tales are told of other heroes, among them the sixth-century Pope Gregory, whose life was farcically re-told by Thomas Mann under the title of *The Holy Sinner.*

But not many gods or heroes belong wholly to the realm of the absolute comic, and Hermes' marvelous childhood is equaled in that respect only by Rabelais' giant tricksters, Gargantua and Pantagruel. We are told of Gargantua that he cried out "as soon as he was born . . . not like other children: 'Mies! Mies!' but 'Drink! Drink! Drink!', as if inviting the whole world to drink, and so loud that he was heard through all of the lands of Booze and Bibulous (RG: 52). . . . And to quiet the child they gave him enough to drink to break his larynx. . . . And they ordered for him seventeen thousand nine hundred and thirteen cows . . . for his every-day supply of milk" (RG: 53). Hermes is presented as having an appetite al-most as ravenous, for he claims that he stole the cattle because he was "craving meat," employing an image Homer used to describe the lion. While the *Homeric Hymm to Hermes* deals only with the first days of its hero's life, Gargantua's rapid growth is displayed from infancy to manhood and even fatherhood. We learn that he spent the time "from his third to his fifth year in the same manner as the other children of that country; that is to say in drinking, eating, and sleeping; in eating, sleeping, and drinking; in sleeping, drinking, and eating," (*RG:* 62), but prov-ing even at this tender age to be a "little lecher" (*RG:* 63). Soon he is on his way to Paris and studies at the university, where people stare at him and he avenges himself by flooding the city, as he undoes his magnificent codpiece and brings out his "john-thomas" (RG: 74). It is also in Paris (whose etymology is given as *par ris* (by way of laughter), that Gargantua steals the great bells of the cathedral having decided that they would "serve very well for cowbells to hang on the collar of his mare" (RG: 75). Rabelais clearly establishes an atmosphere of make-believe and admits gaily that he does not care whether his readers believe him or not (RG: 53).

The *Homeric Hymn to Hermes* partakes of the same spirit of make-believe, as it presents the marvelous child's adventures on the first two days of his life. Norman Brown's summary beautifully conveys the non-mimetic and triumphant character of these adventures:

> As he crossed the threshold on Mount Cyllene in Arcadia where his mother lived, he (Hermes) found a tortoise. Realizing at once the use to which he could put this find, he fashioned it into a lyre, thus becoming the inventor of the tortoise-shell lyre. After accompanying himself on this new instrument in a song about the love of Zeus and Maia—by which he was begotten— he left the lyre in his cradle and, feeling hungry, proceeded on his way after the cattle of Apollo (ll. 20–62). These he found in the region of Mount Olympus, with the cattle of the rest of the gods. It was night time by now. Hermes drove away fifty cows of Apollo's herd, taking many precautions to throw the pursuit off the scent: he drove the cattle backward so that their foot-prints would point to the meadow from which he had stolen them, and he made himself a pair of sandals so constructed as to cover up his own footprints. On his way back to Arcadia he met only one person, an old man working in the vineyard at Onchestus in Boetia; Hermes advised him that if he knew what was good for him he would keep his mouth shut about what he had seen (ll. 63–93).
>
> Upon reaching the ford across the Alpheus . . . he foddered the cattle and put them away in a cave. Then he collected some wood and lit a fire with firesticks, thus becoming the inventor of this method of creating fire. Next he dragged two of

the cows out of the cave, threw them on the ground, and made a sacrifice, dividing them into twelve portions. After throwing away his sandals, he smoothed the sand and returned to his mother's home . . . without being observed. He entered the house through the keyhole, like a wisp of cloud, and nestled down in his cradle, tucking the tortoise-shell lyre under his arm, like a baby with his toy (ll. 94–153). But he had not fooled his mother. She asked him what he had been up to, and she took a pessimistic view of his chances of getting away with his first venture on a career of thievery. "Alas," she sighed, "when your father begot you, he begot a deal of trouble for mortal men and for the immortal gods." Hermes' reply was definitely in character: "Why do you try to scare me as if I were nothing but a silly child? I shall follow the career that offers the best opportunities, for I must look after my own interests and yours. . . . Would it not be better to spend our days in ease and affluence like the rest of the gods? I am going to get the same status in cult as Apollo. If my father does not give it to me, I will become the prince of thieves, (ll. 154–181).

Meanwhile Apollo was in pursuit of the thief. . . . He identified the culprit and arrived at Maia's home. When Hermes saw him, he curled up in his cradle and pretended to be asleep. Apollo searched the place for his cattle. Failing to find them, he brusquely ordered Hermes to tell where they were. "Why, son of Leto," Hermes asked, "what means this rough language? I never even saw your cattle. Do I look like a cattle-raider? I am only two days old, and all I am interested in is sleep and warm baths and my mother's milk." "You certainly have won the title of prince of thieves," replied Apollo, as he picked Hermes up. But Hermes also knew about omens; as he was being lifted up, he let out an omen, "an unfortunate servant of the belly, an impudent messenger," and sneezed for good luck. Apollo dropped him at once. . . . the matter was referred to Zeus for judgment (ll. 182–324).

"And what is this fine prize you have carried off?" Zeus asks Apollo as he sees him carrying a new-born baby under his arm. "It is not fair to accuse me of carrying things off," Apollo replied; "he is the thief and a most cunning one too." Then he told Zeus about Hermes' devices for covering up his traces, and how he had pretended ignorance about the stolen cattle. At this point Hermes spoke in his own defense. "Father," he said, "you know I cannot tell a lie. He came to our house looking for some cattle and began threatening me—and he is grown-up, whereas I was born only yesterday. I swear by the gates of heaven that I never drove the cattle to our house, and that I never stepped across our threshold. I will get even with this fellow for so violently arresting me; you must defend the cause of the weak and helpless." Zeus laughed heartily when he heard his dishonest son's ingenious denials; but his judgment was that Hermes should show Apollo where the cattle were (ll. 325–96). (Br*H*: 69–72)

As they come to the cave and Apollo sees the hides of the cows Hermes slaughtered, he is amazed that a mere baby could have done such work. While he is about to lead his cattle away with a rope of withies, he finds that Hermes has made them take root in the ground. Hermes' playing on his lyre fills Apollo, himself a patron of music, with awe. They exchange pleasantries and strike a bargain wherein Hermes gives Apollo his lyre and Apollo shares with him patronage over cattle. They part as friends. Their friendship, Brown maintains, represents the fusion of the two cults, a fusion that came about because of the development in Greece of commerce, of which Hermes was the patron (Br*H*: 73). Commerce was identified with theft, but the Greek terms for trickster and thief also mean accomplishment and skill in the arts and in magic. There is involved here—as Brown rightly suggests—the opposition of power, on the one part, and helplessness on the other. We sense a comical defiance of the haves by the have-nots, especially when Hermes addresses Zeus and directly asks him to "uphold the cause of the young and helpless" (Br*H*: 88).

Contemplating the range of representations of the Greek Hermes figure, Brown concludes that

> depending on the historical circumstances, the trickster may evolve into any one of such contrasting figures as a benevolent culture hero nearly indistinguishable from the Supreme God, a

demiurge in strong opposition to the heavenly powers, a kind of devil counteracting the creator in every possible way, a messenger and mediator between gods and men, or merely a Puckish figure, the hero of comical stories. The extant representations of Hermes cover this entire range: his standard role, derived from the *Odyssey,* is that of a messenger and mediator between gods and men; in Hesiod's story of Pandora he has a role resembling that of the serpent in the Garden of Eden; in the Homeric Hymn he is in revolt against the existing dispensation in heaven; occasionally he is cast in a purely Puckish role, as in a story of how he stole his mother's clothes while she was bathing. (BrH: 48)

The character's diversity may well reflect, as Brown believes, diverse needs generated by changing environments.

The Fox

In Germanic mythology, Hermes' counterpart is the god Loki. But his manifold features—as contradictory as the world of fantasy and carnival—have found expression above all in animal epics, the best known of which is *Reynard the Fox* (AnRF), a Dutch work translated into English at the end of the fifteenth century. The protagonist's trickery—conceived, with regard to psychology, on an exclusively human level—leads him to suffering as often as to triumph, but finally brings him recognition and honor. Indicative of his clever ruthlessness is an episode wherein he is accused of misdeeds, found guilty, and condemned to be hanged, but manages through clever flattery, lies, and ruthless accusations, to endanger his enemies instead. He does not hesitate to implicate even his own father in order to regain the good graces of the King:

> The Fox said: "Now may my heart be well heavy for great dread; for I see the death before mine eyes, and I may not escape. My Lord the King, and dear Queen, and further all ye that here stand, ere I depart from this world I pray you of a boon:

that I may before you all make my confession openly, and tell
my defaults all so clearly that my soul may not be encumbered,
and also that no man hereafter bear no blame for my theft ne for
my treason. My death shall be to me the easier, and pray ye all
to God that he have mercy on my soul!" (An*RF:* 40)

The King gave him leave. Reynard was well glad and
hoped that it might fall better, and said thus: "Now help,
Spiritus Domini, for I see here no man but I have trespassed unto.
Nevertheless yet was I, unto the time that I was weaned from
the teat, one of the best children that could anywhere be found.
I went then and played with the lambs, because I heard them
gladly bleat. I was so long with them that at last I bit one: there
learned I first to lap of the blood. It savoured well; methought it
right good. And after I began to taste of the flesh thereof, I was
dainty; so that after that I went to the gate into the wood: there
heard I the kids bleat—and I slew of them twain. I began to wax
bold after. I slew hens, poultry, and geese wherever I found
them. Thus became my teeth all bloody. After this, I waxed so
fell and so wroth that whatsoever I found what I might over-
[come], I slew all. Thereafter came I by Isegrim, now in the winter, where he hid him under a tree, and explained to me that he
was mine uncle. When I heard him then explain [our] alliance,
we became fellows, which I may well repent. We promised each
to other to be true and to use good fellowship, and began to
wander together. He stole the great things and I the small, and
all was common between us. Yet he made it so that he had the
best share—I got not half my part. When that Isegrim got a calf,
a ram, or a wether, then raged he, and was angry on me; and
drove me from him, and held my part and his too, so good is
he. Yet this was of the least. But when it so lucked that we took
an ox or a cow, then came thereto his wife with seven children;
so that unto me might scarcely come one of the smallest ribs,
and yet, had they eaten all the flesh thereof, therewithall must I
be content—not for that I had so great need, for I have so great
treasure and goods of silver and of gold that seven wains could
not carry it away."

When the King heard him speak of his great goods and
riches, he burned in the desire and covetousness thereof, and
said: "Reynard, what has become of the riches? Tell me that."

The Fox said: "My Lord, I shall tell you. The riches was stolen. And had it not be stolen, it would have cost you your life and you would have been murdered—which God forbid!; and would have been the greatest hurt in the world." (An*RF:* 42)

What Reynard reveals to the King is that he, Reynard, has appropriated the treasure his own father amassed and hid, so as to use it in plotting against the King and making the Bear usurp his place. Reynard learned about the conspiracy from his wife:

"It happed so that on a morrow-tide early when Grymbart, my nephew, was of wine almost drunk, that he told it to Dame Slopecade, his wife, in counsel, and bade her keep it secret. But she anon forgot it, and said it forth in confession to my wife upon a heath where they both went a pilgrimage, but she must first swear, by her truth and by the holy Three Kings of Cologne, that for love ne for hate she should never tell it forth, but keep it secret. But she held it not, and kept it no longer secret but till she came to me; and she then told to me all that she heard, but I must keep it in secret. And she told me so many tokens that I felt well it was truth; and for dread and fear mine hair stood right up, and my heart became as heavy as lead and as cold as ice." (An*RF:* 44)

Accomplished hypocrite that he is, he tells the King about his horror at the news and his resolve to do everything in his power to save the King, even if this means to betray his own kin. His plan was to find out, first of all, where his father hid the treasure:

"I was sore bethought how I might best wit where my father's goods lay. I awaited at all times, as nigh as I could, in woods, in bushes, in fields, where my father laid his eyes: were it by night or by day, cold or wet, I was always by him to espy and know where his treasure was laid.

"On a time I lay down all flat on the ground and saw my father come running out of a hole. Now hark what I saw him

do. When he came out of the hole, he looked closely about if
anybody had seen him. And, when he could nowhere none see,
he stopped the hole with sand, and made it even and plain like
to the other ground by. He knew not that I saw it. And where
his foot-track stood, there stroked he with his tail, and made it
smooth with his mouth, that no man should espy it. That
learned I there of my false father, and many subtleties that I
before knew nothing of. Then departed he thence, and ran toward the village for to do his things; and I forgot not, but
sprang and leapt toward the hole, and how well that he had supposed that he had made all fast I was not so much a fool but that
I found the hole well, and scratched and scraped with my feet
the sand out of the hole, and crept therein. There found I the
most plenty of silver and of gold that ever I saw. Here is none
so old that ever so much saw on one heap in all his life. Then
took I Ermelyn my wife to help, and we ne rested night ne day
to bear and carry away, with great labour and pain, this rich
treasure into another place that lay for us better, under an hedge
in a deep hole. In the meanwhile that mine housewife and I thus
laboured, my father was with them that would betray the King.
Now may ye hear what they did: Bruin the Bear and Isegrim the
Wolf sent all the land about if any man would take wages that
they should come to Bruin and he would pay them their pay or
wages before [in advance]. My father ran all over the land and
bare the letters. He wist little that he was robbed of his treasure;
yea, though he might have dwelt in all the world, he had not
been able to find a penny thereof." (An*RF:* 46)

When Reynard's father finds out that he has been robbed,
he is in despair and hangs himself, a loss bewailed by Reynard
because it adds to his distress at receiving so little recognition
from a King for whom he has sacrificed everything. It is the
Queen rather than the King who "believes" him and convinces
her husband to pardon him. But their real motive is not mercy.
It is rather their hope to win the treasure the Fox has hidden
(An*RF:* 47–48):

The King took up a straw from the ground, and pardoned and
forgave the Fox all the misdeeds and trespasses of his father and

of him also. If the Fox was then merry and glad, it was no wonder; for he was quit of his death and was all free and frank of all his enemies. (An*RF:* 49)

Reynard, not unlike Aristophanes' "good citizen" had his head on the block as it were and saved his life through the use of his wit. Weaker than anyone else under the circumstances, he not only outwitted his stronger opponents who had accused him but also ingratiated himself with the King:

> Then said the King: "Hear ye all that be poor and rich, young and old, that standeth here! Reynard, one of the head officers of my house, had done so evil, which this day should have been hanged, hath now in this Court done so much that I and my wife the Queen have promised to him our grace and friendship. The Queen hath prayed much for him, insomuch that I have made peace with him. And I give to him his life and member-[ship of my Council] freely again, and I command you upon your life that ye do worship to Reynard and his wife, and to his children, wheresoever ye meet them by day or night. And I will also hear no more complaints of Reynard. If he hath heretofore misdone and trespassed, he will no more misdo ne trespass, but now better him. He will to-morrow early go to the Pope for pardon and forgiveness of all his sins, and forth over the sea to the Holy Land, and he will not come again till he bring pardon of all his sins." (An*RF:* 51)

The Fox is only too anxious to go to Rome:

> "My Lord," quoth the Fox, "therefore will I go to Rome as hastily as I may. I shall not rest by night nor day till I be absolved." (An*RF:* 52)

This does not mean, however, that he is repentant. For he provides himself with the shoes he needs for his pilgrimage by cutting them off the paws of his powerful enemy the Wolf, now in disgrace, and leaving him sore and bleeding. He asks of the King that a mass be sung and sermon preached to send him on his way, and the Ram—totally against his will—has to officiate. The Fox receives his blessing, although everyone is aware of his trickery, his hypocrisy, and his total dishonesty and guilt. Yet all animals hasten to pay him homage, as long as he is the favorite of the King and his enemies have been abased. The Fox is never truly a savior figure, yet he always manages to outwit the strong, while he himself is outwitted by the weaker animals he wishes to dupe (An*RF*:xviii). This prevents the tale from becoming a satire and keeps it within the realm of the carnivalesque.

Till Eulenspiegel

A similar series of fantasy triumphs is represented by Till Eulenspiegel's picaresque adventures (An*TE*). Here we are in the face of a person, not an animal, and we are told of his birth, his start as a "miraculous child," his fame as a rogue and scoundrel even in his tenderest years, his roaming through the various provinces of Germany and other countries, and, finally, his death. The tales were published toward the end of the fifteenth century and made their anti-hero famous, although their author remained anonymous. If Reynard the Fox is presented as a courtier outwitting the King of the animals and his court, Eulenspiegel is shown to be a man of the people, dealing with tanners, furriers, weavers, tailors, bakers, and merchants, cheating those that are too wealthy and stingy, and abasing those that are too high and mighty or too narrow-minded and proper for their own good—whether they are scholars, priests, or women. His name Eulenspiegel (literally, *owl mirror*) may well have meant that wisdom was holding up a mirror to mankind. But far from being moralistic, his pranks are above all hilarious, sometimes vulgar, and, like those of Rabelais' characters, show a predilection for excrement and a joy in the needs of the body—with the exception, however, of sex. Eulenspiegel's death and burial were as strange as his life. His coffin slid into the grave in such a way that the corpse was standing upright, and they decided to bury him that way, because his life had been so strange.

The sheer madcap quality of his pranks is perhaps best illustrated by one he committed in the city of Magdeburg. This is how the title reads: "How Eulenspiegel announced that he intended to fly from the roof at Magdeburg, and dismissed his onlookers with abusive language" (An*TE:*viii). Having become famous for his cleverness, he finds himself challenged by the citizens of Magdeburg to entertain them with a trick. He declares his willingness to do so and tells them that he will go up to the town hall and fly off the roof (An*TE:*32). People crowd about to see him, of course, and this is what happens:

> Well Eulenspiegel stood on the roof of the town hall, flapping his arms, and acting as if he really planned to fly. The people stood there, opening their eyes and mouths and thinking he was really going to fly. Eulenspiegel then laughed and said, "I thought there was no greater fool or buffoon in the world than I. But I see very well that this whole city's utterly full of fools. Now if you'd all told me that you intended to fly, I wouldn't have believed it—and you think I'm a fool. How am I supposed to fly? I'm still neither goose nor bird; after all, I've got no feathers, and without feathers or plumes nobody can fly. So you see very well it's all been a lie."
>
> Then he turned, ran off the roof, and left the crowd, one part cursing, the other part laughing and saying, "There goes a charlatan; but still he spoke the truth." (An*TE:*32–33)

That this spirit of the performer defying an audience on which he is totally dependent, this turning upside down of the world in a fantasy triumph, is still alive is reflected in the very language we use. "The stage clown's appetite for vindictive triumph," John Lahr wrote recently in *Prick Up Your Ears,* his biography of Joe Orton, "can be seen in his language for success: he 'kills the audience,' 'lays them in the aisles,' 'slaughters them,' 'knocks them dead' " (La*P:*116). Eulenspiegel's prank seems, moreover, to have inspired one of the most successful playwrights of our time writing in German. In his play *Publikumsbeschimpfung* (Insult to the Audience) (HaP), Peter Handke has his performers insult those who have come to see his play by telling them what fools they are to have come to witness something he will not show them.

In his mixture of cruelty and kindness, Eulenspiegel is as ambivalent as Trickster, Hermes, and Fox. But Till is the opposite of a hypocrite and does not seem to use flattery to further his ends. Nor do Fox or Eulenspiegel share with Trickster and Hermes their preoccupation with matters concerning sex, the penis, or making love to a woman. What all these figures share is roguishness, lying, stealing, triumphing over the stronger and suffering at their hands. Yet it is the trickster as hypocrite, especially in association with piety—so preeminent in the figure of the Fox—and combined with the love for woman, that seems to have fired the imagination of storytellers during the Middle Ages and Renaissance.

The Trickster as Hypocrite: Tartuffe

In the narratives of the Middle Ages the trickster appears, above all, as a hypocrite. He either has dealings with the Church or is a man of the Church. As such he is found in the tales of Boccaccio and Chaucer that, in their turn, were based on oral traditions, sometimes preserved by industrious monks in Latin manuscripts that have come down to us. Boccaccio chose, indeed, a trickster to be the protagonist of the first of the hundred tales he told in his *Decameron*. This story, that as it were, sets the tone for the entire work, for those days of sheer enjoyment the young storytellers spend away from the plague-ridden city of Florence, is given the title: "Ser Cepperello deceives a holy friar with a false confession, then he dies; and although in life he was a most wicked man, in death he is reputed to be a Saint and is called Saint Ciappelletto" (BoD:68).

The story promises to be irreverent, and Panfilo, the young man who tells it, assures us that it is based on the judgment of human beings, not that of God, whose intelligence is beyond human understanding. The mood of the title prevails, however, and it is one of ambivalence and deceit, both heightening as the tale proceeds.

An Italian merchant on business in France is obligated to return to his country. It is Ser Cepperello, his compatriot, whom he appoints to collect for him a sum of money owed him in France. Ser Cepperello is a man of good appearance and careful dress but has been chosen for the task because he is reputed to be villainous, a notary who takes delight in drawing up false documents and giving false testimony—and one therefore to win every case. We are told that he is a blasphemer, a killer, a man who goes to all sorts of trouble to stir up enmity among friends. We learn, moreover, that "of women he was as fond as dogs are of a good stout stick; in their opposite he took greater pleasure than the most depraved man on earth" (BoD:71). Having accepted the job offered him, he takes lodging at the house of two brothers, Florentines who honor him for the sake of his employer. But while in their house, he falls ill and is pronounced by the doctors summoned as "going each day from bad to worse" (BoD72). The two brothers are in a quandary: they cannot turn out a man so sick but fear that no priest will confess him before his death. Cepperello, aware of their deliberations, reassures them, asking them to look for the ablest and holiest friar to confess him, and maintains that he has done the Lord so many injuries while alive that "to do Him another now that I am dying will be neither here nor there" (BoD:73). The "Confession" of Ser Ciapelletto (it was thus that the French understood and pronounced his name) was as "truthful" as was that of Hermes claiming that he never brought Apollo's cattle to his house (having hidden them in a cave) and that his feet had not crossed the threshold (since he let himself into his mother's house through the keyhole). But the saintly friar who confesses Ser Ciapelletto is convinced that he has been a saint and, upon his death, has the chapter-house bell rung in his honor. The monks say prayers, and he himself, in his sermon, preaches such "marvellous things about Ser Ciapelletto's life, his fasts, his virginity, his simplicity and innocence and saintliness," that "the fame of his saintliness, and of the veneration in which he was held, grew to such proportions that there was hardly anyone who did not pray for his assistance in time of trouble, and they called him, and call him still, Saint Ciappelletto. Moreover it is claimed that through him God has wrought many miracles, and that He continues to work them on behalf of whoever commends himself devoutly to this particular Saint (Bo*D:* 80–81). Panfilo's judgment of the man corresponds completely to the justice prevailing in society and religion, when he vents his feeling "that this fellow should . . . be in Hell, in the hands of the Devil" rather than being received in God's kingdom (Bo*D:* 81). But the justice of the absolute comic, in particular that meted out to the trickster, is of a different nature. Ordinary standards of morality do not apply to Ser Ciappelletto. He falls into the ancient pattern of trickster and saint. God, not unlike Zeus who laughed about his dishonest son Hermes, seems to smile upon the wicked sinner for having outwitted the friar in his simplicity.

A different kind of trickster is found in the fifth tale of the *Decameron*'s Second Day. Here the protagonist Andreuccio, a simpleton, at first experiencing serious hardship, ends up by being exceptionally lucky in the manner of Stupid Hans in the fairy tale. Andreuccio goes from Perugia to a fair in Naples where he wants to buy horses and, being inexperienced and stupid, makes a display of his bulging purse to prove that he is serious about buying. A young Sicilian woman, quite beautiful and "willing to do any man's bidding for a modest fee," is fascinated by Andreuccio's purse and stupidity alike and wonders how she can take advantage of both, when fate comes to her aid. It turns out that the woman servant accompanying her recognizes in Andreuccio an old acquaintance from Perugia, where they had been neighbors. Through questioning her, the

Sicilian learns much about the young man's life and secretly
decides upon a plan. She sends another servant to the inn where
he stays, with the message that a "gentlewoman of the city
wished to make his acquaintance." Feeling honored and flat-
tered, he comes to her house, and she convinces him that he is
her long-lost brother. Strange as the story seems to him at first,
he is convinced by her knowledge of details concerning his
family.

Having been wined and dined by his "sister," he wishes to
leave but is offered lodging and retires, lying in bed stripped to
his doublet because of the heat. The servant assigned to stay
with him shows him the door to the place where he can "relieve his belly" but, upon stepping on the plank that is loosely
placed across an alley, he falls from a goodly height and into
"the filthy mess with which the place was literally swimming"
(BoD:147). Not unlike the Indian Trickster, he falls thus into
excrement. His attempts to get back into the house meet with
mockery, so that, almost naked and covered with filth, he has
to wander through the streets of the nightly city, not knowing
where to turn. In this disarray he chances upon two thieves on
their way to plunder the tomb of the Archbishop of Naples,
known to have just been buried with many valuables, among
them a large ruby ring. They enlist Andreuccio in their services, fully intending to add new sorrows to those he has reported to them. But first they must get rid of the stench he
emits and, having found a well, the two let him down into it.
There they abandon him when they see two officers of the
guard arrive who want to drink from the well. But the officers,
in their turn, run away in full flight when, instead of a bucket
full of water, they pull up Andreuccio, whom they believe to
be a ghost. Thus a cleansed Andreuccio rejoins his thieving
companions and all three continue their way to the tomb.
There it is his lot to climb into it and thrust out the valuables it
contains. But he, too, has now become "wiser" and, claiming
that he cannot find the greatest treasure, the ruby ring, is determined to keep it for himself. Yet his new cleverness is to no

avail: having collected their loot, the two thieves run away, closing the lid of the tomb. Andreuccio is in despair until, to his surprise, he hears a new group of thieves arrive, led by a priest. To allay their fears of the corpse, the priest tells them that the dead do not bite. Still, they are afraid to enter the tomb and it is finally the priest himself who does so. Andreuccio, at once, does bite him, and the three thieves flee in terror, giving Andreuccio a chance to get out of the tomb and take home his precious loot, the Archibishop's ring (BoD: 154–55). Andreuccio's story is a remarkable one: he was wealthy but lost his money because of his vanity, stupidity, and gullibility; he fell into the depth of mire and excrement; he was cleansed by water and rose from the well, almost by a miracle; he descended into a tomb and, by another miracle, was freed from it, so that he is almost like one arisen from the dead, one resurrected. His story is that of a young man who has mastered his naive stupidity to become shrewd and ready to cope with the greed and selfishness of the world. In the spirit of the absolute comic, he becomes victorious by virtue of becoming a rogue, a trickster. Yet the structure of his experience equals that of a saint or savior. He was destined to be the scapegoat, but the scapegoat has learned to outwit the clever rogues, and no one questions his moral right to keep the ring of the Archbishop. Upon his return to Perugia, he tells the "truthful" story—that he invested in the ring "the money with which he had set out to purchase horses."

The protagonists of these two tales are not men of the Church, although their activities bring them in contact with it. But often a trickster is himself a man of the Church. In the eighth story of the *Decameron*'s Third Day, it is an Abbot who plays the part of the trickster, and Lauretta, the tale's narrator, describes him as a "veritable saint of a man in all his ways except for his womanizing, a hobby he pursued so discreetly that very few people suspected . . . it" (BoD: 295). We are told that one of the Abbot's closest acquaintances was "a very wealthy yeoman called Ferondo, an exceedingly coarse and unimaginative fellow whose company he suffered only because Ferondo's simple ways were sometimes a source of amusement" (BoD: 295). Ferondo's beautiful wife has suffered immensely from her husband's stupidity and jealousy and, having chosen the Abbot as her confessor, asks his advice about how to deal with her problem. He promises her that he will "cure" Ferondo of his jealousy, if not his stupidity, by putting him in purgatory, if in return she will let him make love to her (BoD: 297). Her surprise, her scruples, and her hesitation are all conquered by the Abbot's clever arguments that mingle the sacred with the profane:

> Do not be so astonished, my treasure," said the Abbot. "No loss of saintliness is involved, for saintliness resides in the soul, and what I am asking of you is merely a sin of the body. But be that as it may, your beauty is so overpowering that love compels me to speak out. And what I say is this, that when you consider that your beauty is admired by a Saint, you have more reason to be proud of it than other women, because saints are accustomed to seeing the beauties of heaven. Furthermore, even though I am an Abbot, I am a man like the others, and as you can see I am still quite young. It should not be difficult for you to comply with my request; on the contrary, you ought to welcome it, because whilst Ferondo is away in Purgatory, I will come and keep you company every night and provide you with all the solace that he should be giving you. Nobody will suspect us, because my reputation stands at least as high with everyone else as it formerly did with you. Do not cast away this special favour which is sent to you by God. . . . Moreover, I possess some fine, precious jewels, and I intend that you alone should have them." (BoD: 297–98)

Having won over Ferondo's wife by putting a jewel on her finger, the Abbot now busies himself with putting Ferondo in purgatory: he invites him to take a glass of wine, into which he has slipped a powder that will make his guest sleep for three days. Ferondo is believed to be dead and put into a tomb. His widow mourns for him. When he awakens in utter darkness, he is told that he is in purgatory and is administered a beating for having mistreated his wife. In the meanwhile the Abbot, wearing Ferondo's clothes, visits the "widow" as frequently as possible, and those who see him go to her house, believe him to be her husband's ghost. But, after ten months of pleasurable visits, the Abbot learns that Ferondo's wife is with child and that he must decide to summon him back from purgatory. Ferondo's joy at the news that his wife will bear him a child and that he will be permitted to return to her from purgatory exceeds all bounds, and he is fully "cured."

As ambiguous as any trickster, the Abbot is both saint and sinner. He has put himself in the service of Love, whose sovereignty he has acknowledged. He has cured the bad husband. In the light of carnivalesque justice, he is free of all guilt. Morally, however, he is a hypocrite who breaks his vows of chastity and seduces, moreover, a married woman. Yet the story never criticizes or condemns him for such sins. The spirit of the absolute comic prevails in this tale, as Nature triumphs over religious and social laws. But trickster priests are not always shown in a light as agreeable. They sometimes exploit women with much more ruthlessness. Panfilo tells such a tale on the *Decameron*'s Eighth Day. Here we encounter a priest, more interested in women than in books and a man of great ease in conversation (B*oD:* 591). His heart goes out to Monna Belcolore, "a seductive-looking, buxom wench, married to a farm worker," who can sing and dance to perfection. Seeing that her husband is on his way to town, the Priest decides to visit her and try to win her favors. But Monna strikes a hard bargain: her Sunday dress is at the pawnbroker's and she needs five pounds to retrieve it. Anxious to make love to her, he agrees to pay the money and, as security, leaves his own black cloak. But once she has done his bidding, he changes his mind about the money. To retrieve his cloak, he sends a messenger to borrow her stone mortar he needs to prepare a sauce. The sacristan who returns the mortar the following day requests that she give back the black cloth the priest left her "as security." Since the request is made in front of her husband, who is dismayed at her having asked for security, she reluctantly complies, swearing that she will never lend the priest her mortar again. The priest, however, upon hearing her reply, laughs uproariously, dwelling gleefully on the sexual implications of mortar, pestle, and the preparation of a sauce. But even this totally selfish hypocrite is neither censured nor punished. His tricks are accepted in the mood of carnival and the exuberance of storytelling. If the priest of this story, though not unlike "hende" Nicholas of the *Miller's Tale,* who so cruelly tricks Alison's jealous husband, remains unscathed, this simply proves that the "punishment" in such tales is totally unrelated to the crime (in any moral sense of the word). Nicholas's being scalded by Absolon does not correspond to any prevailing sense of comic justice but is rather as accidental as the Indian Trickster's eating or being deprived of the food he has acquired in a manner that would be unlawful according to any social justice. This fact is also demonstrated by Chaucer's *Shipman's Tale,* whose amorous trickster priest by the name of Daun John [Don Juan?] is a ruthless hypocrite, betraying a most generous friend but getting off scot-free.

Daun John is very much befriended by a wealthy merchant whom he calls "dear cousin" and who provides him with exquisite hospitality. The merchant's wife is unusually beautiful but spends her husband's money so lavishly that he finds himself in financial straits. He invites Daun John to his house to inform him that, in order to straighten out his finances, he has to journey to Belgium. But Daun John is also taken aside by the merchant's wife who talks about what she believes to be her husband's meanness and confides in Daun John that she is in need of money to pay a debt. Joining her in maligning his "dear cousin," he promises to lend her the money, if she will do his bidding. But he actually borrows the needed sum from her husband, who does not hesitate to deprive himself of it in spite of his own difficult circumstances. Upon his return from a successful business trip, the merchant stops on his way home at the house of Daun John, not to ask for his money but to tell

him of his good fortune; he is, nevertheless, given to understand that all that was owed him was returned to his wife in all
fairness. The merchant could not but understand and see "there
was no remedye/ And for to chide it were but follye / 'Sith that
the thing may not amended be / Now wife,' he said, 'and I
foryive it thee / But by thy life, ne be namore so large / Keep
bet my good, this yive I thee in charge' " (Ch*CT*:213–14).
Again, no moral judgment is meted out to the trickster, either
for his betrayal of the merchant's friendship and the love he
swore the merchant's wife or for his breaking of the laws of
hospitality. He is an out-and-out hypocrite, although, in a
moralistic sense, one might conclude that the spendthrift wife
has been taught a lesson. Or was it rather the good husband
who was not only cuckolded but cheated of his money?

Having looked at these versions of the trickster figure as
fool, scoundrel, hypocrite and lover, we cannot but be surprised at the curious reception given Molière's *Tartuffe* (Mo*T*)
by Church officials in seventeenth-century France, although the
comedy's protagonist is but a polite and elegant avatar of a medieval literary tradition that was clearly still in vogue during
Molière's lifetime. The play's first performance, in 1664, at the
end of sumptuous entertainments at the King's court in Versailles, is said to have met with much applause from the King
and his following, who found it highly amusing. Its protagonist is clearly as much a hypocrite and glutton as the medieval
men of the Church we have passed in review, and he displays a
way of adjusting his concerns with poverty and chastity that
resembles theirs. Unfortunately, we will never know the comedy's original text. For Molière admittedly altered it on being
refused permission to present it at the Paris theater, the Palais
Royal, because of intervention by the ruling secret society, the
Compagnie du Saint Sacrement. As a consequence the playwright and his troupe had suffered a moral and financial set-
back, and his frustration had reached such dimensions, and the
hypocrisy he mocked in his comedy (no more than had been
traditional in the realm of the absolute comic) had become to

him so intense and frightening a reality, that he had come to consider it a vice he seriously had to crusade against.

In a petition to Louis XIV, Molière, the carnivalesque mocker, seemed to be on his way to becoming a moralist; he attacked those, who so relentlessly persecuted him, as "false coiners of devotion who seek to ensnare their fellow men by means of a counterfeited zeal and a sophistical charity," designating their machinations as "covert rascality" (MoT: 105). In the Preface to the play that he published five years later, he accused them of hypocrisy, maintaining that they were unable to stand a joke. (Rabelais would have condemned them as *agelasts*.)

In this Preface of 1669, Molière wrote:

> This is a comedy, about which a great deal of fuss has been made and it has long been persecuted. The people it makes fun of have certainly shown that they command more influence in France than any of those I have been concerned with before. Noblemen, pretentious women, cuckolds, and doctors have all submitted to being put on the stage and pretended to be as amused as everyone else at the way I portrayed them, but the hypocrites would not stand for a joke: they took immediate alarm and found it strange that I had the audacity to make fun of their antics or to decry so numerous and respectable a profession. For them, it was an unforgivable crime and they united in furious attacks on my play. They were at pains not to retaliate on the points which touched them most nearly. . . . Following their laudable custom they used the cause of Godliness to conceal their own interests and according to them *Tartuffe* is a play which offends against true religion. . . : every single syllable is blasphemy; the very gestures of the actors are criminal. (MoT: 99)

Today we can judge the play only by the text that has come down to us, although we have certain indications as to what alterations Molière may possibly have made in order to get permission to stage it—something he and his company so urgently needed. From a contemporary letter describing an early performance we get some idea of what the effect of its opening scene must have been. The comedy did then, and does now, open with old Madame Pernelle about to leave her son Orgon's household; she is scolding his son and daughter, his young second wife, and her brother, as well as the servant Dorine for what she considers their levity and immoral behavior. As she acts the judge supreme, she clearly divides the members of the household into two opposing camps: on the one side are the sinners who also happen to be young; on the other, her son Orgon, his friend Tartuffe, and herself, so that we become aware of the traditional youth/old-age opposition of the commedia dell'arte and comedy in general. Tartuffe, who stays at the house by special invitation of her son, is admired by her because of his piety, his unselfishness, his self-imposed poverty, and his impeccable morality. "Try to visualize," the letter describing the comedy suggests, "at first an old woman onstage, whose appearance and dress would hardly suggest that she is the mother of the master of the house, if it were not for the respect and deference shown her by a number of elegant and well appointed people. Her words and her mimicry equally express her desire to leave a place where, as she bluntly puts it, *she can no longer stay in view of the kind of life people are leading there"* (MoŒc4:437; my translation). It is not without interest that her part was actually played by an old man.

Madame Pernelle's views on morality and the high qualities of Tartuffe are not in the least shared by the younger members of the household (Orgon has not yet returned from a journey), so that Tartuffe is both praised and declared an hypocrite long before he makes his own appearance onstage. Indeed, we learn infinitely more about his privileged position in the family and his obvious hypocrisy through a dialogue that ensues between the returning master of the house and his servant Dorine during which he inquires, above all, about Tartuffe, whom he loves and admires well enough to wish to have him marry his own daughter by an earlier marriage. Orgon is ready even to disinherit his son, and to make over the family fortune to this hypocrite, who, in turn, not only enjoys all the pleasures of Orgon's generous hospitality but also tries to seduce his host's young second wife Elmira.

Tartuffe's behavior is quite in keeping with what we have learned to expect of the trickster in the realm of the absolute comic, and a number of critics have assumed that the comedy, known to have consisted at first of only three acts, ended with Tartuffe's seduction of Elmira and the gullible Orgon's total defeat. As a husband who declares his willingness to abandon his family in order to follow the precepts of Tartuffe ("Yes, under his influence I'm becoming another man. He's teaching me how to forgo affection and free myself from all human ties. I could see brother, children, mother, wife, all perish without caring that much!" (MoT: 117) he tells his brother-in-law), Orgon deserves to be cuckolded according to the laws of the absolute comic. His fate would, indeed, have corresponded to that of similar characters in the playwright's repertoire, George Dandin, for instance. But the conclusion of the play as we now know it is almost tragic and seems to contradict the spirit in which the characters were conceived: the hypocrite's clever appropriation of all of Orgon's wealth and his ruthlessness seem to reflect the bitterness Molière experienced during his long fight for the right to stage the play. By the fourth act the Hypocrite has so cleverly insinuated himself into Orgon's family, and evil seems to triumph over gullibility and decency in such a way that only the intervention of the King can resolve the situation. However, the King's Messenger, in declaring Tartuffe a long sought after criminal and Orgon an honored servant of the King, introduces an element of real justice into the realm of the absolute comic, where it is totally out of place. The Messenger's arrival at the conclusion of the comedy is more contrived than was usual even for a comedy, and must be considered as startling in the work of the playwright as are the many lengthy exchanges of the young lovers—usually avoided by the author but treated here with particular charm. Much of this appears to have been added by the author, both to expand the original three acts and to counteract the impact of the role of Tartuffe.

The need for such strategies becomes perhaps more obvious when we realize that Tartuffe—quite in keeping with the tradition of the hypocrite in the realm of the absolute comic—at first seems to have appeared onstage dressed as a man of the Church.

Having at last received permission to stage *Tartuffe* publicly in 1667 and subsequently deprived again of this privilege after only two performances, Molière addressed a second petition to the King to plead his cause, explaining in this *deuxième placet* that he had removed from the comedy all that might have been offensive to religious sensitivities: that he had not only changed its title and the name of its protagonist (first called Panulphe) but had also "disguised" him by giving him the appearance of a man of the world with an elaborate hairdo, a small hat, a large collar, an abundance of lace, and a sword (un petit chapeau, de grands cheveux, un grand collet, une épée, et des dentelles sur tout l'habit). The word "disguised" is significant, of course. It indirectly confirms the testimony of some of the author's contemporaries who maintained that Panulphe had looked like a priest. In fact, if one were to reverse the changes described by Molière—as some critics have done—one would have to conclude that Panulphe first wore his hair short, had a large hat, a small collar, no sword, and no lace trimmings. To seventeenth-century audiences, his appearance thus would have suggested that he belonged to a group of young hopefuls mockingly known as *abbés* (abbots) who—though not of the Church—dreamt of some day receiving from it a comfortable living. We are told that none less than Boileau and Racine had belonged to that group and, when young, had signified through their dress and behavior their devotion and dedication to a life of austerity, though waiting for their day of reward and recognition. (See MoŒcc 1:833–81.)

Furetière's Dictionary—that Webster of seventeenth-century France—lists *petit collet* (small collar) as synecdoche for a man of austerity and devotion: " 'Small collar' is used as designation for a man who has decided to reform and become more devoted, because men of the Church, out of modesty, wear small collars, while men of the world wear their collars large and trimmed with lace." (On appelle petit collet un homme qui s'est mis dans la réforme, dans la dévotion, parceque les gens d'Eglise portent par modestie de petits collets, tandis que les gens du monde en portent de grands ornés de points et de dentelles.") Furetière, writing after Molière's *Tartuffe,* was possibly inspired by that comedy when he added that sometimes hypocrites were referred to as "small collars" because they feigned modesty by wearing them. Disguised as a man of the world, Tartuffe no longer differed from any other seventeenth-century Frenchman; he became a contemporary of the playwright and his king. As the "small collar," his existence was more ambivalent and conjured up that comic character of long standing in the tradition of the absolute comic, the abbot or monk. Writing about the comedy a century or so later, Voltaire mentions the fact that the Italian commedia dell'arte actors staged in Paris, at the same time, a much less memorable play with a similar character. The Italian comedy was called *Scaramouche ermite* (Scaramouche the Hermit), and its protagonist, a hermit dressed as a monk, climbs up to the window of a married woman, disappears, and reappears from time to time to announce: "Questo è per mortificar la carne." (This is for the mortification of the flesh.) Voltaire quotes on that occasion a quip attributed to one of the courtiers of Molière's time: "The Italian actors offended only God, the French offended hypocrites" (Mo*Œ*4:369). Molière's infinitely more subtle Tartuffe, though falling into the same tradition, looked to some of the playwright's contemporaries like a parody of themselves or their friends; to others he represented a carnivalesque defiance of authority that, in the light of the quarrels within and against the Church, was felt to be threatening. The laughter provided by *Tartuffe* was no longer considered impersonal, but something aimed rather by an individual at individuals. This shift in receptivity, that is, in notions of what could be considered laughable, may well explain why the comedy, when presented in Versailles, was thought "highly amusing," whereas it was condemned from the pulpit and declared dangerous by members of the secret Compagnie du Saint-Sacrement (Company of the Holy Sacrament). The Company's reaction, though obviously prompted by politics of Church and State, seems to have been cause and result of the growing incomprehension of carnivalesque laughter as reflected in the decline of Rabelais' fame.

Suggestive though Tartuffe's garb may have been, the comedy's text alone—even in the form in which it is known to us today—must have conjured up in the minds of seventeenth-century audiences, still familiar with medieval traditions of parody through tales and *sotties,* those many gluttonous and lecherous trickster figures of abbots and monks preaching and acting out notions of love that were closer to the cult of Venus than to the Christianity they professed to represent. I have already made reference to the legend of the gluttonous Abbot who considered his belly divine and therefore protected it from the harm a hair shirt might do it, treating it with the loving care that only soft shirts and good food and drink could provide. As if in response to such associations, Tartuffe, before entering upon the stage, is heard to order his servant Laurent: "Put away my hairshirt and my scourge and continue to pray Heaven to send you grace. If anyone asks for me I'll be with the prisoners distributing alms" (MoT: 134). This is added to Dorine's previous description of Tartuffe as a man who at table is given the seat of honor and who, always treated to the best his host has to offer, eats enough for six. In an outrageously comical dialogue with Orgon, just returned from his journey and inquiring after the well-being of Tartuffe rather than that of his own wife who has been ill, Dorine portrays Tartuffe clearly as the hypocritical glutton of parody, whose ascetic demeanor contrasts as sharply with his devotion to food and drink as did that of the Abbot of the divine belly. While Elmira could not eat at all, Tartuffe, supping with her, "devoutly de-

voured a couple of partridges and half a hashed leg of mutton."
While high fever prevented Elmira from sleeping, Tartuffe,
"feeling pleasantly drowsy, . . . went straight to his room,
jumped into a nice warm bed, and slept like a top until morning" (Mo*T*: 116). When Elmira, having been bled, finally
found some sleep, Tartuffe "dutifully kept up his spirits, and
took three or four good swigs of wine for breakfast to fortify
himself against the worst that might happen and to make up
for the blood the mistress had lost." No wonder, "he's very
well; hale and hearty; in the pink" (Mo*T*:116–17).

But, like the hypocritical Abbot, Tartuffe is more than a
glutton. The Abbot's devotion to food and drink culminated in
his desire to find a woman to whom he could whisper: "You
alone please me, you will lie with me tonight." Tartuffe
equally yearns for the pleasures of the flesh, and, contrary to
comic tradition, it is not his host's daughter but his host's wife
Elmira who tempts him. He seems to have listened to all the
arguments of all of Boccaccio's clever men of the Church, for
like them, he tries to convince Elmira not only of the legiti-
macy of his love for her but also of the smiles God would be-
stow upon them, since, in her, Tartuffe would adore God's
creation. Says Tartuffe:

> "A passion for the beauties which are eternal does not preclude a
> temporal love. Our senses can and do respond to those most
> perfect works of Heaven's creation, whose charms are ex-
> emplified in beings such as you and embodied in rarest measure
> in yourself. Heaven has lavished upon you a beauty that dazzles
> the eyes and moves the hearts of men. I never look upon your
> flawless perfections without adoring in you the great Author of
> all nature and feeling my heart filled with ardent love for that
> fair form in which He has portrayed Himself." (Mo*T*:137)

He grants that he thought at first his love for her might be an
obstacle to his salvation,

> "but at length I came to realize, O fairest among women, that
> there need be nothing culpable in my passion and that I could

reconcile it with my virtue. Since then I have surrendered to it heart and soul." (MoT: 137)

Admonished by Elmira to stand more firmly against temptation, he counters:

"Confronted by your celestial beauty one can but let love have its way and make no demur. . . . I'm not an angel."

He blames her "enchanting loveliness" for his conduct and promises her a "devotion beyond compare," were she to deign to notice his "insignificance" (MoT: 138). But he assures her, above all,

"Moreover, your honor runs no risk with me; at my hands you need fear no danger of disgrace; these courtly gallants that women are so fond of noise their deeds abroad; they are forever bragging of their conquests. . . . But men of our sort burn with discreeter fires; our secrets are forever sure; our concern for our own reputation is a safeguard for those we love, and to those who trust us we offer love without scandal, satisfaction without fear." (MoT: 138)

Faithful to her husband, or at least unmoved by Tartuffe's wooing, Elmira breaks off their tête-à-tête, only to provoke another, this one consciously designed to be witnessed by her husband, who is to be shown Tartuffe as the scoundrel he really is:

ELMIRA: How can I consent to what you ask without offending Him whose name is ever on your lips?

TARTUFFE: If fear of Heaven is the only obstacle to my passion, that is a barrier I can easily remove. That need not restrain you.

ELMIRA: But they threaten us with the wrath of Heaven.

TARTUFFE: I can dissipate these foolish fears for you. I know the way to remove such scruples. . . . There are ways and means

of coming to terms with Heaven, of easing the restraints of
conscience according to the exigencies of the case, of re-
dressing the evil of the action by the purity of the intention. I
can instruct you in these secrets, Madam. Only allow yourself
to be led by me. (MoT:150–51)

While Tartuffe's arguments echo those of medieval abbots and
monks in similar situations, they are so cleverly couched in the
language of Jesuit and Jansenist theology that some of his critics
accused him of mocking one, others of slighting the other of
the two quarreling religious groups. At the same time, Tartuffe's declarations of love are replete with a poetry that is of
the seventeenth century, whereas his position in the Elmira-
Orgon triangle corresponds to that of an adulterous monk,
whose story told and retold survives in Latin manuscripts still
extant in libraries from Oxford to Rome, Paris to Prague.

The effort to discover where Molière might have found his
inspiration for Tartuffe has led to mention of numerous likely
and unlikely "sources," but none are convincing. For we know
almost nothing of the playwright's reading habits or the books
he perused. Even the Rabelaisian echoes that permeate his work
may be proof not of his intimate knowledge of that author but
rather of Rabelais' popularity that made certain of his ideas and
expressions a common cultural property of the times. It is quite
certain that a number of medieval traditions and patterns of
thought and speech were very much alive in seventeenth-century France, when the Middle Ages were often looked down
upon. There are numerous and unmistakable traces of a comic
medieval heritage to be found in Molière's own work, for instance, the "erotic grammar" of the Jealous Clown, or the Imaginary Invalid's pretended death—to mention but an early farce
and the author's final comedy. But we are not so much interested in tracing any possible influences as in the nature and structure of Molière's laughter, and it is here that we find that his
Tartuffe shares its absolute comic with that of a popular medieval story—the tale of the Adulterous Monk.

In one of its many versions—of which manuscripts are extant at Besançon, Cambridge (England), and Oxford, and which was transcribed by Lehmann (Le*P*)—the monk's tale is presented in the form of a "joyous sermon," whose author professes reluctance but shows obvious relish in reporting the gruesome adventures of a lecherous monk coveting a married woman to whom he promises his "immense wealth" in order to gain her favors. In this variant, the woman is a caricature: no longer young but eager to submit to the monk's amorous advances, she uses all possible cosmetics to conceal the blemishes of age and to put a blush upon her cheeks (so as not to blush for the pallor of her face and for her rattling teeth). She is willing to drug her husband so that she can spend the night with her monkish lover, but she has scruples about his religious habit, scruples he willingly removes by removing his cloak and "placing himself between her and God." Their lovemaking is interrupted, however, by the husband's untimely arrival. The monk, stark naked, hides in a basket but is discovered by the husband and his servants because his tonsured head sticks out. The husband's interrogation of him is filled with erotic double entendre, and the monk is finally nailed down (his body in the position of the cross) and made, as the Latin text puts it delicately, to "mourn forever the loss of his twins (Le*P*:224–31). The monk's castration is of the same order of cruelty as the death of Fliptail and represents a similar fantasy triumph of ordinary humanity over the arrogance of the mighty clergy.

The mood of carnivalesque degradation of the sacred is sustained by the fact that the language used in telling the tale is a composite of passages from the Bible, the Psalms, and the Gospels, grotesquely travestied to assume vulgar and erotic meaning. The title of some fifteenth-century variants of the story, "Passio cuiusdam monachi" (The Passion of a Certain Monk) is obviously reminiscent of "Passio Domini Nostri Jesu Christi" (The Passion of Christ) and is at the same time a pun on *passion* in the sense not only of suffering but also of love. Some of the variants begin, moreover, like a Gospel reading, using the formula "In illo tempore" (at that time it came to pass). As a matter of fact, we are told that narrators exerted every effort to make the sacred language they used clash as strongly as possible with the carnivalesque manner that turned its original meaning upside down. The large numbers in which these Latin manuscripts have been preserved prove the enjoyment the clergy derived from them, and it is worth repeating here that Rabelais' work, which abounds in such travesties of sacred language, was neither censured nor found offensive in France before the late seventeenth century. Bakhtin rightly refers to Friar John, one of Rabelais' outstanding characters, as "the incarnation of the mighty realm of travesty of the low clergy. He is a connoisseur of 'all that concerns the breviary' (en matière de bréviaire); this means that he can reinterpret any sacred text in the sense of eating, drinking, and eroticism, and transpose it from the Lenten to the carnival 'obscene' level." He can, as we have noted earlier, use Christ's last words on the cross, "sitio" (I thirst) and "consummatum est" (It is finished) as if they were mere expressions referring to food and drink, and he feels no qualms about obscenely parodying Psalm 121: "I will lift up mine eyes" as "Ad formam nasi cognoscitur ad te levavi" (by the shape of the nose it will be known to you how I lift up).

But the association, in the tale's title, of the castrated monk with Christ seems more than a play on words, more than a degradation of a sacred test. It makes his punishment paradoxical, suggesting the very ambiguity of this monk figure. His is the ambiguity of the trickster as both wounder and wounded of which Jung was so strongly aware. As one who brings love to a woman neglected by her husband, he serves the powers of Nature. Bakhtin, in fact, refers to the story in order to stress its positive shrovetide value. As the adulterer, the monk is the wounder, yet he is wounded by a cruel and stupid husband. In some versions of the tale the husband is presented as being so churlish as to ask the naked monk why he has come without his wedding suit. The monk is confronted with a dilemma without a solution, with what Jung has called the "quaestio crocodiliana," and explains as follows:

> A crocodile stole a child from its mother. On being asked to give it back to her, the crocodile replied that he would grant her wish if she could give a true answer to his question: "Shall I give the child back?" If she answers "Yes," it is not true, and she won't get the child back. If she answers "No," it is again not true, so in either case the mother loses the child. (RaT:271)

The monk is both right and wrong, and much of the story's effect depends on the delicate balance between the three characters involved: the woman's degree of wantonness (in one variant she has a list of lovers amounting to 144,000), her age, her beauty or the lack thereof; the husband's stupidity and jealousy; the monk's cleverness.

Without a doubt, Molière's *Tartuffe* has all the ingredients, all the structural elements of the medieval monk's tale. Though replete with the genius and wit of one of the greatest writers of comedy and written for the *honnêtes gens,* the polite society of seventeenth-century France, it equally parodies religious thought and speech. Its language is more complex, more elegant, its composition more imaginative. Mood and circumstances are those of seventeenth-century France. Yet there is the married woman wooed by a monk (even though "disguised"). There is the adulterer—lecherous, gluttonous, hypocritical—who is caught by her husband in flagrante as he makes love to her, at least in word, if not in deed. There is the churlish husband, incapable of appreciating his wife, or of putting himself in the service of Love. Only Elmira deviates from the medieval pattern in that she is neither ugly nor old or wanton. Nor is she "the woman on top," willing to deceive her husband. A perfect lady, she "invites" Tartuffe and encourages him to speak his mind freely, merely to expose his hypocrisy. Her impeccable morals lift her above the plane of the absolute comic. And yet, for the space of a scene, she too assumes the role of a trickster (a woman trickster at that). To make the Hypocrite drop his mask, it is she who manipulates "characters," "setting," and "situation," bidding her husband hide underneath the table, Tartuffe to meet and talk to her of his love, and Orgon to interrupt and confront him. It is then that she gains "sovereignty," though in a way that is totally unselfish: she wants to help Marianne, her stepdaughter (whom Orgon has destined to marry Tartuffe), her stepson Damis (whose inheritance is to go to Tartuffe), and she wants her husband to understand how badly his "friend" and guest has deceived him. Her "sovereignty" reveals Orgon as the comic fool he is. As he sits underneath the table, listening to Tartuffe's daring propositions to Elmira but lacking the courage to confront him, Orgon is clearly a figure of the absolute comic; he reminds us of old man Géronte's hiding in Scapin's sack to "escape his enemies." (See later section called The Trickster as Servant.) Elmira's plot reveals her husband as the comic scapegoat he deserves to be, according to the laws of carnivalesque laughter—if only for his offense against the power of Nature and Love, the tyranny he exerts over his children, and the disregard he has for his lovely young wife. In other moliéresque comedies as well as in farce it is such selfish old men that become the butts of laughter as young lovers are united, and it may well be, as many critics have surmised, that the comedy ended with Orgon's "total victimization" and Tartuffe's triumph—before Molière altered it.

It is easy to imagine an earlier version of the comedy without the present ending, so extraneous to all notions of the absolute comic: with an Elmira less virtuous, and tempted to play the woman on top; with the roles of the young lovers reduced and that of the reasonable Cléante, Elmira's brother the *raisonneur,* weakened or totally omitted. The play's delightful romantic scenes, so much more elaborate than is Molière's wont, ultimately remain hors-d'oeuvres, and the role of the *raisonneur* seems to assume proportions seldom found in the playwright's work. Even if lack of documentation does not permit us to conclude that these are later additions, we cannot but feel that Tartuffe, the trickster, firmly holds the center of the stage, although he does not make his entrance upon it before the third act. He is by no means the "blocking character" Northrop Frye declares him to be. If he prevents the union of the young lovers this is not at all his doing but rather that of Orgon. His amorous attentions are exclusively centered upon Elmira, so that the comedy's central concern is that of the monk as adulterer, glutton, and lecher. If he is a hypocrite, this is, above all, because he has to accommodate his desires to his religion and overcome the scruples of the woman he wishes to seduce, not unlike the medieval monk who places himself between the woman and God to shield her from being seen by Him. Tartuffe's reasoning is not too remote either from that of Boccaccio's Abbot who convinces Ferondo's wife that it is an honor to have one's beauty admired by a saint accustomed to the beauties of Heaven. It is, in fact, not Tartuffe the adulterer but Tartuffe the criminal that is punished, at the play's present conclusion, by what one senses to be a sleight of hand on the part of the author and something extraneous to its spirit.

Tartuffe's hypocrisy is of a more complex nature, however. It is displayed not only in his relationship to Elmira but also in his exploitation of those who are gullible and naive, whether in questions of faith or trustworthiness. It is here that he assumes qualities we associate with the Spanish *pícaro,* the trickster par excellence. One is not surprised, therefore, to find some of his most ruthlessly deceptive moments foreshadowed in a Spanish picaresque tale. Its trickster is not a man but a woman—which may account for the linking of exploitation and love. The story was probably known to Molière, if not in the original, at least in a French adaptation made by his famous older compatriot Scarron and entitled *Les Hypocrites* (The Hypocrites) (ScN). Whereas this title conceals the true nature of the protagonist, the original unashamedly announces it to be a woman: *La ingeniosa Elena, la hija de Celestina* (Ingenious Helen, the Daughter of Celestine) (SaE). In the literature of Spain,

Celestine is a name that represents the hypocrite of all hypocrites, the greatest trickster of them all. The scenes in *Tartuffe*
that are thought to have been inspired by *Ingeniosa Elena* are
those concerning his false piety and those wherein, accused of
heinous crimes, he is deemed innocent because of the clever
way in which he admits to them. There seems to exist a direct
kinship between Reynard the Fox, Elena, and Tartuffe—even
to the extent that their hypocrisy leads to an increase in wealth
and honor—at least temporarily. What earlier tricksters do not
share, however, is the linking of foxiness and sex. Amorous
abbots were after women, not wealth; the Fox was after
wealth, not sex. Could it be that—like Tartuffe—the female
trickster is after both? What, then, is a woman trickster?

The Woman as Trickster

If literature seems to indicate that it is "sovereignty" over men
that women most desire and that they often attain in the realm
of the absolute comic, we would expect to encounter a variety
of female tricksters who not only cherish such sovereignty
when it comes their way but also actively try to obtain it. But
evidence seems to contradict this. In almost all the literature of
the absolute comic it is a male character who is the prime
mover, although the woman, responding to his love, may well
support him in his efforts to outwit her husband. She may ad-
minister the necessary sleeping potion or tell the appropriate
lie. The goddess Iris, who was the messenger of the Greek
gods before Hermes took over her function, was, according to
Norman O. Brown (Br*H:* 50), never known in the *Iliad* as a
trickster figure. Nor are there women who act as tricksters in
the well-known Trickster and animal cycles of the North
American Indians, the medieval animal epics, or the Eulenspiegel stories. All these tales have male characters as their protagonists. It is true that, for a period in his life, the Indian
Trickster assumes the form and function of a woman, cheating

a male partner into marrying him and bearing a child, but he transcends this experience and returns to his maleness.

Yet the woman trickster was ruling in carnivalesque European festivities, and the *Mère folle* or *Mère sotte* (mothers of foolishness) acquired at least as much fame as the Lords of Misrule. Brueghel's mysterious canvas *Malle Griet* (Mad Mag) surely represents a female trickster. In literature, this Lady of Misrule has found her most glorious existence in Stultitia (Stupidity) praising folly in Erasmus's *Praise of Folly*. Because she accepts the premise that all are fools, she herself is, of course, a fool. Yet it is she who praises folly. Does a fool praising folly induce us to reject it as foolish or seduce us with her praise into accepting it? Stultitia remains a joyful mystery, as she praises the joys of life that God has provided for us and condemns those men that are too prudent to *live* because of the dangers which might ensue: prudence that eschews life is folly. Wisdom lies in rejoicing in God's world. Yet she who preaches such wisdom is Folly herself—Stultitia. Folly praising Folly is two-faced. She is a paradox, in particular when she declares herself willing to condone those lies men live by and to accept a certain amount of hypocrisy. For life is but a play and men are but players on a stage. Created by Erasmus in 1511, Stultitia, Folly, preaching foolishness to an imaginary audience she assumed to be fools (all men are fools), was equaled in subtle brilliance only by Rabelais speaking as author in his Gargantua and Pantagruel novels, written about two decades later. To consider Stultitia a female trickster would itself be the height of folly, however. She not only reflects the views of her author Erasmus but is, above all, an allegory, owing her female sex mainly to grammar (Latin *stultitia,* like all nouns of this kind, is feminine). She resembles, it is true, the Foolish Mothers of French popular festivities, but these were, of course, men elected to the post by their fool societies and dressed up as women because it was felt that women were by nature foolish and "lyked . . . to speake streight what so ever laie on [their] tongues ende" (Kai*PF*).

Yet literature has known powerful women tricksters, among the strangest of whom is Celestine, the "mother" of Helen. She looms large as protagonist of a curious Spanish work, a dramatic tale, written at the end of the fifteenth century by the Spaniard Fernando de Rojas and entitled *Comedia* (later: Tragicomedia) *de Calisto y Melibea* (RoC). Calisto and Melibea are the names of the tale's young lovers, but it did not take long before the character of Celestine, the go-between who brought them together, began to be considered so prominent that the work has been referred to as *La Celestina*. As such it was almost at once translated into French and English, and in 1631 James Mabbe rendered its spirit in a felicitous translation he entitled *Celestine or the Tragick-Comedie of Calisto and Melibea*. Celestina is described in Mabbe's version as

> an old bearded woman, a sorceresse, suttle as the Divill, and learned in all the fopperies and villanies that the world can affoorde. Her name is *Celestine,* one who in her lyfe, I thinke in my Conscience, hath made and vnmade 100000 virginityes in this Citye. Such a power she hath, what by her persuasions and other her coninge devices, that none can escape her. She will move harde Rockes yf she list, and at her pleasure provoke them vnto Luxurie. (RoC: 130)

Celestine is a bawd, a witch, a procurer, a medicine (wo)man, a receiver of stolen goods; her doings are remembered with horror by young Parmeno, who, as a child, had been left with her by his mother and had served her:

> "I wente in to the markett-place and fetcht her vittailes; I waited on her in the streetes and supplied her want in some other the like services, as far as my poore sufficiencie and slender force was able to performe. So that, though I were but a little whiles with her, yet I remember euery thinge as fresh as yf it were but yesterdaye, and remaines still in so newe a rememberance that old age hath not bene able to weare it out. This good honest whore, this matron, forsooth, had at the verie ende of the Citye, amongst your Tanners' close by the water's side, a loue howse,

somewhat separated from neighbours, halfe of it fallne downe, the rest ill-contrived, and worse furnished. Now, for to gett her liuinge, you must vnderstande, she had 6 trades. She was a *semster, a perfumer, a farder of faces, a virgin maker or mender of crack't Virginities, a Baude,* and some little relishe she had of *witcherie.* Her first trade was a Cloke to all the rest, vnder collour whereof manie younge wenches which were all at her commaunde came to her howse to learne to worke, some on smokes, some on gorgettes, and others on manie other thinges. But not one of them that came thither but brought with her either bacon, wheate, flower, or a Iar of wine, or some other like provision, as they could conveniently steale from their Mistresses. And some other theftes they committed of greater qualitie, makinge her howse (for she was the Receaver and kept all thinges close) the Randeuous of all their Roguerie." (RoC: 135)

But she is also portrayed by Parmeno as the hypocrite, never missing mass because the church is her marketplace where her love bargains are made:

"She was a great frende to *schollars, stewards* and *Abbots' pages.* To theise she sold the blood, the innocent blood of theise poore sillie fooles, who did easilie aduenture their virginityes, drawn on by her fayre promises and the amendes that should be made them. Naye, she did proceede so *farr,* that by their meanes she had to doe with your *Recluses* and your *votaries,* and neuer mist of your purpose. And what tyme doe you thinke shee chose, when she would deale with anie of theise? An honest and holie tyme, as when they walkt their *stations,* or wente on their night processions, at your midnight *Masses* and your morninge *Mattens* and such other their seacret deuotions. Manie of them haue I seene come into her howse disguised and masked because they would not be knowne. And with them manie an holie Fryar, bare-footed, breechlesse, and mufled all ouer the face; which went in thither to bewayle their sinns. Now, what were her marchandize, thinke you? She faind her selfe skillfull in curinge of little Children, she would take flaxe from one howse and putt it fourth to spinn in an other, that she might therby haue the freer accesse vnto all. One would crye «Heere, Mother!»,

and an other «There, mother!». Looke where the old woman
is: so that this old Trott, this Mistres, forsooth, or this
Nurse, yf so you will haue it, was well-knowne to them all. For
all theise her troubles, though she still wente from place to
place, yet for all this did she neuer misse her *Masses,* nor her
Vespers, nor yet omitt to visitt the *Monasteries* of your *fryars,* nor
your *Nunneries.* And her reason for it was verie good, for there
she had all her *Alleluias:* it was her only markett, where she
made all her bargaines." (RoC: 135–36)

In spite of Parmeno's serious warning, however, rich
young Calisto, madly in love with rich, young, and well-
guarded Melibea, wishes to engage Celestine's services. She, in
turn, is willing to work her tricks and arrange for a rendezvous, if the financial rewards will measure up to the young
man's wealth. Her first attempt fails, and Calisto is rejected by
Melibea. But Celestine, knowing the weakness of the human
heart and the power of love, will not give up as long as money
is coming her way

"*Melibea* is fayre, *Calisto* fonde, and withall verie franke. He
cares not to spare his purse, nor I my paynes. He is willinge to
spende, and I, yf I can, to speede him in his purpose. Lett his
monie walke and lett his suite hange as longe as it will. Monie
can worke anie thinge: yt breaketh harde rockes, it passeth ouer
Riuers on dry foote. There is not anie place so high, whereinto
an *Asse* laden with gold is not able to reach vnto. His inconsid-
erate follie and ferventnes in affection is sufficient to marr him,
and to make vs. This is all that I knowe. ——— And this is that
whervppon we must make our profitt. Well, now must I goe to
Pleberio's howse. *Sempronio,* farewell. For though Melibea doth
now brave it, and standes so high vppon their [sic] pantofles, yet
(as god would haue it) she hath not bene the first that I haue
made to leave her cacklinge in my dayes. They are all of them
ticklish and skittish; the whole generation of them is giuen to
winchinge and flinginge, but after that they haue once consented
and yealded to their riders, sufferinge themselues to be sadled in
the opposite part to their Reynes and to be strongly girzed in the

inside of their loynes, they will neuer be made to giue ouer: the feilde must be theirs. I am not able to expresse vnto thee the greate impression of that sweetenes which the primarie and first kisses of him they love leaveth imprinted in their hartes. They are enimies of the meane and wholly sett vppon extreames." (RoC:163)

The Spanish tale ends in tragedy. Induced by Celestine's shrewd and hypocritical arguments, Melibea agrees to return the love Calisto bears her. But what seems paradise soon turns into chaos and death. Unwilling to share her rich reward with one of Calisto's servants to whom she had promised his due, Celestine is murdered, and the ensuing disorder disrupts the lovers' meeting and causes Calisto to fall to his death in a hasty retreat. Having lost her lover, Melibea kills herself. Avarice has destroyed youth, beauty, and love. Celestine's trickery is that of the serpent in paradise; her work that of the Devil; and, worse than the Fall, the result is death.

Death is here "real," as it were. It lacks the light-heartedness of make-believe and is therefore tragic rather than comic.

Fatality, indeed, seems to cling to women tricksters in literature. Though they are often "women on top," they rarely profit by their enterprise. Zeus does not laugh at their misdeeds the way he laughed at the lies and thievery of Hermes. Their enterprise is, moreover, usually concerned with sex and the acquisition of wealth, or rather escape from poverty. Unlike Celestine, however, the female tricksters of literature are often beautiful. Like her Greek namesake Helen, Elena, the "daughter of Celestine" (SaE) whose brand of hypocrisy seems to have inspired Molière's Tartuffe, is such a type. We learn that her natural grace added to the beauty of her face is such that she soon comes to possess money proportionate to her attraction. Her eyes are black, lively, sweet, huge, and apt to create "victims" all around her. No one can help but love her. By birth, however, she is extremely poor. Her mother having been "charitable" to all sorts of men, married her father, at forty,

making him believe that she was a virgin. Her mother's
Moorish name had been Sara, but she changed it to Mary and
was given the nickname "Celestine" as a badge of honor. Elena
is thus doubly the "Daughter of Celestine": daughter of her
mother, so nicknamed; and the spiritual daughter of the Celestine of legend, whose hypocrisy she "inherited," as it were.
Truth was something that has never crossed her lips, we are
told. She knows how to use her beauty and tears to move the
hearts of men and is capable of inventing incredible sob stories
to make them open their purses. Her tricks force her to move
from city to city, in the manner of Spanish *pícaros,* and all she
hears and sees she ingeniously weaves into a stratagem to win
more loot. It is she who is the prime mover, serving and ruling
over her picaresque lover Montufar. But even her love for him
must give way when she comes to realize that beauty is bound
to fade and that a woman should be married to a rich man
before she is thirty. They cannot part, however, united as they
are by their mutual fear of poverty and his need for her beauty
to provide them with a livelihood.

Having heard that a wealthy man is marrying off his
nephew Sancho because of the young man's wild adventures
with women, Elena succeeds in convincing the rich uncle that
the young man has wronged her and in extorting from him
money to "seal her lips." Once the trick is discovered, the
young Sancho sets out to pursue the criminal but is so struck
by her beauty that his goal becomes love rather than justice. To
escape pursuit of any kind, the outlaws become hypocrites.
They dress and act like saints, live a life that appears to be
simple, visit prisons, teach hymns and catechism to children,
preach, and pray, thereby not only gaining the town's admiration but also receiving alms to be distributed among the poor.
Betrayed by an old acquaintance, Montufar admits to all he is
accused of, only to be admired for his humility and to see his
accuser almost killed for having wronged a "saint" (Sa*E:* 99).
Believed to be a saintly brother and sister, Elena and Montufar
live a life of luxury until they are denounced by a spiteful ser-

vant. It is then that disgrace befalls them. In the Spanish tale, the trickster's adventures end thus unhappily.

In Scarron's French adaptation (Sc*N*), however, Hélène climbs to new heights, as she and Montufar escape to Madrid. A jealous Montufar sees her give of her favors too freely to one of the many lovers she entertains with his full approval. He is out to kill the young lover but is stabbed to death by him instead. The young man ends up in prison, and Hélène, leaving her house in despair, stumbles into the house of young Sanche who still loves her; she leaves with him for the Indies to start a new life. There they live happily ever after. Scarron wrote his tale in 1655. One is reminded at once of Defoe's *Moll Flanders* (De*MF*), published in 1683, wherein Moll and her highway-robber husband end up in North America to conclude their picaresque lives in peace and respectability.

Moll Flanders is, of course, the female trickster, the *pícara*, par excellence. She does not have the sinister qualities of a Celestine. But she is beautiful, irresistible to men, clever, ambitious, determined to use her tears and her beautiful eyes to "become a fortune." Her origins are as humble and criminal as those of all *pícaros*. She never knew either father or mother, having been born in prison and her mother having been deported rather than executed because she could "plead her belly." Her name "Moll" is a name traditionally given to female thieves and prostitutes. It is truly pseudonymous, yet it is, as she claims, "well known in the records and registers at Newgate, and in the Old Bailey" (De*MF:* 1). Her life is a struggle for existence which can be won only through trickery: she must either make a rich marriage or become adept at thieving; both require cleverness, dishonesty, and true skills. She prides herself on her adroitness at spotting and appropriating valuables. Thieving, in spite of the certain death that is its reward when one is caught, becomes her occupation when she believes herself too old to find a husband. Until she reaches that age, all her skills are used to get married, only to find herself widowed or abandoned by husbands who, having spent her money, have to escape from justice. The only man who does not abandon her is deserted by her because she discovers that he is her brother.

But while Moll finds happiness at the end, her life of trickery never seems to be as carefree as that of the Spanish Elena, even though Elena's ends in misery. Nor is the tale of either woman told as roguishly as is Scarron's version of that of Elena. For Scarron alone does not introduce a sense of morality and maintains fully that mood of the absolute comic that is beyond good and evil. Defoe, on the contrary, dwells on the evil of social institutions, the misery of prisons, the threat and problems of deportation, the lives of prostitutes and thieves, even the role of women in his society. "I would fain," he has Moll assert, "have the conduct of my sex a little regulated in this particular, which is the thing in which of all the parts of life, I think at this time we suffer most in; 'tis nothing but lack of courage, the fear of not being married at all, and of that frightful state of life called an old maid, of which I have a story to tell by itself. This, I say, is the woman's snare; but would the ladies once but get above that fear and manage rightly, they would more certainly avoid it by standing their ground, in a case so absolutely necessary to their felicity, than by exposing themselves as they do; and if they did not marry so soon as they may do otherwise, they would make themselves amends by marrying safer" (DeMF:76). Yet it is this desire to get married (marriage often being seen as a means to raise them from poverty to riches) that seems to inspire female tricksters, above all in the fiction that follows. There is the Marianne of Marivaux and the Becky Sharp of Thackeray, who have enriched literature as precious examples of female trickery with its ultimate aim of a rich marriage. Unforgettable among their accounts is that of the heroine in Marivaux's *Life of Marianne* (MarM), of her going to mass in a new dress, with the desire of being noticed by marriageable young men:

> "I went to church, at whose entrance I found a crowd. But I did not stay there. My new dress and my appearance would have been lost there; and, sliding softly through the crowd, I tried to get to the front of the church where I noticed some well-dressed

people: dressed up women, some quite ugly. There were also a
number of young good-looking men, belonging either to the
army or the Church." (MarM: 58–59; my translation)

Marianne watches them and interprets each and every one of
their gestures. She believes she understands them fully. She is
sure of her own graces and soon finds the eyes of all young
men centered upon her, whereas all women present become
diminished as she outshines them. Her sense of power is immense: she has become the prime mover. All that happens
henceforth will depend on her (MarM: 62).

It would be wrong, nevertheless, to see the woman as
trickster only as adventuress intent on making a fortune and
possibly doing it by marrying well. As Natalie Davis rightly
suggests, Jeanne d'Arc, in her men's clothes, followed the example of many transvestite saints (DazSC: 145), and is clearly
the trickster as saint; and the many women of romance as they
abandon home and security in quest of the one man they love,
don men's garb in order to avoid adventure. In *As You Like It*
(ShA,), Rosalind, about to leave her villainous uncle's house,
sighs:

"Alas, what danger will it be to us,
Maids are we, to travel forth so far!
Beauty provoketh thieves sooner than gold."

And when Celia suggests that they wear old clothes and be-
smirch their faces, it occurs to Rosalind that she might dress up
as a man:

"A gallant curtleaxe upon my thigh,
A boar-spear in my hand, and—in my heart
Lie there what hidden woman's fear there will—
We'll have a swashing and a martial outside,
As many other mannish cowards have
That do outface it with their semblances." (Act *III*, sc.3)

But doublet and hose not only make it impossible for her to shed a woman's tears; they also prevent her from being recognized by her beloved, until she uses her "magic" to turn herself back into a woman. Viola in *Twelfth-Night; or, What you Will* can serve the Count, whom she loves, disguised as a man, whereas he would never have admitted to his house a woman other than the beloved and unattainable Olivia. Quite aside from the fact that Viola's disguise offers Shakespeare the opportunity for much witty dialogue, it shows proud Olivia falling in love with Viola, a man only in appearance—and all ends happily only because Viola has a twin brother. Variations on such themes are to be found in all the romances of Italy, Spain, and France, and it is perhaps only in Shakespeare's *Merchant of Venice* (Sh*MV*) that a woman disguised as a man proves so superior in wit that she can cut a knot no one else is able to untie. Portia's victory is a fantasy triumph as she makes the spirit of the law win out over its letter. It is in this manner that she turns tragedy into comedy, replacing what might have been a "real" scapegoat with one of make-believe in the realm of the absolute comic.

The truly lighthearted female trickster is found mainly, however, in the comedies of Molière. We have mentioned before Elmira's felicitous manipulations and interference in *Tartuffe,* designed to unite the young lovers by putting to ridicule their gullible father, who blocks their marriage in favor of Tartuffe, whom he believes to be a saint. Elmira, as we have seen, is an unselfish trickster figure. She is abetted and even guided, however, by the servant Dorine, more clever and less selfish yet, whose role in that sense is both traditional and highly original.

The Trickster as Servant

Brown, when outlining the history of the Hermes figure within Greek mythology, noticed a development from independence and autonomy to subordination. Hermes, the insubordinate and sly trickster, becomes the messenger and the servant-in-chief of Zeus the King. According to Brown, the Homeric poems actually give evidence of this change: whereas, in the *Iliad,* Hermes enjoys the same independence as the other "free" gods, such as Athena and Apollo, he has come in the *Odyssey* to assume the function of messenger, formerly performed by Iris (BrH: 50). Now, it is in the guise of messenger, slave, or servant that tricksters most frequently make their appearance in European theater: Greek comedy, the Italian and later the French commedia dell'arte, and the Spanish *comedias.* The independent trickster, male or female, is perpetuated mainly in narratives; the female trickster as transvestite populates romances and Shakespearean comedies; the trickster servant is a veritable Lord of Misrule on the stage. In this sense, Dorine is part of a tradition. What makes her original is her being a woman, not a manservant. No wonder that this role has attracted some of the greatest actresses on the French stage! It is important, versatile, and brilliantly alive. For Dorine plays adversary to a character as subtly shrewd as Tartuffe. If Elmira unmasks him, this is due to Dorine's prompting and masterminding. An outspoken, level-headed, and resourceful trickster, she is able to outwit the hypocrite, himself full of trickery. Indeed, hers is in a certain way a fantasy triumph over hypocrisy, against which she has rebelled, leading in tow not only Orgon's family but also the audience. If she does not win out over Tartuffe altogether, this is only because of the complexity of his character and its many facets. Her spirited provocations of her master Orgon, her narrow escapes from being beaten by him, her witty repartee, dramatically bring to life what might have remained otherwise a mere description of Tartuffe, who is both reviled and praised in superlatives before he himself appears onstage.

Yet Dorine is but the first of Molière's prominent women servants to usurp the role of the trickster, usually reserved for manservants or slaves. Toinette, in the later *Malade imaginaire*

(Imaginary Invalid) (Mo*II*), outshines her in sheer slapstick antics. She, too, dares outwit her master Argan, who so thoroughly enjoys his imagined ill health that he not only spends a fortune on doctors and medicine but also wants his daughter to marry a physician. It is Toinette who, in her loyalty, mocks him to the point where she is threatened with a thrashing. It is she who makes possible a rendezvous between the two young lovers and who sets the stage for and devises the plot that will unmask the Invalid's grasping, hypocritical wife. Toinette is truly the trickster of the absolute comic when she announces the arrival of a famous doctor who wishes to see Argan, the famous patient, and, rapidly donning a doctor's garb, alternately plays her own part and the part of that famous physician. Her swift change of costume and character, together with the absurdity of her "cure," grotesquely mock both the patient and his healers:

> TOINETTE: I'm a travelling physician . . . seeking opportunities for the exercise of my talents, patients worthy of my attention. . . . I scorn to bother with the dull ordinary run of minor ailments, rheumatism, coughs, fevers, vapours, headaches, and suchlike. I want serious illnesses. . . . I only wish, sir, you had every malady I've just mentioned, that you were given up for lost by all the doctors, despaired of, at death's door, so that I could demonstrate the excellence of my remedies and my anxiety to be of service to you. . . . Let us have your pulse! . . . Who's your doctor?
>
> ARGAN: Mr. Purgon.
>
> T: He's not on my list of the great physicians. What does he say is wrong with you?
>
> A: He says it's my liver—others say it's my spleen.
>
> T: They are all ignoramuses. Your lungs are the trouble.
>
> . . . .
>
> A: I have headaches from time to time.
>
> T: Exactly. Lungs!
>
> A: Sometimes I seem to have a sort of mist before my eyes.

T: Lungs!

> . . . What the deuce are you doing with this arm?

A: How d'ye mean?

T: I should have that arm off at once if I were you . . . it takes all the nourishment and prevents the other one from thriving. . . . I should have that right eye out too if I were in your place. . . . Don't you see how bad it is for the other one? . . . Take my advice, have it out. . . . (Mo*II:* 267–68)

Though always referred to as being very young, Toinette does not play the part in the comedy that tradition reserved for young women, namely, that of an inane girl in love. Hers are, instead, all the qualities of the mature trickster: wit, imagination, cleverness, the ability to tell a lie in such a way that she can claim she has never told one, and the cunning to devise plots for others and change her own dress and behavior to assume a different role. She is in a certain sense also the go-between for the young lovers and creates opportunities for them to meet. She is, in fact, the comedy's prime mover. It is finally she who, together with the Invalid's brother Béralde, conceives and stages the carnivalesque scene which concludes the comedy and wherein she has assigned to her master—without his knowing it—the principal part. She has devised for him a fantasy triumph whereby he seems to outwit Death by becoming a physician and having immortality bestowed upon him. In the world of the absolute comic, this seems to be the only occasion when Death seems outwitted, and it is done in so topsy-turvy a manner that all involved know—all, except the Imaginary Invalid—that the scene is make-believe, not demanding, even for the fraction of a second, a suspension of disbelief, but rather defying all that is mimetic.

Molière is among the first in the history of the theater to present women as servant tricksters of such importance. Dorine and Toinette appear in almost every scene of their respective plays. Each proves, moreover, superior in wit to the master in whose pay she is. Each invents and directs plots, each acts, play-acts, and makes others act. Both are unselfish saviors and, while devoting themselves to the task of helping the young and setting the world aright, are often threatened with beatings—though never truly beaten. But, in spite of the importance each has as prime mover of the action, neither Dorine nor Toinette is the protagonist of her play. It was rather to a manservant that Molière entrusted the role of trickster as protagonist: to Scapin in *Les Fourberies de Sapin* (That Scoundrel Scapin) (MoSS), a role he himself played in performances during his lifetime. Scapin seems a direct descendant of Hermes the Thief, and it is not accidental that French *fourberie* is English "trick."

With Scapin, Molière returns to the trickster as the clever, intriguing servant figure whose survival depends on his ready wit and whose master can always—bodily as well as verbally— lash out at him for his very wit and inventiveness. What Scapin declares to be his "petite philosophie," his guiding principle in life, is to expect always the worst and thank his lucky stars when it does not happen (MoSS:83). Scapin is the typical *pícaro*, lending himself to all the laughter the absolute comic has at its command, and it is not surprising that even the critic Boileau, Molière's friend and admirer, found him too farcical to do justice to the playwright's exquisite taste. Boileau praised Molière for his most "classical," that is, "least farcical" comedies, thus preferring wit and the significative comic to the absolute comic, whose joyful spirit was doomed to be suppressed for centuries to come. And yet the absolute laughter of Scapin has survived, and his complexity as the trickster even today captures our imagination. Scapin is the comedy's central figure in more than one sense: as the guardian of two young men whom their two old fathers, away on business, have more or less left in his charge, he invents complicated stratagems, directs their execution, assumes various roles and disguises. As he goes about his business of guiding, protecting, and providing for his two charges, he is determined to set the world aright. He helps his penniless young wardens at the expense of their stingy elders, thoroughly enjoying his fantasy triumphs over authority. So devoted and dedicated is he to his work, so proud of his skill as a rogue, so unselfish in the service of others, that—paradoxically—he resembles a saint and a savior. Yet his pride is also that of a Mephistopheles, as he fancies himself a wheeler and dealer, powerful, indispensable, capable of overcoming any and all obstacles, and, like Mephistopheles, is shown ultimately to be expendable and unnecessary. His is the fate of the trickster who heals, wounds, and is himself at last mortally wounded. As jester, he is the plaything of jest.

Scapin, a French version of Italian Scappino, is a well-known commedia dell'arte mask, whom Callot included in his sketches entitled "Balli di Sfessania." The name Scappino was derived from Italian *scappare* (to flee, to escape), and the character was conceived as a coward, a swift-footed "starling," ever ready to skim away, swoop back, twitter and warble, pilfer right and left, and yet forever returning. He was traditionally bereft of all logic, creating confusion everywhere, forgetting everything, and always holding out his hand for a gratuity. (See, e.g., Du*IC:* 168, *passim*). He was also established as a Don Juan type, falling in love with any servant girl rather than a king's daughter, and as a born liar. As a type, he had been conceived and created by the Milanese commedia dell'arte actor and scenario writer Niccolo Barbieri, whose stage name was Beltrame and who had both composed the scenario and written the comedy *L'Inavvertito overo Scapino disturbato e Mezzetino travagliato* which had served as a model for Molière's *L'Etourdi,* an earlier version of *That Scoundrel Scapin.* (Du*IC,*34n3). Molière obviously changed the character of Scappino, giving him almost the same importance that he had conveyed upon Tartuffe, the hypocritical monk, and upon Don Juan, the trickster who defied the dead.

The comedy's orchestration of characters corresponds to the tradition of the commedia dell'arte. Two young men, Octave and Leander, who like to live well but are financially dependent on their wealthy fathers, have fallen in love with two young women and have married them secretly in the absence of their fathers, while the two old men (Argante, father of Octave, and Géronte, father of Leander) have made their own wedding plans for their sons. The young men's valets (Silvester and Scapin), in whose charge they were left when their fathers departed on business, assist them in their troubles, and, of the two valets, it is Scapin who excels in the ingenious strategems and intrigues that are meant to bring about their happiness.

In the true tradition of the trickster, Scapin is not only a rogue but a prime mover, and it is his almost total commitment to the young, whose fantasy triumph would involve the degradation of their elders, that inspires him. Danger does not frighten him: "It amuses me to tackle things where there is a little risk involved," he boasts (MoSS:95). He despises timid souls who dare not engage in anything because they foresee how dire the consequences might be. In order to get the better of the two authoritarian fathers, he invents hilariously grotesque stories and the most improbable *lazzi*. Among the figures of Latin comedy, he is comparable to the parasites of Terence and the braggart soldiers but he is also a mixture of loyalty and innate roguery vis-à-vis his own young master. While he takes such pride in his métier that he will never give up until his battles are won, this very vainglory makes him use his cleverness in situations where it is not called for, thereby invariably complicating them and getting himself into trouble.

His trickery is aimed at the two old men, Argante and Géronte, and he likes to triumph over them, apparently for no selfish purpose, but in order to serve the two young men, his master and his master's friend. His inventions are extravagant, and he can rightly boast, each time a problem presents itself that he has already found the solution and that "the plot is already laid" (MoSS:83). He will admit with the utmost modesty:

> "Well, to tell the truth, there isn't much I can't manage when I'm put to it. There's no doubt about it. I've quite a gift for

smart ideas and ingenious little dodges. Of course, those who can't appreciate them call 'em shady, but boasting apart, there are not many fellows to equal yours truly when it comes down to scheming or something that needs a little manipulation. I had built up a pretty good reputation for that sort of thing, but it's like everything else today—credit goes to anyone but those who have earned it! I got into trouble over a certain little matter, and since then I've sworn I'll give it all up." (MoSS: 66–67)

Scapin's predecessor Mascarille had shouted in the same playwright's *L'Etourdi* (The Scatterbrain): "Vive la fourberie et les fourbes aussi!" and had had visions of having his portrait painted and adorned with the gold inscription: "Vivat Mascarillus, fourbum imperator!" (Long live Mascarille, the Emperor of scoundrels!) Yet fate outtricks both tricksters. In the case of Mascarille, his young master's naiveté foils every ingenious plan he devises to help him. In the case of Scapin, Molière's later and more experienced version of the trickster servant, all the brilliant fireworks of his ingenuity come to naught because it appears at the comedy's conclusion that the young women the fathers had destined to be their daughters-in-law are precisely the ones their sons had secretly married. Whereas they were consciously opposing one another, they were unwittingly in complete agreement, and had Scapin been less clever, all would have been much more simple. It is he, the trickster, who turning order into disorder, created difficulties where there were none at all. The machines his subtle mind designed and set in motion—beautiful, intricate, and ingenious—proved not only superfluous but also a hindrance. And yet without him there would have been no comedy, no carnivalesque laughter—no more than there would have been a *Tempest* without Prospero or Shakespeare. All is imagination, all play. Yet it is Scapin the trickster who is excluded from the gaiety that prevails at the comedy's end, once all its characters have recognized each other for what they really are and all misunderstandings have been cleared up. It is then that Scapin's tricks no longer seem those of a savior but rather those of a crook and a rogue: what the old men remember are the extortions, the lies, the blows he dealt out to them, the degrading situations he devised for them, and their own shameful gullibility in paying heed to him. Géronte threatens to kill him, and it is only through another daring ruse that Scapin can save his life: Pretending that he has been mortally wounded by a falling brick, he has himself carried onstage, a dying man with his head grotesquely bandaged. This ancient trick, this commedia dell'arte *lazzo,* forces Géronte to grant him his pardon during the wedding feast honoring the two couples. At the same time, it prevents Scapin from partaking of the food, lest his trick be discovered. Scapin is saint and sinner, a servant and yet by virtue of his wit the prime mover; a devil and a savior, he is crucial in creating that climate wherein comedy triumphs.

For what truly counts in this comedy—as indicated by the fact that the trickster supplies the play with its title—are Scapin's inventions and enterprises, his activities and the plots he devises for others, even though they ultimately misfire. It is as if Scapin were writing the play as his brain creates situations and fabricates solutions that lead to new complications necessitating further plotting (cf. Hu*M, passim*). Much of the plotting has to do with the money his young masters need and that their old fathers possess in abundance without wishing to part with it. Scapin, like many tricksters, takes from the rich to give to the poor, although it is cunning rather than force that makes him succeed in his robberies. His only selfishness seems to consist in the pride he takes in his art as a rogue. Having convinced Argante that his son was forced by the girl's ruffian brother to marry her, Scapin, relishing the old man's distress, suggests as a possible remedy a large payment to be made to the brother. It is to extort money that Scapin spins his marvelous yarn of madcap make-believe:

"I've just been to see the brother of the girl your son has married. He's a professional blackguard, one of these fellows who are free with their swords, talk of nothing but cutting people to pieces, and think no more of killing a man than tossing off a glass of wine. I led him on to the question of this marriage, and I made him see how easy it would be to get it dissolved on a plea of violence and your strong position as a father and the influence you would bring to bear in court of law by reason of the justice of your cause, your money, and your friends. Eventually, I influenced him to the extent that he began to listen to the possibility of settling it for a sum of money . . . , provided you will make it worth his while." (MoSS:84)

Argante, who begins to be intrigued by this possibility and wants to know how much the brother might be willing to take, is appalled at the suggestion that it might be several hundred pounds. But as Scapin breaks down the sum, inventing the brother's willingness to take less because he will soon have to go to war and needs a horse and saddle, a servant, a donkey, uniforms, and weapons, Argante, though arguing madly about every additional item, finally agrees to pay two houndred pounds so as to save—as Scapin has proved to him— one hundred and fifty pounds in legal costs that might otherwise ensue. Yet Scapin's arguments ultimately assume their full weight because the "brother"—Scapin's fellow servant, carefully costumed and coached by him with regard to the gestures and language to be used—makes his threatening appearance upon the stage and frightens Argante into submission. The rich and powerful Argante, upon seeing the "brother" in cloak and dagger, hides behind Scapin, thus providing a double fantasy triumph: he humbles himself before Scapin and even more so before the audience that is aware of the extent to which he has been outwitted. Scapin's is a fantasy triumph as well as the triumph of fantasy over narrow materialism.

In the case of old Géronte, Scapin's exertion of his imagination is even wilder and his triumph still greater. He tells the gullible father that his son was kidnapped by Turks who are holding him prisoner on their ship and, though they invited him there to be their guest, will not free him without a handsome ransom. Utterly distraught and a prey to his growing anger, Géronte cries out over and over again, "What the devil was he doing on that ship?" But there is no escape. According to the way in which Scapin presents matters, the old man must pay. He distractedly pulls out his purse and just as distractedly puts it back before Scapin can get hold of it. Such stinginess, in the trickster's view, cries out for revenge, and he hits upon the device of telling Géronte that the Turks are after him and out to kill him. Géronte's only escape is to hide in a sack the servant happens to carry. With the dignified old miser in his sack, Scapin engages in lengthy imaginary conversations, impersonating Géronte's "enemies" who want to find and kill him, and defending him in response in his own voice. In the course of these conversations, the sack is dealt many a kick by Scapin who is thanked afterwards for having "saved" his master's father.

But for all the loyalty with which he serves his young master, Scapin does not manage to be totally honest with him, especially when questions of food and drink are involved. His treachery is revealed when Leander, sword in hand, bids him confess his "crimes" and Scapin, not knowing what aroused his master's anger, admits to all sorts of wrongdoing the young man never suspected.

> LEANDER: I'll make him confess to me here and now. Yes, you scoundrel, I know what tricks you've been up to. I've just heard. I expect you thought I shouldn't find out. But I'll have the confession from your own lips, or I'll run my sword through your guts. . . . Out with it, then.
>
> SCAPIN: Something I've done, master? . . . I assure you I can't think of anything.
>
> L (*threatens to strike him*): You can't think of anything?
>
> S: Well then, master, since you will have it, I confess that I and a few friends drank that small quartern cask of Spanish wine someone gave you a few days ago. It was I who made the hole in the cask and poured water on the floor to make you think the wine had run out.
>
> L: So that was you, you dog! You drank my Spanish wine and

were the cause of my abusing the servant girl, thinking she was to blame?

s: Yes, master—I ask your forgiveness.

L: I'm glad to know about that—but it's not what I'm after.
. . . It's something much more serious than that, and I'm going to have it out of you. . . . (*threatening to strike him*). . . .

s: Yes, master, I confess that one evening about three weeks ago you sent me with a watch to the young gypsy girl you are in love with and I came home with my clothes torn and my face covered with blood and I told you I'd been beaten and robbed. It was me, master—I'd kept the watch for myself!

L: You kept my watch for yourself?

s: That's it, master—to tell the time by!

L: We *are* finding things out. A fine faithful servant I have, I must say. But that still isn't what I want.

s: That isn't it?

L: No you scoundrel—there's something else yet you have to own up to.

s: The devil there is!

L: Quickly! I'm in a hurry. . . . (*about to strike*).

s: All right, then, master. You remember the apparition you met one night, about six months ago, that beat you up and nearly made you break your neck running away and falling into a cellar. . . .

L: Well———

s: That was me, master. I was the apparition.

L: You were the apparition, were you, you scoundrel!

s: Yes, sir, just to give you a bit of a scare and to cure you of having us running round after you every night as you used to. (MoSS: 79–81)

Scapin, who is the prime mover of all events, seems also in charge of the play. Like Molière himself, he is, as has been pointed out, playwright, director, and actor. At every turn of the comedy he not only invents new plots and stratagems that result in new dramatic situations, he not only himself assumes various roles, but he also coaches the other characters in roles he invents for and assigns to them. We have mentioned the fact that his fellow servant Sylvester is directed by him to play the part of the gangster brother who is willing to annul his sister's marriage for a bribe sufficiently large to buy horse, harness, and fighting equipment. No sooner has Scapin grasped that Argante will try to annul his son's marriage than he thinks of a countermove. "Leave it to me," he tells Sylvester. "The plot is laid. I'm just trying to think of a reliable man to play a part I need," and, scanning his chum with the eye of an experienced director, he exclaims: "Wait—stop a minute—stick your hat at an angle and look like a blackguard! Limp a bit with one leg! Hand to your side! Scowl! Strut like a tragedy king! Good. Follow me! I can show you how to disguise your face and your voice" (MoSS:76). To prepare the young man for his dreaded encounter with his father, soon to return from his voyage, Scapin rehearses with him, playing himself the part of the father and inventing appropriate dialogue for both father and son:

> SCAPIN: What *you* have to do now is to prepare to stand up to meeting your father.
>
> OCTAVIO: I must admit that the idea makes me tremble already. I have a sort of natural diffidence I just can't get over.
>
> S: Well, unless you stand firm from the outset he'll take advantage of that natural diffidence to treat you like a child. Come, try to pull yourself together. Make up your mind to answer him firmly whatever he says to you.
>
> O: I'll do what I can.
>
> S: We'll better practise a little to get you used to the idea. We'll put you through your part and see how you get on. Come now, a resolute air, head up, firm glance.
>
> O: Like this?
>
> S: A bit more yet.
>
> O: That it?

s: Right. Now imagine I am your father coming in. Answer me boldly as if I were he. 'Now, you scoundrelly good for nothing! You disgrace to a decent father! How dare you come near me after what you have done while I have been away? Is this what I get for all I've done for you, you dog! Is this the way you obey me? Is this how you show your respect for me?'— Come on, now—'You have the audacity, you rascal, to tie yourself up without your father's consent and contract a clandestine marriage? Answer me, you rogue, answer me! Let's hear what you have to say for yourself?' What the devil—you seem completely nonplussed!

o: Yes—you sound so much like my father.

s: Well, that's the very reason why you mustn't stand there like an idiot. . . .

o: I'll be more determined this time. I'll put a bold face on it.

s: Sure?

o: Certain.

s: That's good then, for here comes your father!

o: Heavens! I'm done for! (*Runs off.*) (MoSS: 71–72)

Falstaff

The scene is reminiscent of that between Falstaff and the young Prince Hal in Shakespeare's *1 Henry IV* (ShH-1), where Falstaff warns the young man: "Well, thou wilt be horribly chid tomorrow when thou comest to thy father. If thou love me, practise an answer," and where the Prince replies: "Do thou stand for my father and examine me upon the particulars of my life." (act II, sc. 3, ll. 351–54) If both Shakespeare and Molière, living in different countries at different times, used the device with such skill and to such good purpose, we may well assume that it was well known to men of the theater. To speak of influences would be as absurd as it is futile. But an awareness of the similarity in pattern permits us to recognize more clearly each author's dramatic genius and intent. Having looked at Molière's scene, we should therefore glance at Shakespeare's.

Falstaff, having agreed to play the part Hal has assigned to him, declares:

> FALSTAFF: This chair shall be my state, this dagger my sceptre, and this cushion my crown.
>
> PRINCE: Thy state is taken for a join'd-stool, thy golden sceptre for a leaden dagger, and thy precious rich crown for a pitiful bald crown.
>
> FAL: Well, an the fire of grace be not quite out of thee, now shalt thou be moved. Give me a cup of sack to make my eyes look red, that I may be thought I have wept; for I must speak in passion, and I will do it in King Cambyses' vein.
>
> PRINCE: Well, here is my leg.
>
> FAL: And here is my speech. Stand aside, nobility.

The Prince and Falstaff have as audience the inn's hostess, who admires their art and enjoys the good sport, comparing it to that of the "harlotry players."

> FAL: . . . . Harry, I do not only marvel where thou spendest thy time, but also how thou art accompanied. For though the camomile, the more it is trodden on, the faster it grows, yet youth, the more it is wasted, the sooner it wears. That thou art my son I have partly thy mother's word, partly my own opinion, but chiefly a villainous trick of thine eye and a foolish hanging of thy nether lip that doth warrant me. If then thou be son to me, here lies the point: why, being son to me, art thou so pointed at? Shall the blessed sun of heaven prove a micher and eat blackberries? A question not to be ask'd. Shall the son of England prove a thief and take purses? A question to be ask'd. There is a thing, Harry, which thou hast often heard of, and it is known to many in our land by the name of pitch. This pitch, as ancient writers do report, doth defile; so doth the company thou keepest. For Harry, now I do not speak to thee in drink, but in tears; not in pleasure, but in passion; not in words only, but in woes also: and yet there is a virtuous man whom I have often noticed in thy company, but I know not his name.

PRINCE: What manner of man, an it like your Majesty?

FAL: A goodly portly man, i' faith, and a corpulent; of a cheerful look, a pleasing eye, and a most noble carriage; and, as I think, his age some fifty, or, by'r Lady, inclining to three-score; and how I remember me, his name is Falstaff. If that man should be lewdly given, he deceiveth me; for, Harry, I see virtue in his looks. . . . Him keep with, the rest banish. And tell me now, thou naughty varlet, tell me where thou hast been this month?

PRINCE: Dost thou speak like a king? Do thou stand for me, and I'll play my father. . . . Well, here I am set.

FAL: And here I stand. Judge, my masters.

PRINCE: Now, Harry, whence come you?

FAL: My noble lord, from Eastcheap.

PRINCE: The complaints I hear of you are grievous.

FAL: 'Sblood, my lord, they are false! . . .

PRINCE: Swearest thou, ungracious boy? Henceforth ne'er look on me. Thou art violently carried away from grace. There is a devil haunts thee in the likeness of an old fat man; a tun of man is thy companion. Why dost thou converse with that trunk of humours, that bolting hutch of beastliness, that swoll'n parcel of dropsies, that huge bombard of sack, that stuff'd cloakbag of guts. . . , that reverend vice, that grey iniquity, that father ruffian, that vanity in years? Wherein is he good but to taste sack and drink it? Wherein neat and cleanly but to carve a capon and eat it? Wherein cunning, but in craft? Wherein crafty, but in villainy? Wherein villainous, but in all things? Wherein worthy, but in nothing?

FAL: I would your Grace would take me with you. Whom means your Grace?

PRINCE: That villainous abominable misleader of youth, Falstaff, that old white-bearded Satan.

FAL: My lord, the man I know.

PRINCE: I know thou dost.

FAL: But to say I know more harm in him than in myself were to say more than I know. That he is old (the more the pity) his white hairs do witness it; but that he is (saving your rever-

ence) a whoremaster, that I utterly deny. If sack and sugar be
a fault, God help the wicked! If to be old and merry be a sin,
then many an old host that I know is damn'd. If to be fat be
to be hated, then Pharaoh's lean kine are to be loved. No, my
good lord. Banish Peto, banish Bardolph, banish Poins; but
for sweet Jack Falstaff, kind Jack Falstaff, true Jack Falstaff,
valiant Jack Falstaff, and therefore more valiant being, as he is,
old Jack Falstaff, banish not him thy Harry's company, banish
not him thy Harry's company. Banish plump Jack, and banish
all the world!

PRINCE: I do, I will. (act II sc. 4, ll. 350–453)

Prince Hal and Falstaff are avowedly playing a game, but
what is said by the Prince in jest is, within the reality of the
play, meant in earnest. The reasoning he presents as being the
King's is truly his own. His assessment of Falstaff's character
and the role he plays in the Prince's life give proof of an understanding that Hal's behavior seemingly belies. Seemingly,
though not really: for the notion of Falstaff's banishment,
which becomes a reality at the end of the play's second part, already seems to have taken root in the Prince's mind at a time
when Falstaff was still among his closest companions.

In terms of literary tradition, the scene clearly establishes
Falstaff as an avatar of the trickster figure, although he is a nobleman rather than a traditional servant. He is as much a liar as
Molière's Scapin, except that he boasts mainly about his brav-
ery in war and, thereby, comes close to being the typical
braggart soldier. His lies are so coarse and obvious that they are
beyond belief. At the end of *1 Henry IV,* Falstaff, as genuine a
coward as any traditional braggart soldier that ever presented
himself on a stage, pretends to have been mortally wounded at
the very moment he is challenged in battle. Prince Hal, believing him dead, includes him in his lament over his enemy Hotspur, whom he has vanquished in a fierce duel. Once Falstaff
knows himself safe because Hotspur has been killed, he coura-
geously arises to stab the corpse and, shouldering it, does not
hesitate to boast before an astonished Prince Hal that he had

come to life again and, in an hour-long battle, had killed Hotspur. Deception is so much a part of his existence that he unflinchingly declares even death to be counterfeit:

> 'Sblood, 'twas time to counterfeit, or that hot termagant Scot had paid me scot and lot too. Counterfeit? I lie; I am no counterfeit. To die is to be a counterfeit; for he is but the counterfeit of a man who has not the life of a man; but to counterfeit dying when a man thereby liveth, is to be no counterfeit, but the true and perfect image of life indeed. (act v, sc. 2, ll. 112–119)

Falstaff is as capable as Scapin of betraying his beloved sovereign or master, and both are invariably found out in spite of their cleverness. Sir John Falstaff's stealing, however, is done on a much grander scale than that of the French servant: purse-taking is his "vocation" and the tales of his robberies even reach the ear of the King. Scapin's clever appropriation of his master's casket of Spanish wine seems naive compared to Sir John's lifelong love of sack that makes him detest all those, especially the King's good son John, who do not know the pleasure of good wine and food. We might recall Falstaff's famous remarks in *2 Henry IV* (Sh*H-2*):

> "I would you had but the wit. 'Twere better than your dukedom. Good faith, this same young sober-blooded boy doth not love me; nor a man cannot make him laugh. But that's no marvel; he drinks no wine. There's never none of these demure boys come to any proof; for thin drink doth so over-cool their blood, and making many fish-meals, that they fall into a kind of male greensickness; and then, when they marry, they get wenches. . . . A good sherris sack has a twofold operation in it. It ascends me into the brain; dries me there all the foolish and dull and crudy vapours which environ it; makes it apprehensive, quick, forgetive, full of nimble, fiery, and delectable shapes, which delivered o'er to the voice, the tongue, which is the birth, becomes excellent wit. The second property . . . is the warming of the blood. . . . It illumineth the face . . . : skill in the weapon is nothing without sack, for that sets it awork; and

learning a mere hoard of gold kept by a devil, till sack commences it and sets it in act and use. . . . If I had a thousand sons, the first humane principle I would teach them should be to forswear thin potations and to addict themselves to sack." (act IV, sc 3, ll. 83–120)

In *2 Henry IV,* Prince Hal's fat companion is as proud of his wit as Scapin is of his clever plotting. "I am not only witty in myself." he boasts, "but the cause that wit is in other men" (act I, sc. 2, ll. 8–9). Yet, like the servant Scapin, the nobleman Falstaff is rejected and banished at the end. When young Prince Hal becomes Henry V and Falstaff clownishly hastens to reap the rewards of their long friendship, he is told with dignity but firmness: "I know thee not. . . . / Presume not that I am the thing I was/ For God doth know . . . / That I have turn'd away my former self/ So will I those that kept me company/ When thou dost hear I am as I have been/ Approach me, and thou shalt be as thou wast/ The tutor and the feeder of my riots/ Till then I banish thee, on pain of death" (act v, sc. 5, ll. 45–62). This speech would reveal the new King to be an *agelast,* had he not earlier proved himself capable of being a rogue in his own right, though one who knows when it is time to play and when to be serious. Thus both the nobleman and the servant are not only prime movers but also sufferers and martyrs to their causes. Theirs is the ambivalence of the trickster. But despite the traditional characteristics they share, their creators shaped them to their will and imagination. Molière's Scapin is gossamer compared to the fat and monstrous Falstaff, the companion of Shakespeare's future King. Molière's comedy is meant to be madcap entertainment in its wild play of the imagination and its enjoyment of utter improbabilities. Shakespeare's *Henry IV,* on the other hand, combines its clownishness with great seriousness and has, therefore, been a challenge to critics of different eras, two of whom at least touch so closely upon our conception of Falstaff as the trickster figure that it is a particular pleasure to refer to them here.

C. L. Barber is of the opinion that Shakespeare, in his Falstaff comedy, fused two saturnalian traditions, "the clowning customary on the stage and the folly customary on holiday" (BarS: 195). To this critic, Falstaff is the Lord of Misrule who, contrary to Prince Hal, would like to extend unduly the space of festivities that by its very nature has to be limited, as the Prince reminds him, in *1 Henry IV:*

> "If all the year were playing holidays,
> To sport would be as tedious as to work;
> But when they seldom come, they wish'd for come." (act I, sc. 2, ll. 87–90)

Barber identifies Falstaff as the scapegoat of the saturnalian ritual who, in being sacrificed, brings to the reign of the young King that purification he needs to free himself and his country from the crimes perpetrated by his predecessors: "So the ritual analogy suggests," Barber maintains, "that by turning on Falstaff as a scapegoat, as the villagers turned on their Mardi Gras, the prince can free himself from the sins, the 'bad luck,' of Richard's reign and of his father's reign, to become a king in whom chivalry and a sense of divine ordination are restored" (BarS: 207).

Barber assures us, however, that "we do not need to assume that Shakespeare had any such ritual patterns consciously in mind; whatever his conscious intention, . . . these analogues illuminate patterns which his poetic drama presents concretely and dramatically." He concludes that "Hal's final expulsion of Falstaff appears in the light of these analogies to carry out an impersonal pattern, not merely political but ritual in character": Falstaff is but the figure of carnival traditionally buried at the end of a period during which the world could be turned upside down with impunity (BarS: 206). Interesting though Barber's view may be, it is, above all, Walter Kaiser who, in his *Praisers of Folly* (KaiPF), has recognized the full ambiguity of both the Falstaff figure and its function—so like what Jung thought essential to the trickster of carnival and legend.

Kaiser considers the literary topos of a prince and his companion particularly well suited to the spirit of folly and finds in the juxtaposition of such contrasting and complementary characters an irony that enhances the trickster concept. He has in mind such servant companions as Sancho Panza, Pantalone of the commedia dell'arte, and precisely Falstaff—all invariably fatter and more foolish than their masters. But he does not exclude Sganarelle, companion to Molière's Dom Juan, or even Joyce's Leopold Bloom, father-friend to Stephen. "This ironic paradox," Kaiser maintains, "informs the comradeship of Hal and Falstaff throughout *Henry IV*, but nowhere is it more clearly demonstrated or more fully realized than in the famous mock-trial scene in Act II of *Part One*" (Kai*PF:*254). Kaiser brilliantly analyzes this scene (which I have quoted above), stating that

> we realize at once that the fool is longing to play the king; indeed, it is the fool's natural desire to put down the mighty from their seat and to climb into that seat himself. The fool, the epitome of *homo ludens,* also wants simply to play, and his favorite game is to mock by imitation his enemies. Because his most dangerous enemy is the law, his favorite game is the mock trial—a traditional sport of fools that achieves its most terrible form when Lear's fool sits in judgment upon the mad king's filial joint-stool. The game is an illusion, as the etymology of the word implies ["illusion" meaning *in ludo,* in a game, playfully], but within the illusion lies the reality. That is to say, the game is played in jest, and hence is an illusion; but the same game will soon be played in earnest, and hence is a reality. That reality, however, is as complex as the complexities of the illusory game, where the partners change places. . . . When Falstaff the companion plays first the king and then the son in order to praise himself (whom both king and son would censure), when Hal the prince plays first himself and then the king in order to censure Falstaff (rather than be censured himself—which was the original point of the game), and when that playing is also serious . . . , it is play within a play, and there are games within games, mirrors reflecting mirrors . . . , the totality of the performance's endless variations. (Kai*PF:*255).

As Kaiser suggests, the lusory character of the scene is emphasized from the outset: the ridiculous props, Falstaff's pretense that the Hostess, who applauds the game, is playing the part of his queen and that the tears of laughter and merriment brought to her eyes are regal tears of sorrow, so that he comforts her: "Weep not, sweet queen, for trickling tears are vain." Such emphasis on play-acting by all involved in this Shakespearean scene compels us, we easily agree, "to see the validity of Falstaff's point of view. In one sense, we agree that banishment of the companion would be banishment of all the world, and therefore the prince has lost as well: he is left without a world to rule. This is not to claim that we do not recognize the justice of the censure of Falstaff or the bogus nature of his self-praise. Nevertheless, the game makes it possible for us to see that there may be a kind of virtue in the old fool" (Kai*PF:* 257). Falstaff himself is seen in this light as sinner and saint.

One might, however, go further still, and consider Falstaff the double of Prince Hal, following the lead of Otto Rank and Freud, who believed that world literature, and especially the theater of Shakespeare, is full of divided characters, each part of which is incompletely understood unless the two are combined into a unity (Ran*DJG:* 17 and Ran*DL passim*). In this perspective, the Prince-Falstaff figure would represent more strongly yet the ambivalence of the trickster as both sinner and saint, wounder and wounded. Hal's enjoyment of the prank he plays on Falstaff, as he gleefully robs him of the gold obtained from the merchants he waylaid, is as genuine as it is roguish. Though not an outright thief, the Prince does, in a holiday mood, turn the world upside down and scoff at the laws he should have upheld. We are reminded of Jung's allusion to the "daemonic features exhibited by Yahweh in the Old Testament" that seem to him reminiscent of "the unpredictable behaviour of the trickster, . . . his senseless orgies of destruction and his self-imposed sufferings, together with the same gradual development into a saviour and his simultaneous humanization." In the eyes of Jung, "it is just this transformation of the meaningless into the meaningful that reveals the trickster's compensatory relation to the 'saint' " (Ju*TF:*256). In this sense, the ultimate banishment of Falstaff must be understood, as it has been by many critics, as Hal's inner development from the young prankster and trickster into the "saint," a development that cannot come about without suffering affecting both parts of the personality: that which banishes and that which is banished, the wounder and the wounded.

It is not accidental that Rank discussed this doubling device in literature in connection with the Don Juan figure. Though it did not occur to him to speak of Don Juan as a trickster (especially since he had in mind above all Mozart's Don Giovanni), he assigned to him and Leporello all the qualities essential to the trickster figure. And this is not as surprising as it might seem. After all, the Spanish priest Tirso de Molina, who created the Don Juan character that set fire to the imagination of so many playwrights, composers, and even film makers, had entitled his work *El Burlador de Sevilla,* The Trickster of Seville (Ma*DJ:* 50–99). The root of *burlador* is *burla* (trick or joke), also that of burlesque. Rank's point of reference is Mozart's masterpiece, the opera *Don Giovanni,* whose lyrics were written by Da Ponte. Because of Mozart's romantic stress on Don Juan as the lover—a considerable shift from Tirso's conception—the figure has been seen in this light ever since, and Rank's perspective is determined by it. This is regrettable, and one might wish that Rank had chosen for his deliberations the *Dom Juan* of Molière—preceding *Don Giovanni* by more than a century—because in it master and servant (Dom Juan and Sganarelle) partake of the absolute comic in a way no longer felt appropriate to Don Giovanni and Leporello, their eighteenth-century counterparts. This trend away from the absolute comic had started, as we have observed, in the seventeenth century so that, even at that time, Sganarelle's carnivalesque antics were already frowned upon.

Molière may not have read Tirso's *comedia,* written about half a century before his own play, but he was undoubtedly familiar with its plot. There had been at least two French adaptations of the *comedia* before his own, and there were in existence a number of commedia dell' arte scenarios. Tirso's plot has maintained itself throughout the centuries but varying emphasis has imbued it with different meaning: Don Juan has been the religious sinner, the trickster offending the dead, the lover in pursuit and pursued, a man obsessed to live up to the essence bestowed upon him, a man in heaven and a man in hell. Fundamentally, however, the servant-master relationship remains the same, so that Rank's description of it in *Don Giovanni* seems universally valid:

> The creation of a Don Juan figure with its carefree, frivolous, devil-may-care attitude would be impossible if the other part of Don Juan were not split off in the person of Leporello, who represents the disapproval, the fear and the conscience of the hero. This gives us the key to the question why Leporello must represent his master only in particularly difficult situations and why he is allowed to criticize him; he supplies, so to speak, the conscience which our hero lacks. On the other hand we can now better understand the magnitude of Don Juan's wickedness—made possible by the fact that the restraining elements of his personality have been split off. (Ma*DJ*: 631)

Rank considers the psychological unity of these two characters a poetic product, and the figure of Leporello a necessary part of the artistic representation of Don Juan himself (Ma*DJ*: 630).

We are at once aware of the analogy with the Prince Hal-Falstaff couple, and this analogy also points up significant differences. Falstaff, though a nobleman, is socially inferior to Prince Hal, and it seems quite proper that the trickster figure should be of a lower rank. Molière's Sganarelle is Dom Juan's servant, without any claims to nobility, yet it is the master who is the trickster, while the servant, a blundering, blustering simpleton, serves as his master's conscience. Sganarelle thus becomes, in the archetypal sense of the term, his master's double, and to some extent his complement. In that sense he is, in the words of Rank, a powerful

> consciousness of guilt which forces the hero no longer to accept the responsibility for certain actions of the ego, but to place it upon another ego, a double, who is either personified by the devil himself or is created by making a diabolical pact. This detached personification of instincts and desires which were once felt to be unacceptable, but which can be satisfied without responsibility in this indirect way, appears in other forms of the theme as a beneficent admonitor . . . who is directly addressed as the conscience of the person. . . . As Freud [Rank refers to Freud's essay on Narcissism] has demonstrated, this awareness of guilt, having various sources, measures on the one hand the distance between the ego-ideal and the attained reality; on the other, it is nourished by a powerful fear of death and creates strong tendencies toward self-punishment, which also imply suicide. (Ran*DL:*76–77)

Rank's definition of doubleness would apply as readily to the Shakespearean Hal-Falstaff relationship as to innumerable other literary doubles. In Molière's *Dom Juan,* Sganarelle might be considered his master's "beneficent admonitor" were it not for the occasion of a grotesque reversal of roles between master and servant and the playwright's obvious intent to turn the servant's admonition of his superior into an absolute comic that would prevent them from sounding too serious or too pompous. At the same time Molière succeeded in preserving an underlying interplay of fear and guilt.

In Da Ponte's *Don Giovanni* (Ma*DJ:*278–315), Leporello not only dreams of being like his master but also serves on occasion as Don Giovanni's substitute, so that he is not only his alter ego but also is taken to be identical with him. He confides to the audience, in the very first lines of the opera, "I'd like to act the gentleman myself, and give up the servant life. My good master is inside with a servant girl, needless to say, while I play the sentinel" (Ma*DJ:*288). Leporello is, in fact, given the chance to exchange clothes with his master and to hold in his arms Giovanni's mistress Elvira, whose maid is momentarily his master's favorite. Clothes are exchanged to dispel the maid's suspicions, and the trick is made possible because Elvira, trusting the dulcet tones of her lover's voice, believes in his "repentance" and descends to meet him in the night garden. Leporello plays his part so well that she believes him to be Don Giovanni. Molière's Sganarelle, however, secretly despises his master, and, although he serves him loyally, would never wish to be like him or lead a similar life. Nor would his appearance and demeanor allow him to substitute for his master—not even in the darkest night. He is rather the simpleton who, not unlike Don Quixote's Sancho Panza, possesses a natural shrewdness and understanding and, without adherence to lofty principles of any sort, is governed by concepts of sensibility that his master spurns.

Rank is also of the opinion that Don Juan was not, to begin with, the "frivolous heartbreaker," and as he wonders what drama and legend could detect in this figure to imbue it with such powerful existence, he arrives at the conclusion that "the typical sensualist and lover—even one of this grand style—could have been easily and perhaps even better represented by a different figure. On the other hand, the drama of the Christian hell, loaded with all the guilt feelings of original sin, would by now seem as foreign and outdated to us as all the other ecclesiastic medieval morality plays, were it not that so great a man and artist as Mozart liberated his Don Juan (as Goethe liberated Faust from the religious puppet-play concerning a magician, and Shakespeare liberated Hamlet from the ghost stories of his precursors) by recapturing the basic human values from a clutter of trivia, and expressing them in eternal symbols" (MaDJ: 626). The psychoanalyst believes, in other words, that the figure's appeal to popular imagination rests on Mozart's expansion of "the ancient but painfully tragic motif of guilt and punishment" to include that of the young lover's quest for "the irreplaceable mother" in defiance of his "unconquerable mortal enemy, the father" (Ma*DJ:* 627). In spite of its ingenuity, this interpretation underestimates those elements of the absolute comic that, though no longer preserved in Mozart's opera with its eighteenth-century mood, are powerfully present in Molière's comedy (Ma*DJ*) and provide it with overtones as reminiscent of medieval fools as of such modern madmen as Beckett's Lucky and quite as serious in their questioning of God and human existence.

> SGANARELLE: I feel in the mood for arguing with you. You remember I am allowed to argue as long as I don't preach at you.
>
> DON JUAN: Very well, then.
>
> SG: I'd like to find out what your ideas are. Do you really not believe in Heaven at all?
>
> D.J.: Suppose we leave that alone.
>
> SG: That means that you don't. And Hell?
>
> D.J.: Eh?
>
> SG: No again! And the Devil, may I ask?
>
> D.J.: Yes, yes. . . . Ha! Ha! Ha!
>
> SG (*aside*): This chap will take some converting! (*To D.J.*) Now just tell me this—the Bogy Man—what do you think about him?
>
> D.J.: Don't be a fool!
>
> SG: Now I can't allow that. There's nothing truer than the Bogy Man. I'd go to the stake for that. A man must believe in something. What *do* you believe?
>
> D.J.: . . . I believe that two and two make four, Sganarelle, and that two fours are eight.
>
> SG: Now that *is* a fine sort of faith. As far as I can see then, your religion's arithmetic. What queer ideas folk do get into their heads! And, often enough, the more they have studied the less sense they have! Not that I've studied myself, master, not like you have, thank the Lord! Nobody can boast that he ever taught me anything, but with my own common sense and using my own judgment I can see things better than books,

and I know very well that this world we see around us didn't
spring up of its own accord overnight—like a mushroom! I
ask you who made these trees, these rocks, the earth and sky
above, or did it all come of its own accord? Take yourself, for
example! You exist! Are you a thing of your own making or
was it necessary for your father to beget you, and for your
mother to bring you into the world? Can you look on all the
parts of this machine which make up a man and not wonder
at the way one part is fashioned with another, nerves, bones,
veins, arteries, lungs, heart, liver, and all the other things
which go to— Oh, for goodness' sake do interrupt me! I can't
argue if I'm not interrupted. You are keeping quiet on purpose and letting me run on out of sheer mischief.

D.J.: I am waiting until you have finished what you are trying
to say.

SG: What I'm trying to say is that there's something wonderful
in man, say what you like, and something that all your
learned men can't explain. Isn't it remarkable that here am I
with something in my head that can think of a hundred different things in a moment and make my body do whatever it
wants; for example, clap my hands, lift my arms, raise my
eyes to heaven, bow my head, move my feet, go to the right
or the left, forward or backward, turn around—— (*in turning
round he tumbles over.*)

D.J.: Good! And so your argument falls to the ground! (Mo*DJ:*
222–24)

Sganarelle's arguments, so lacking in logic, are not in the
least foreign to modern writers, whether they call themselves
believers or atheists. One cannot but detect in Sganarelle's
words that profound anguish that echoes through a theater we
now often call "absurd," although, like this simpleton's speech,
it employs the medieval form of the *coq-à-l'âne* to eff the ineffable:

"This is more than I can stand, master. I can keep quiet no
longer. You can do what you like to me: beat me, knock me
down, kill me, if you like, but I must open my heart to you and

tell you what I think, as a faithful servant should. You know, master, the pitcher can go to the well once too often, and, as some writer very truly said—who he was I don't know—men in this world are like the bird on the bough, the bough is part of the tree and whoever holds on to the tree is following sound precepts; sound precepts are better than fine words; the court is the place for fine words; at the court you find courtiers, and courtiers do whatever's the fashion; fashion springs from the imagination and imagination springs from the soul; the soul is what gives us life, and life ends in death; death sets us thinking of Heaven; Heaven is above the earth; the earth's different from the ocean; the ocean's subject to tempests, and tempests are a terror to ships; a ship needs a good pilot and a good pilot needs prudence; young men have no prudence, so the young should be obedient to the old; old men love riches; riches make men rich; the rich aren't poor; poor men know necessity and necessity knows no law. Without law men live like animals, which all goes to prove that you'll be damned to all eternity!" (Mo*DJ*: 245)

One is reminded not only of Lucky's speech in *Godot* but also of medieval *sotties* and passages in Rabelais, such as Lord Suckfizzle's ramblings on behalf of Pantagruel:

"Sometimes we think of one thing, but God does the other; and when the sun is set all beasts are in the shadow. . . . I am no scholar to catch the moon in my teeth; but in the butter-pot where they sealed the volcanic instruments, the rumour was that the salt beef made one find the wine at midnight without a candle, even if it were hidden at the bottom of a collier's sack, . . . and that is just what it says in the proverb, that it is good to see black cows in burnt wood, when one enjoys one's love. . . . My lords, do not believe that at the time when the said good woman caught the spoonbill with birdlime the better to make the younger son's portion for the record of the sergeant, and when the sheep's pudding took detours round the usurer's purses, there was nothing better to preserve us from the cannibals than the rope of onions tied up with three hundred turnips. . . ." (RG:209–10)

The same "logic" that leads Pantagruel to conclude at the end of his speech that they now must make peace (a conclusion that always seems justified), leads Sganarelle to believe that Dom Juan will be damned by all the devils in Hell, should he decide to become a hypocrite as he had threatened to do. Like Lucky's outburst in *Waiting For Godot,* Sganarelle's outburst is but another proof that "the ineffable cannot be effed"—as one of Beckett's characters would maintain—and that logic is out of place where matters of great importance to man are concerned.

The Fools of medieval *sotties* share with Rabelais' Lord Suckfizzle, Molière's Sganarelle, and Beckett's Lucky—some Ionesco characters might be included here as well—a disregard for the platitude that language is meant to convey meaning through logic. Either playfully or with serious intent, they therefore turn the realm of words upside down and make it part of carnival and the absolute comic. Language freed from the laws of logic may become sheer playful sound; as Brueghel's canvas *Proverbs* illustrates, understood literally and envisioned out of context proverbs portray a world that is topsy-turvy and grotesque. If regarded closely, however, the chaos created reveals new meanings underneath the pretense of playfulness, or at least seems to ask important questions concerning man's place in the universe and vis-à-vis God that a serious questioner dare not ask. In the case of Sganarelle we cannot but recognize the juxtaposition of the precariousness of man's existence, which he compares to that of a bird on the branch of a tree, with the assertion that he who lives lawlessly will be damned by all the devils in Hell. It is only the carnivalesque form chosen for such a mixture of philosophy and morality that preserves the dignity of the argument, as it assigns it to the realm of the absolute comic.

Quite similar is the impact upon reader or audience of Sganarelle's halting reply to his master's cynical declaration that he believes in nothing but that two and two make four and four and four, eight. It was bruited about, when Molière's *Dom Juan* was presented, that a well-known prince had actually made such a statement on his deathbed. Sganarelle's demonstration of the smooth functioning of his body and brain as "proof" of the existence of God would be embarrassingly simplistic, were it not for the comic clumsiness of his body and mind and his master's exclamation "so your argument falls to the ground" at the very moment Sganarelle tumbles. Dom Juan, too, has turned language upside down by taking a metaphor literally. It seems, indeed, that Dom Juan and Sganarelle complement one another as if they were two sides of one and the same character, neither of which can be understood fully without the other. But one might also maintain that Dom Juan, within himself, combines the aspects of saint and sinner in a manner similar to that conceived by Tirso when he created his *burlador,* and in which the character has survived in manifold guise throughout the ages.

Although *Dom Juan* is among those rare moliéresque comedies that lack the character orchestration of the commedia dell'arte—that is, the two or more old men as well as the young lovers and their servants—, the work's episodic nature is appropriate to the protagonist's mercurial and picaresque qualities as a trickster. In a moment of frankness, Sganarelle tells Gusman, who is Elvira's servant, what he thinks of his master and describes him as "the biggest scoundrel that ever cumbered the earth, a madman, a cur, a devil, a Turk, a heretic who believes neither in Heaven, Hell, nor werewolf" (Mo*DJ:* 300). He makes him out to be an atheist, calling him "a swine of an Epicurean. . . , shutting his ears to every Christian remonstrance, and turning to ridicule everything we believe in." (Mo*DJ:* 200). To Gusman's disclosure that Dom Juan not only promised marriage to his mistress Dona Elvira but actually married her, Sganarelle retorts: "Believe me, to satisfy his passion he would have gone further than that, he would have married you as well, ay, and her dog and her cat into the bargain! Marriage means nothing to him. . . . If I were to give you the names of all those he has married in one place and another, the list would take till tonight. That surprises you!

What I'm saying makes you turn pale, but this is no more than the outline of his character: it would take me much longer to finish the portrait. Let it suffice that the wrath of Heaven is bound to overwhelm him one of these days and that, for my part, I would sooner serve the Devil himself. . . . A nobleman who has given himself over to wickedness is a thing to be dreaded. I am bound to remain with him whether I like it or not: fear serves me for zeal, makes me restrain my feelings and forces me often enough to make a show of approving things that in my heart of hearts I detest" (Mo*DJ:* 201).

Winning the heart of a woman is for Dom Juan nothing but a sport, and he chalks up his victories as so many rewards for expertise in his art, taking the same pride in them that Scapin took in his skill as manipulator, strategist, and deviser of plots. Emotionally, he is totally detached from his conquests. He has none of the passionate involvement of an Arnolphe or a Tartuffe. In his concern for victory at all costs, he employs therefore not the language of love but that of war, as the following passage illustrates:

> "How delightful, how entrancing it is to *lay siege* with a hundred attentions to a young woman's heart; to see day by day, how one makes slight *advances;* to pit one's exaltations, one's sighs and one's tears, against the modest reluctance of a heart *unwilling to yield;* to surmount step by step, all the little *barriers* by which she *resists;* to *overcome* her proud scruples and bring her at last to consent. But once one succeeds, what else remains? What more can one wish for? All that delights one in passion is over and one can only sink into a tame and slumbrous affection—until a new love comes along to awaken desire and offer the charm of new *conquests.* There is no pleasure to compare with the *conquest* of beauty, and my *ambition* is that of all the great *conquerors* who could never find it in them to set bounds to their ambitions, but must go on for ever from *conquest to conquest.* Nothing can restrain my impetuous desires. I feel it is in me to love the whole world, and *like Alexander still wish for new worlds to conquer."* (Mo*DJ:*203, italics added)

Dom Juan's victories are not fantasy triumphs; for, aloof and strong, he reduces the weak to slavery. At the same time his victories are absurd, since he never has time to enjoy his conquests but, like a lowly *pícaro,* is forever on the run. The very excess of his behavior turns him forever from pursuer into one pursued. As a result of having tricked two simple country women, he is hunted by their lovers, as well as by the brothers of Elvira, and forced to flee, disguising his identity. Not even he can face twelve men on horseback who are after his very life, although he is brave enough to rescue a stranger from robbers who attack him. The stranger, who happens to be Elvira's brother, cannot but admire Dom Juan's courage and generosity. Yet, though a nobleman, Dom Juan is as homeless and hunted as any *pícaro* or trickster.

Particularly striking, among the picaresque episodes, is Dom Juan's encounter with Francisque, the Poor Man, a hermit who, though praising God for providing for all his creatures, is forced to beg for alms. His name is undoubtedly meant to allude to St. Francis who decided to live among God's creatures because he was unwilling to compromise his faith for the sake of money. In the mode of the trickster who loves to turn the world upside down, Dom Juan promises the Poor Man a gold piece if he will swear, rather than praise God. Such a request, though totally in conformity with the spirit of the absolute comic and quite acceptable to Sganarelle, who encourages Francisque to swear a little, ill befits a nobleman, a *grand seigneur.* He ultimately surrenders the coin, if not for the love of God, at least "for the love of mankind."

It is not surprising that those of his contemporaries who had condemned Moliére's absolute comic in his *School For Wives* and *Tartuffe* were even more appalled by his *Dom Juan.* Yet the playwright had carefully retained for his protagonist those qualities of the trickster that Don Juan's Spanish creator had had in mind. In fact, the French playwright heightened the character's stance as a trickster by conferring upon him all the wit and cleverness the commedia dell'arte usually reserved for servants: he clearly engages in *lazzi,* even when dealing with women and at moments when young masters in love are expected to be at their most romantic. Molière's Dom Juan, when winning his victories over the two peasant girls Charlotte and Mathurine, for instance, skillfully plays the double role assigned to servants in the playwright's earlier farces and customarily assumed by a *zanno* in the commedia dell'arte. Harlequin was famous for having transformed himself, in front of an audience, from a man selling soft drinks into a woman displaying lingerie for sale. He achieved this grotesque effect through clever costumes and miming. Even today, such rapid transformations from one persona into another are used by famous mimes with great success. It is this trick of the absolute comic that is employed also by Dom Juan, *grand seigneur,* though not with the help of any change of costume, but merely through quick turns of the head from one woman to the other and even more stunning mental gymnastics. He declares his love to each woman, one on either side of him, and each believes that he will marry her and that he has only scorn for the rival and for that person's claims to his love. The hilarious episode ends with Charlotte's request that he openly declare her his fiancée and put Mathurine in her place—a request to which he assents with arrogant double talk:

> "What do you want me to say? You both claim that I have promised to marry you, but don't you each know the truth without any need for me to explain? Why make me go over it once more? Surely the one I have really given my promise to can afford to laugh at the other. Why need she worry so long as I keep my promise to her? All the explanations in the world won't get us any further. We must do things, not talk about them. Deeds speak louder than words. There's only one way I can hope to reconcile you. When I do marry, you will see which one I love. (*Aside to Mathurine*) Let her think what she pleases! (*Aside to Charlotte*) Let her amuse herself with her fancies! (*Aside to Mathurine*) I adore *you.* (*Aside to Charlotte*) I am devoted to

you. (*Aside to Mathurine*) There is no beauty like yours. (*Aside to Charlotte*) Since I have seen you I have no eyes for anyone else. (*To both*) I have some business I must attend to. I will be back in a quarter of an hour." (*He goes out.*) (MoDJ:219)

Dom Juan's departure is followed, as is to be expected, by a comic fight among the two women, whose gullibility and vanity are great enough to justify their comic victimization.

What enhances the carnivalesque mood of the scene and others preceding it is the very fact that peasants are onstage and speak their dialect. The meanings acquired by English "clown" and French *"villain"*—both originally designations of peasants or village dwellers—indicate the low esteem in which these people were held and the laughter they were apt to arouse. While regional dialects had been used by actors of the commedia dell'arte and while Molière had earlier used peasant speech in other comedies, their scenes in *Dom Juan* are more elaborate and given more importance. Seen through their eyes and imagery, the world of the nobleman begins to look absurd, whether with regard to dress, behavior, or notions of love. Yet Dom Juan is better equipped and more skilled than any comic *zanno* when it comes to turning the world willfully upside down. When the merchant Dimanche—merchants were also comic figures per se—comes to collect the money Dom Juan owes him, the nobleman trickster simulates such friendship for him and pretends so skillfully that they are social equals that Dimanche, overwhelmed with gratitude, leaves without daring to be so "vulgar" as to ask for his money—although he has no such qualms with regard to what Sgnarelle owes him. If Dom Juan here plays the role of hypocrite with the skill of a trickster, we may not assume, however, that this is his true face. Like any great trickster figure he has two faces, and many of his actions are prompted by his dislike for that hypocrisy that seems to govern all sorts of commerce among human beings (and here he is, undoubtedly, the mouthpiece of the playwright smarting from the vicious attacks against his *Tartuffe*):

"Hypocrisy alone is an art, the practice of which always commands respect, and though people may see through it they dare say nothing against it. All other vices of mankind are exposed to censure and anyone may attack them with impunity. Hypocrisy alone is privileged. It stills the voice of criticism and enjoys a sovereign immunity. Humbug binds together in close fellowship all those who practise it, and whosoever attacks one brings down the whole pack upon him. . . . It is under shelter of this pretence I intend to take refuge and secure my own position. I shall not abandon my pleasures, but shall be at pains to conceal them and amuse myself with all circumspection. So, if by any chance I am discovered, the whole fraternity will make my cause their own and defend me against every criticism." (Mo*DJ*: 243–44)

According to the logic of the comedy and that of its predecessors, Dom Juan is not punished at the end for any specific misdeed other than that he dared to challenge the dead.

It is interesting, nevertheless, to speculate on what basis the play was either attacked or defended by Molière's contemporaries. Its protagonist was found wanting, not because he outwitted simple peasant women or a humble merchant creditor, but because he had seduced Elvira, preventing her from becoming a nun. Almost all criticism was centered upon similar questions concerning religion and filial piety: that the Hermit was promised money, provided he deny God; that religion was reduced to a belief that two and two make four, and four and four eight; and that a son showed no respect for his father. Dom Juan was declared to be an atheist and a hypocrite, and Sganarelle to be a libertine. On the other hand, the comedy was also justified on moral grounds: for the protagonist was after all struck dead by lightning at the end.

Not one of Molière's critics, neither friend nor foe, recognized in Dom Juan the trickster figure—still so much alive among the people and the clergy—that the playwright had imbued with his genius. No one gave Molière credit for his ingenious reversal of the traditional master/servant relationship that, nevertheless, preserved the character of each. Yet it is in the Dom Juan figure that Molière again gives evidence of his profound sense of the absolute comic which can direct its laughter even at Death, though realizing that this power of Nature will ultimately be victorious. The Don Juan we usually think of today—the Don Juan who loves and abandons women because he is in quest of an ideal that is not of this world; the Don Juan ultimately saved by a virtuous "Gretchen" figure who intercedes for him in Heaven—is but a figment of Romantic imagination. He is an indication of the changeability of taste and the concepts that inform it and thereby affect the meaning with which author and audience imbue literary plots. He should alert us to the necessity of understanding both the universal and the temporal grammar of a genre, if we wish to do justice to an author's imagination and accept his guidance, as we react with tears, dismay, laughter, or ambivalence. With regard to the absolute comic, a prolonged ignorance of its idiom has deprived centuries of its liberating enjoyment and laughter as well as of its deeply comforting philosophy.

Summary

How, then, are we to summarize the phenomenon of the trickster figure in (European) literature and the absolute comic?

In his ambivalence, the trickster seems to be of the very essence of the absolute comic and of farce, personifying in his own person the genre's proximity to laughter and tears. He always seems to be the prime mover, that which makes the world go round: the serpent that made man lose his paradise and strive to regain it, the Mephistopheles that makes Faust lose his innocence and be condemned, though ultimately saved. We may laugh with him or at him. As the "ape of God," instrumental in eliciting either laughter or tears, the trickster also is vulnerable: as often wounded as he wounds. He is usually a man who succeeds in winning the favors of women. If a servant, he may, through plotting, lying, and thieving, win such favors for his young master. He may prove to be his master's evil double, denied by him as soon as he is no longer needed (as in the case of Falstaff and Mephistopheles) but also, carrying the full responsibility of his master's guilt, become his scapegoat. As a male figure—whether independent, messenger, or servant—the trickster seems to be a direct descendant of Hermes the Thief. Yet he assumes the stature of a nobleman in the paradoxical figure of Don Juan who, like the "low-born villain" of the Spanish ballad, defies Death and the dead as well as Love. As the trickster himself is a paradox, so the comic justice meted out to him is ambivalent. He is sometimes triumphant and often defeated—almost always, in some form, a scapegoat.

Though most trickster figures in narrative and on the stage are male—seemingly direct descendants of Hermes—literature also knows female tricksters. They indulge in the same serpent- or fox-like hypocrisy to gain their ends, mainly those of the evil go-between or the whore. As such they bring unhappiness and even death to those they serve, as in the case of Phaedra and Celestine. Yet they, too, may suffer in the end. After the Renaissance, however, the female trickster sheds her ugliness to become, as *pícara,* the beautiful temptress hunting for security in the form of wealth and a rich lover or husband. She whores and thieves and escapes the gallows only because she knows how to move men by her beauty and her ready tears, or sometimes by her superior wit. Later centuries have transformed her into the Moll Flanderses, the Mariannes, and the Beckys, who succeed in concealing their fortune hunting beneath feigned gentility. But the "woman as trickster" is "on top" mainly when she is in men's clothes, as in some Shakespearean comedies, where she is in quest of her beloved, or when, as in some of Molière's comedies, she is clever, witty, versatile, inventive, and unselfishly devoted to uniting the young lovers, leading them to triumph over their stingy old fathers. In these comedies, female tricksters are prime movers, true "delight-makers," and a source of liberating laughter. Although they are women, they seem to share Hermes' desire to oppose society and its gods whenever these favor the strong and disregard the weak. Yet their triumphs as well as their defeats like those of all tricksters—belong to the realm of fantasy and imagination and are far from being mimetic. They kill and are "killed" by laughter, not by the sword.

In modern literature tricksters have reappeared in many guises: as a child drummer, a schoolboy degrading a medal of honor, a holy sinner, a confidence man, a petitioner outwitting military and civilian authority, a woman defying the restrictions of a bourgeois society, to mention but a few. Though they may change their external appearance to accord with changing mores, they are as eternal as the laughter of farce they elicit whenever they turn the world upside down in the service of a justice prevailing *sub specie aeternitatis,* a justice less individual and more universal than that of society, as it sees man in the light of myth. Thomas Mann might have had in mind the absolute comic and its ambivalent trickster figure when he wrote in his essay "Freud and the Future":

> While in the life of the human race the mythical is an early and primitive stage, in the life of the individual it is a late and mature one. What is gained is an insight into the higher truth depicted in the actual; smiling knowledge of the eternal, the ever-being and authentic; a knowledge of the schema in which and according to which the supposed individual lives, unaware, in his naive belief in himself as unique in space and time, of the extent to which his life is but formula and repetition and his path marked out for him by those who trod it before him. . . . His dignity and security lie all unconsciously in the fact that with him something timeless has once more emerged into the light and become present; it is a mythical value added to the otherwise poor and valueless single character; it is native worth, because its origin lies in the unconscious. (ManE: 318)

Originating in that mythical stage of the human race and its subconscious, the trickster figure provides us, indeed, with insights that reach beyond life as we daily live it. By turning the world playfully upside down, by putting down the mighty from their seats and—though only in jest—exalting them of low degree, the trickster makes apparent the frailty of human existence and the proximity of laughter and tears. Quintessence of the absolute comic, he transports us into worlds where imagination and make-believe triumph. Because he makes scapegoats of pompous authoritarians, he is himself sacrificed for daring to be both Satan and savior. But though it is mixed with sadness, the laughter he elicits is liberating in its ambivalence: while it makes us realize that we are but spokes in the great wheel of existence, it makes us cherish the moment of infinity allotted to us.

References

(The letter symbols preceding each listing are those used in the text.)

AmDF   Amado, Jorge. *Dona Flor and Her Two Husbands*. Harriet de Onis, tr. New York: Avon, 1977.

AnRF   Anon. "Reynard the Fox," *The Epic of the Beast*. Caxton tr., modernized by William S. Stallybrass; William Rose, ed. London: Routledge, 1924.

AnTE   Anon. *A Pleasant Vintage of Till Eulenspiegel*. Paul Oppenheimer, tr., from 1515 edition. Middletown, Conn.: Wesleyan University Press, 1972.

AphA   Aristophanes, "The Acharnians." In Whitney J. Oates and Eugene O'Neill, Jr., eds., *The Complete Greek Drama*, vol. 2. New York: Random House, 1938.

AstP   Aristotle, *On the Art of Poetry*. Lane Cooper, ed., Ithaca, N.Y.: Cornell University Press, 1967.

AthW   Atherton, James S. *The Books at the Wake*. London: Faber and Faber, 1959.

AtwJ   Atwater, Nathaniel B. "Poetic Justice and the *Miller's Tale*," *The CEA Forum* (April 1978), 8:4.

BakR   Bakhtin, Mikhail. *Rabelais and His World*. Helene Iswolsky, tr. Cambridge: M.I.T. Press, 1968.

BanD   Bandelier, Adolphe F. *Delight Makers*. New York: Dodd, Mead, 1960.

BarS   Barber, C. L. *Shakespeare's Festive Comedy: A Study of Dramatic Form and Its Relation to Social Custom*. Princeton, N.J.: Princeton University Press, 1959.

BatM   Bateson, Gregory. "Metalogue About Games and Being Serious," *Steps to an Ecology of Mind*. New York: Norton, 1955.

BatP   Bateson, Gregory. "A Theory of Play and Fantasy," *Steps to an Ecology of Mind*. New York: Norton, 1955.

BauL   Baudelaire, Charles. "On the Essence of Laughter," *The Mirror of Art*. Jonathan Mayne, tr. Garden City, N.Y.: Doubleday, 1956.

BeMD   Beckett, Samuel. *Malone Dies*. New York: Grove Press, 1956.

BeWG   Beckett, Samuel. *Waiting for Godot*. New York: Grove Press, 1954.

BeWt   Beckett, Samuel. *Watt*. New York: Grove Press, 1959.

BerL   Bergson, Henri. "Laughter," *Comedy*. Wylie Sypher, ed. Garden City, N.Y.: Doubleday Anchor, 1956.

BoD   Boccaccio, Giovanni. *The Decameron*. G. H. McWilliam, tr. Harmondsworth: Penguin, 1977.

BrH   Brown, Norman O. "The Homeric Hymn to Hermes," *Hermes the Thief: The Evolution of a Myth*. New York: Vintage, 1969.

CaH   Campbell, Joseph. *The Hero With a Thousand Faces*. New York: Meridian, 1956.

CeJE   Cervantes, Miguel. "The Jealous Extramaduran," *Exemplary Stories*. C. A. Jones, tr. Harmondsworth: Penguin, 1972.

ChCT   Chaucer, Geoffrey. *The Canterbury Tales*. Donald R. Howard, ed. New York: New American Library, 1969.

DapDG   Da Ponte, Lorenzo. "The Punished Libertine or Don Giovanni." A. M. Schizzano and Oscar Mandel, trs. In Oscar Mandel, ed., *The Theatre of Don Juan*. Lincoln: University of Nebraska Press, 1963.

DazSC   Davis, Natalie Zemon. *Society and Culture in Early Modern France*. Stanford, Calif.: Stanford University Press, 1975.

DeMF   Defoe, Daniel. *Moll Flanders*. New York: Pocket Books, 1952.

DuIC   Duchartre, Pierre Louis. *The Italian Comedy*. Randolph T. Weaver, tr. New York: Dover, 1966.

EuB   Euripides. "The Bachae," Gilbert Murray, tr. In Whitney J. Oates and Eugene O'Neill, Jr., eds., *The Complete Greek Drama*, vol. 2. New York: Random House, 1938.

FreJ	Freud, Sigmund. *Jokes and Their Relation to the Unconscious.* James Strachey, tr. New York: Norton, 1963.
FreTT	Freud, Sigmund. *Totem and Taboo.* A. A. Brill, tr. New York: Moffat, Yard, 1918.
FryAC	Frye, Northrop. *Anatomy of Criticism.* Princeton, N.J.: Princeton University Press, 1957.
GiPB	Girard, René. "Perilous Balance: A Comic Hypothesis," *Modern Language Notes* (1927), 87:811–26.
GiVS	Girard, René. *La Violence et le Sacré.* Paris: Grasset, 1974.
GrCM	Grass, Günter. *Cat and Mouse.* Ralph Manheim, tr. New York: Signet, 1964.
GrF	Grass, Günter. *The Flounder.* Ralph Manheim, tr. New York and London: Harcourt Brace, 1978.
GrTD	Grass, Günter. *The Tin Drum.* Ralph Manheim, tr. New York: Vintage, 1962.
HaP	Handke, Peter. *Publikumsbeschimpfung.* Frankfurt: Suhrkamp, 1966.
HeC	Heller, Joseph. *Catch-22.* New York: Dell, 1978.
HuHL	Huizinga, Johan. *Homo Ludens: A Study of the Play Element in Culture.* Boston: Beacon, 1950.
HuM	Hubert, J. D. *Molière and the Comedy of Intellect.* Berkeley and Los Angeles: University of California Press, 1962.
IoM	Ionesco, Eugène. *Macbett.* Paris: Gallimard, 1972.
JeP	Jekels, Ludwig. "Zur Psychologie der Komödie," *Imago* (1926), 12:328–35.
JuTF	Jung, Carl G. "On the Psychology of the Trickster Figure." In *The Collected Works,* vol. 9, pt. 1. New York: Bollingen, 1959.
KaC	Kafka, Franz. *The Castle.* Edwin and Willa Muir, trs. New York: Knopf, 1965.
KaiPF	Kaiser, Walter J. *Praisers of Folly.* Cambridge: Harvard University Press, 1963.
KeCM	Kern, Edith. "Concretization of Metaphor in the Commedia dell' Arte and Modern Literature," *Actes du IVe Congrès de l'Association Internationale de Littérature Comparée.* The Hague: Mouton, 1965.
KeGD	Kern, Edith. "The Gardens in the *Decameron* Cornice," *Publications of the Modern Language Association of America*

(1951), 66:505–23. Reprinted (in German translation) in *Boccaccios Decameron,* Peter Brockmeier, ed. Darmstadt: Wissenschaftliche Buchgesellschaft, 1974.

KiEO   Kierkegaard, Søren. *Either/Or.* David F. and Lillian Marvin Swenson, trs. Princeton, N.J.: Princeton University Press, 1971.

LaP   Lahr, John. *Prick Up Your Ears.* New York: Knopf, 1978.

LahH   Lancaster, Henry Carrington. *A History of French Dramatic Theory,* pt. 3, vol. 3. Baltimore: Johns Hopkins University Press, 1936.

LanM   Lanson, Gustave. "Molière et la farce." In Henri Peyre, ed., *Essais de Méthode de Critique et d'Histoire Littéraire.* Paris: Hachette, 1965.

LeP   Lehmann, Paul. *Die Parodie des Mittelalters.* Stuttgart: A. Hersemann, 1963.

LiD   Littré, Emile. *Dictionnaire de la Langue Française.* Paris: Hachette, 1873.

MaDJ   Mandel, Oscar. *The Theatre of Don Juan.* Lincoln: University of Nebraska Press, 1963.

ManCK   Mann, Thomas. *The Confessions of Felix Krull, Confidence Man.* Denver Lindley, tr. New York: Vintage, 1969.

ManE   Mann, Thomas. *Essays.* H. T. Lowe-Porter, tr. New York: Knopf, 1957.

ManHS   Mann, Thomas. *The Holy Sinner.* H. T. Lowe-Porter, tr. New York: Knopf, 1951.

MarM   Marivaux, Pierre Carlet. *La Vie de Marianne.* F. Deloffre, ed. Paris: Garnier, 1963.

MauP   Mauron, Charles. *Psychocritique du genre comique.* Paris: José Corti, 1964.

MoDJ   Molière. *Don Juan or the Statue at the Feast,* in *The Miser and Other Plays.* John Wood, tr. Harmondsworth: Penguin, 1974.

MoGD   Molière. *George Dandin ou le mari confondu.* In *Œuvres complètes,* vol. 2. Maurice Rat, ed. Paris: La Pléiade, 1947.

MoII   Molière. *The Imaginary Invalid.* In *The Misanthrope and Other Plays.* John Wood, tr. Harmondsworth: Penguin, 1974.

MoJ   Molière. *La Jalousie du Barbouillé*. In *Œuvres complètes*, vol. 1. Maurice Rat, ed. Paris: La Pléiade, 1947.

MoŒ   Molière. *Œuvres*. Les Grands Ecrivains de la France. Paris: Hachette, 1876.

MoŒc   Molière. *Œuvres complètes*. Gustave Michaut, ed. Paris: Imprimerie Nationale de France, 1949.

MoŒcc   Molière. *Œuvres complètes*. Georges Couton, ed. Paris: Bibliothèque de la Pléiade, NRF, 1971.

MoSS   Molière. *That Scoundrel Scapin*. In *The Miser and Other Plays*. John Wood, tr. Harmondsworth: Penguin, 1974.

MoSW   Molière. *The School for Wives*. Morris Bishop, tr. In *Eight Plays by Molière*. New York: Modern Library, 1957.

MoT   Molière. *Tartuffe*. In *The Misanthrope and Other Plays*. John Wood, tr. Harmondsworth: Penguin, 1974.

MoWG   Molière. *The Would-Be Gentleman*. In *The Miser and Other Plays*. John Wood, tr. Harmondsworth: Penguin, 1974.

MrP   Moser-Rath, Elfriede. *Predigtmärlein der Barockzeit*. Berlin: De Gruyter, 1964.

NaL   Nabokov, Vladimir. *Lolita*. New York: Capricorn, 1972.

NeOC   Neumann, Erich. *The Origins and History of Consciousness*. Bollingen Series. Princeton, N.J.: Princeton University Press, 1973.

NiZ   Nietzsche, Friedrich. *Thus Spake Zarathustra*. Thomas Common, tr. New York: Modern Library, 1929.

PA   Perrucci, Andrea. *Dell'Arte rappresentativa, premeditata ed all'improvviso* (Naples, 1966). Reprinted in Enzo Petraconne, *La Commedia dell'Arte*. Naples: Ricciardi, 1927.

PeT   Petit de Juleville, L. *Répertoire du Théâtre comique en France au Moyen-Age*. Paris: Cerf, 1886.

PiS   Picot, Emile. *Recueil général des sotties*. Paris: Firmin-Didot, 1902–12.

RG   Rabelais, François. *Gargantua and Pantagruel*. J. M. Cohen, tr. Harmondsworth: Penguin, 1972.

RaT   Radin, Paul. *The Trickster: A Study in American Indian Mythology, with Commentaries by Karl Kerényi and C. G. Jung*. London: Routledge and Kegan Paul, 1956.

RanD*J*   Rank, Otto. "The Don Juan Figure." Walter Bodlander, tr. In Oscar Mandel, *The Theatre of Don Juan.* Lincoln: University of Nebraska Press, 1963.

RanD*JG*   Rank, Otto. *Die Don Juan-Gestalt.* Leipzig, Vienna and Zürich: Internationaler Psychoanalytischer Verlag. 1924.

RanD*L*   Rank, Otto. *The Double in Literature.* Harry Tucker, Jr., tr. and ed. Chapel Hill: University of North Carolina Press, 1971.

Ro*C*   Rojas, Fernando de. *Celestina; or the Tragick-comedie of Calisto and Melibea.* James Mabbe, tr.; Guadelupe Martinez Lacalle, ed. London: Tamesis, 1972.

Sa*E*   Salas Barbadilla, Alonso J. *La ingeniosa Elena, Hija de Celestina, novela picaresca del siglo XVII.* Barcelona: Horta, 1946.

Sc*N*   Scarron, Paul. *Nouvelles tragi-comiques.* Paris: Editions Stock, 1948.

Sch*S*   Schneegans, Heinrich. *Geschichte der grotesken Satire,* Strasbourg: Trübner, 1894.

Sh*A*   Shakespeare, William. *As You Like It.* G. L. Kittredge, ed. Waltham, Mass.: Blaisdell, 1967.

Sh*H-1*   Shakespeare, William. *1 Henry IV.* G. L. Kittredge, ed. Waltham, Mass.: Blaisdell, 1966.

Sh*H-2*   Shakespeare, William. *2 Henry IV.* G. L. Kittredge, ed. Waltham, Mass.: Blaisdell, 1966.

Sh*MV*   Shakespeare, William. *The Merchant of Venice.* G. L. Kittredge, ed. Waltham, Mass.: Blaisdell, 1966.

V*Œ*   Voltaire. *Œuvres complètes,* vol. 3. Louis Moland, ed. Paris: Garnier, 1877–85.

W*F*   Welsford, Enid. *The Fool: His Social and Literary History.* London: Faber and Faber, 1935.

Index